WE WANT MILES

MILES DAVIS

cité de la musique PARIS
THE MONTREAL MUSEUM OF FINE ARTS
Skira Rizzoli NEW YORK

WE WANT MILES

MILES DAVIS VS. JAZZ

Sun Life Financial is proud to partner once again with the Montreal Museum of Fine Arts in presenting the exhibition *"We Want Miles": Miles Davis vs. Jazz* and thus play a vital role in promoting art in all its many forms to as broad an audience as possible.

Through this multimedia retrospective, visitors will have a chance to experience the highlights of the life and career of Miles Davis in a setting designed in its entirety around the brilliant sounds of his legendary music. Photographs, film clips, paintings and music combine in this multidimensional journey of sight and sound that pays tribute to an artist who is still widely admired and continues to be an inspiration to so many.

Sun Life Financial recognizes and commends the important contribution of this exhibition, which blurs the lines between music and the visual arts and promises to take visitors far beyond the boundaries of jazz and the legend that is Miles Davis. We are proud to play a part and to help make the arts more accessible through this exhibition and its catalogue.

With culture, life's brighter!
Life's brighter under the sun.

Sun Life Financial

WE WANT MILES
MILES DAVIS VS. JAZZ

This exhibition was initiated and organized by the Cité de la Musique, Paris, with the support of Miles Davis Properties, LLC, in association with the Montreal Museum of Fine Arts.

Musée de la Musique, Paris
October 16, 2009 to January 17, 2010

The Montreal Museum of Fine Arts
Jean-Noël Desmarais Pavilion
April 30 to August 29, 2010

Exhibition Curator
Vincent Bessières

Exhibition Design
Projectiles

Sound Design
Philippe Wojtowicz

In Montreal, the exhibition is presented by Sun Life Financial, in collaboration with Sony Music Entertainment.

The Montreal Museum of Fine Arts wishes to thank the Festival International de Jazz de Montréal, Archambault, Air Canada and its media partners *La Presse*, *The Gazette*, Astral Media and the Société Radio-Canada. Its gratitude also extends to Quebec's Ministère de la Culture et des Communications for its ongoing support.

The exhibition benefits from funding provided by the Volunteer Association of the Montreal Museum of Fine Arts.

The Museum wishes to thank the Association of Volunteer Guides of the Montreal Museum of Fine Arts for their unflagging support. The Museum is also grateful to its VIPs and the many corporations, foundations and individuals for their contributions, and, in particular, the Fondation Arte Musica, led by Pierre Bourgie.

The Montreal Museum of Fine Arts' International Exhibition Programme receives financial support from the Exhibition Fund of the Montreal Museum of Fine Arts Foundation and the Paul G. Desmarais Fund.

EXHIBITION – PARIS
Associate Curator
Éric de Visscher
Exhibitions Department
Isabelle Lainé
Project Coordinators
Marion Challier
Wissam Hojeij
Exhibition-design Oversight
Olivia Berthon
Dictino Ferrero
Graphic Design, Exhibition
Laurent Meszaros
Audiovisual Coordinators
Matthias Abhervé
Romane Olmedo
Intern
Guillaume Fouquart
Preventive Conservation
Stéphane Vaiedelich
Marie-Anne Loepper Attia
Works Registrar
Laurence Goux
Technical Team
Rui Chaves Palhares
Philippe Vieira
Liaisons and Access
Delphine de Bethmann
Caroline Bugat
Sophie Valmorin
Caroline Jules

EXHIBITION – MONTREAL
Coordination in Montreal
Executive Assistant – Special Exhibitions
Anne Eschapasse
Technical Support
Sylvie Ouellet

Registrar and Head, Archives
Danièle Archambault
Head, Membership
Jean-Sébastien Bélanger
Head, Computer Services
Gaétan Bouchard
Head, Security, Visitors Services and Admission
Sophie Boucher
Head, Editorial Services and Graphic Design
Emmanuelle Christen
Head, Library
Joanne Déry
Head, Exhibitions Production
Sandra Gagné
Head, Conservation
Richard Gagnier
Manager, Boutique and Bookstore
Christine Hamel
Head, Publishing
Francine Lavoie
Head, Development
The Montreal Museum of Fine Arts Foundation
Thierry-Maxime Loriot
Head, Purchasing and Auxiliary Services
Francis Mailloux
Head, Education and Community Programmes
Jean-Luc Murray
Head, Exhibitions Management
Pascal Normandin
Head, Financial Control and Accounting
Guy Parent

CATALOGUE
The first edition of this book was published in French by Éditions Textuel / Cité de la musique, Paris, 2009, in conjunction with the presentation of the exhibition at the Musée de la Musique, Paris.

Under the editorship of
Vincent Bessières
Principal Author
Franck Bergerot
Coordination
Marion Challier
Manon Lenoir
Marianne Théry
Publishing Oversight
Jessica Mautref
Graphic Design
Caroline Keppy
Sandrine Roux
Illustrations Oversight
Wissam Hojeij
Revision
Alexis Diamond
Translation
Alexis Diamond
Clara Gabriel
Keith Marchand
Donald Pistolesi
Katrin Sermat
Proofreading
Jane Jackel
Typesetting
Guy Pilotte
Production
Sandrine Pavy
Copyright
Linda-Anne D'Anjou
Publishing Assistant (Montreal)
Sébastien Hart
Publisher (Montreal)
Francine Lavoie

ISBN MMFA: 978-2-89192-342-2
www.mmfa.qc.ca
ISBN Skira Rizzoli: 978-0-8478-3528-7
Library of Congress Control Number : 2010922543
www.rizzoliusa.com
Legal deposit: 2nd quarter 2010
Bibliothèque et Archives nationales du Québec
National Library of Canada

PRINTED IN ITALY

Also published in French under the title:
We Want Miles. Miles Davis: le jazz face à sa légende
© MMFA 2010
ISBN MMFA: 978-2-89192-343-9

ACKNOWLEDGEMENTS

We would like to thank the photographers for their involvement in this project, in particular: Anton Corbijn, Annie Delory, Didier Ferry, Marcel Fleiss, Lee Friedlander, Claude Gassian, Don Hunstein, Marvin Koner, Guy Le Querrec, Annie Leibovitz, Jean-Pierre Leloir, Herman Leonard, Fred Lombardi, Kirsten Malone, Mark Patiky, Jan Persson, Christian Rose, André Sas, Susumu Shirai, Chuck Stewart, Shigeru Ushiyama, Baron Wolman, as well as the late Irving Penn, Willy Ronis, Vincent Rossell, Dennis Stock, Bob Willoughby.

We express our sincere gratitude to all those who lent their assistance and made this project possible:

Lars Annersten
Anton Corbijn Limited: Monica Axelsson, Stijn Claassen
Geraldine Baum
Bibliothèque nationale de France: Françoise Simeray, Anne Legrand
The Blanton Museum of Art: Meredith D. Sutton
Johanne Bougie
The Broad Art Foundation: Vicky Gambill
Dave Brolan
Carnegie Museum of Art
Cinémathèque française: Jacques Ayrolles, Isabelle Regelsperger
Eleana Cobb
Contact Press Images: Dominique Deschavanne
Conversation and Co Ltd: Sashiko Nakanishi
Chip Cronkite
Michael Cuscuna
Eagle Rock France: Marie Waldt
ESPN Classic: Virginie Bernon, Alex Lowe, Damion Potter
Festival International de Jazz de Montréal: André Ménard, Alain Simard, Jacques-André Dupont, Denyse McCann, Myrianne Bertrand, Serge Lafortune, Julie Martel, Isabelle Normand
Fine Art Shipping: Betsy Dorfman
Fondaction Boris-Vian: Nicole Bertolt
Bonnie Foster
Fraenkel Gallery: Peter Colon
French Ambassador to the United States, Cultural Department: Emmanuel Morlet, Armelle Pradalier
Maxine Gordon
Frederick Hoffman
Honda Motor Europe: Richard Mathiau
Institut national de l'audiovisuel: Emmanuel Hogg, Pascal Rozat, Sylvie Richard, Bernadette Gazzola-Dirrix
Laboratoire Gorne: François David
Edward Gottlieb
Ngoc Suong Gras
Bibi Green
Lionel Guyon
Teppei Inokuchi
Emma Lavigne
Médiathèque de Villefranche-de-Rouergue: Daniel Alogues, Patrick Brugel
Dany Michel
Nederlands Fotomuseum: Carolien Provaas
The New York Public Library for the Performing Arts: Stephan Saks, Deborah Straussman
Niki Charitable Art Foundation: Jana Shenefield
Dale Parent
Stéphane Paudras
Ludovic Perrot
Les Poissons volants
Olivier Pouzin
Projectiles: Réza Azar, Hervé Bouttet, Clémence Dupuis Delamarzelle, Daniel Meszaros
Michael Randolph
Rencontres photographiques d'Arles: Alice Martin, Pascale Giffard
Rhino Entertainment Company: Kristopher E. Ahrend, Kristina Groennings, Cheryl Pawelski
Rogers & Cowan: Karen Sundell
Richard Rothman
Norman Saks
Samething for Miles: Nancy and Lélia Campbell
Susan Scofield
Cynthia Sesso/CTSIMAGES
Shukat Arrow Hafer Weber & Herbsman: Peter Shukat, Jason Finestone
Sirius XM Radio
Vernon L. Smith II
Sony Music Entertainment Canada: Velma Barkwell
Sony Music Entertainment France: Daniel Baumgarten, Olivier Cochet
Sony Music Entertainment United States: Lyn Koppe, Glenn Korman, Elizabeth Miller, Matthew Plotnik, Jeffrey Schulberg, Che Williams
Steve Music: Nicolas Grégoire
Nancy Taylor, Blair McCoy
Sarah Tenot
WEA Studio Services/Archives: Julie Brunnick, Steve Lang
Frank West
Western Historical Manuscript Collection, University of Missouri: Nancy McIlvaney
Agnès Wolff

In addition to those mentioned above, Vincent Bessières would like to thank Reza Ackbaraly, Vincent Anglade, Bob Belden, Nicolas Brémaud, Paul Buckmaster, Ron Carter, Laurent Coq, Christophe Dal Sasso, Michel Delorme, Jonathan Duclos-Arkilovitch, Alex Dutilh, Bill Evans, Éric Garault, Jean-Noël Ginibre, Frédéric Goaty, François Lacharme, Grégory Lagrange, Olivier Linden, Florence Masson, Takafumi Mimori, Nell Mulderry, Chihiro Nakayama, Martine Palmé, Ronan Palud, Pierrick Pedron, Thierry Pérémarti, Isabelle Rodier, Daniel Soutif, Alain Tercinet, Bertrand Uberall, Doug Weiss, as well as all those who, at one time or another, offered their support or assistance to this project.

LENDERS

This project would not have existed if it were not for the invaluable and generous assistance of Miles Davis' heirs, particularly his children Cheryl Davis and Erin Davis, as well as his nephew Vince Wilburn, Jr. We would like to express our gratitude to them, as well as to Darryl Porter, manager of Miles Davis Properties, LLC, and to Charles J. Biederman, Manatt Phelps & Phillips, LLP.

We also thank the following lenders for their generous support:

CANADA

Montreal
Festival International de Jazz de Montréal
Paul Maréchal
Hugo St-Cyr
Concordia University, Gerald Beasley, Guylaine Beaudry

Ottawa
Bibliothèque et Archives Canada, Robert McIntosh

Toronto
CODA Magazine, Mark Barnes

FRANCE

Bondy
Michèle Codin

Montcuq
Olivier Grall

Paris
Philippe Baudoin
Bibliothèque nationale de France, Bruno Racine
Klaus Blasquiz
Centre d'information du jazz, Pascal Anquetil
Cinémathèque française, Serge Toubiana
Fatras, Eugénie Bachelot
Fondaction Boris-Vian, Ursula Vian-Kübler
Galerie Agathe-Gaillard, Agathe Gaillard
Galerie Albert-Benamou, Albert Benamou
Claude Gassian
Paris Jazz Corner, Arnaud Boubet
Philippe Ghielmetti
Jean-Luc Katchoura
Shaun de Koenigswarter
Roger Lajus
André Martinez and Odile Martinez de la Grange
Jeanne de Mirbeck
Gérard Sibille

GERMANY

Darmstadt
Jazzinstitut, Wolfram Knauer

Offenbach
Günther Kieser

JAPAN
Kohshin Satoh et Yuki, Yuhi Sato
Kiyoshi Koyama

UNITED KINGDOM

London
Anton Corbijn Limited, Anton Corbijn

UNITED STATES

Austin
The Blanton Museum of Art, The University of Texas at Austin, Ned Rifkin

Bloomfield
Wallace Roney

Burbank
Warner Music Group, Edgar Bronfman, Jr.

Franklin
Cherie Willoughby

Greensboro
University of North Carolina at Greensboro (UNCG School of Music), Miles Davis Jazz Studies Program, Steve Haines

Katonah
John Scofield

Los Angeles
Olana DiGirolamo
Darryl Jones
L.A. Jazz Institute, Ken Poston
Cortez McCoy
Miles Davis Properties, LLC, Cheryl Davis, Erin Davis, Vince Wilburn, Jr.
Marcus Miller
Stella Benabou Shapiro and Dorian Shapiro

New York
Cindy Blackman
The Coltrane Family
Frank Driggs
Jo Gelbard
The New York Public Library for the Performing Arts, Music Division, George Boziwick
James Rabito
Amalie R. Rothschild
Robert M. Rubin and Stéphane Samuel
Schomburg Center For Research in Black Culture, New York Public Library, Astor, Lenox & Tilden Foundations, Diana Lachatanere
Annie Leibovitz
Sony Music Entertainment, Rolf Schmidt-Holtz, Adam Block

Newport
Caterine Milinaire

Newark
Institute of Jazz Studies, Rutgers University, Dan Morgenstern

San Francisco
Fraenkel Gallery, Nina Brillant
Wolfgang's Vault, Katherine York

North Hollywood
Devik Wiener

Santa Monica
The Broad Art Foundation, Joanne Heyler

Santee
Niki Charitable Art Foundation, Bloum Cardenas

Studio City
Herman Leonard Photography, LLC

Westbury
Anthony Barboza

Woodstock
Al Foster

Worthington
Foley McCreary

Photo Jean-Pierre Leloir.

WE WANT MILES

LAURENT BAYLE / GENERAL DIRECTOR, CITÉ DE LA MUSIQUE, PARIS
ÉRIC DE VISSCHER / DIRECTOR, MUSÉE DE LA MUSIQUE, PARIS

In 1980, after nearly five years of silence, Miles Davis began to play again in the studio and on stage. The snappy title of one of the first records heralding his comeback was the self-evident statement "*We Want Miles*." Who is this "*we*"? How do you explain that simply saying a first name can conjure up an artist's undeniable power? To understand the universal respect commanded by a figure of this stature, recognized for elevating a fledgling musical genre to a global phenomenon, we need only call to mind the course of his career: Miles Davis got his start playing in big bands in his hometown of St. Louis, enthusiastically embraced bebop, initiated the cool, embarked on a quest for a third avenue between swing and free jazz, and subsequently immersed himself in electric jazz, with occasional forays into soul and rock. Could this also explain how his name became legend, with musicians of every stripe all over the world incessantly chanting "We want Miles" to encourage him to return to centre stage?—a stage he would now take by storm, with numerous records, television appearances, advertising and film projects that transformed him into a genuine media icon. First, Davis became aware of the legend of jazz, which had expanded into a worldwide genre, then of his own legend as a "global" artist who transcended styles, schools and genres to assert himself as a musician, creator and leader of one of the twentieth century's signature musical currents. Although he contributed to the history of jazz in much the same way as Duke Ellington, Charlie Parker, John Coltrane and Thelonious Monk, no other musician embraced its many developments with such boldness and ingenuity. He even anticipated its major turning points, transforming music meant for entertainment and dancing into music that had to be listened to, and he was subsequently criticized for some of his choices by those who shunned progress. As with Serge Gainsbourg, whose name immediately came to mind when the Cité de la musique was considering a first temporary exhibition on French chanson, cult figure Miles Davis instantly occurred to us as soon as the topic of jazz was proposed. In addition to a record title (*You're under Arrest*), these two figures, born in the same year, shared the desire to avoid being confined to any one style, always seeking out new, innovative—and sometimes unexpected—musical avenues. They were inspired by the sense of "the moment" both in the way they related to their era and in their work: Gainsbourg wrote fast, Davis created music on the spot, pushing the art of improvisation to the limit without ever losing the connection with his audience. To quote saxophonist David Liebman from one of the texts in this catalogue, "When Miles went on stage, past and future didn't exist. It was all about the present tense, the essence of true improvisation and what most jazz musicians strive for daily when playing."

It is undoubtedly this "mystery of the present moment" that Miles Davis never ceased to explore, developing both the sounds (his move to electric and amplified instruments is an example of this, as are his collaborative efforts with Gil Evans) and the language of jazz. To do so, he tapped into a fertile source of renewal by working with new musicians. From John Coltrane to Herbie Hancock, the long list of artists who worked with Davis demonstrates his openness to the influences of other sizeable talents—his contemporaries as well as younger musicians. From *Kind of Blue* and *Tutu* to *Porgy and Bess* and *Bitches Brew*, Davis' great albums all bear witness, in various forms, to his quest for the perfect moment.

This is the exceptional journey related in this book—a faithful counterpart to the exhibition first presented at the Musée de la musique and subsequently at the Montreal Museum of Fine Arts—which presents a chronological account by Franck Bergerot supplemented with reminiscences by certain key figures of the time. As for the exhibition, the photographs were chosen with particular care, since it is true that jazz and photography share a common history. Both capture the moment and record contrasts, immortalizing the illustrious heroes and pivotal moments of a musical genre that is quintessentially ephemeral.

Neither the exhibition nor this catalogue would have been possible without the tireless efforts and unfailing ingenuity of curator and editor Vincent Bessières. The project received steadfast support from the Miles Davis Estate, especially Cheryl Davis, Erin Davis and Vince Wilburn, Jr. The many lenders, photographers and institutions that contributed to the exhibition not only made it possible but also ensured its originality. To them, and to the people at the Cité de la musique and at the Montreal Museum of Fine Arts, who helped make it a reality, we offer our heartfelt thanks.

MILES AND MILES OF MILES

VINCENT BESSIÈRES / EXHIBITION CURATOR

Jazz has had its fair share of eccentric personalities, picaresque protagonists, tragic destinies, meteoric careers and dazzling creators. But Miles Davis is still the most fascinating and mysterious of them all. The exhibition *"We Want Miles"* does not claim to be the last word on this artist who left his mark on the twentieth century; rather, it is an attempt to sketch a broad outline, analyze his transformations and follow his evolution. Like the art of Picasso, to whom he is often compared, Davis' music has its periods. In step with the fast-paced century, he set out in a new direction every five years. He lost his audience, found another, lost that one—and won over yet another. When Miles shed his skin, you just had to keep up with him. He sparks both desire and frustration: when you arrive where you expect him to be, he's already gone. What he played one day he would never play again. And yet it's always Miles. His sound may have changed, his bands may have had a high turnover rate, he may have flouted convention and been electrified by electricity, but something remains, making it possible to identify him in just a few notes.

This is the thread running through the exhibition, which seeks to discover this complex and elusive man: Miles the proud young boy, Miles the country bumpkin who dreams of Bird, Miles the epitome of cool, Miles the boxer, arrogant Miles, Miles the down-and-out junkie, Miles who turns his back on his audience, Miles and his kind of blue, Miles as Porgy, Miles as Bess, Miles celebrating the *saeta*, Miles who finally smiles, Miles who questions jazz, Miles the hepcat, Miles the rocker, Miles the show-off, Miles and his bitches' brew, Miles who thinks he's Hendrix, Miles on the corner, Miles who vanishes, Miles who reappears, Miles the star demanding royal treatment, Miles haunted by his ghosts, Miles who never looks back, blue Miles, Miles who stares down the ignorant, Miles the macho, the hero, the leader, Miles with his nerves on edge, Miles beaten by the cops, Miles who shamelessly tells his story, Miles and his trumpets of many colours, Sphinx-like Miles, hip Miles, bop Miles . . . Miles, Miles, Miles. "We want Miles," you say. But which one?

Can we separate the man from his music? Can we understand his work without connecting it to his life? His music has survived him, of course. But in the quintessentially personal medium that is jazz—this intimate art form in conversation with the world—Miles inhabits the music as much as he plays it. Or is it the music that inhabits him? Imagine his silhouette on stage, his body hunched over, his trumpet raised. What did Miles play that he had not experienced? Aside from boxing, nothing else interested him. Miles never stopped looking jazz in the face and confronting it.

Opening new pathways, absorbing trends, surpassing styles, he turned around and gave it back, all the while avoiding clichés, easy recipes and ready-made formulas. His misconduct cannot be dismissed on the grounds that he so often strove for excellence and originality. Who is not a fan of Miles Davis? Who cannot find, in this vast, varied body of work, a piece that speaks to them? Everyone has a favourite Miles Davis album, even Barack Obama, whose election as president of the United States adds symbolic resonance to an anecdote in Davis' autobiography about a White House dinner President Reagan invited him to in 1987.

When another guest, a woman of a certain age, condescendingly asked him what he had done that was important enough to merit an invitation to the hallowed halls of the White House, Miles replied, "Well, I've changed music five or six times." That's enough to warrant an exhibition . . . and this book, which will serve as a lasting record of it. "We Want Miles," and we can never get enough of him.

Photo Festival International de Jazz de Montréal, 1988.

MILES
THE PICASSO OF JAZZ

"I don't know about Picasso . . . maybe in a way I change music and stuff. . . . Yeah, you can say that . . . I do change it . . . but I can't help it, you know. It's not that I'm a genius but it's just that I can't help it."

—Miles Davis, 1985

"In painting, you can try anything. It is even your right. As long as you never do anything over again."

—Pablo Picasso

"Now, nothing in music and sounds is "wrong." You can hit anything, any kind of chord. Like John Cage playing the shit he's playing, making all them strange sounds and noises. Music is wide open for anything."

—Miles Davis

"I stir things up too much, move them around too much. You see me here, and yet I've already changed. I'm already somewhere else."

—Pablo Picasso

"Nothing is out of the question the way I think and live my life. I'm always thinking about creating. My future starts when I wake up every morning."

—Miles Davis

"For me each painting is a study. . . . But as soon as I start to finish it, it becomes another painting and I think I am going to redo it. Well, it is always something else in the end."

—Pablo Picasso

"The music we did together changed every fucking night. . . . Even we didn't know where it was all going to. But we did know it was going somewhere."

—Miles Davis

NATHALIE BONDIL
DIRECTOR, THE MONTREAL MUSEUM OF FINE ARTS

Miles Davis was the "Picasso of Jazz." This oft-repeated honorary title has the virtue of conveying that each of these men was a genius at his art—which is quite true. Both the painter and the jazz musician renewed themselves constantly, never getting locked into a single style, borne throughout their career by a pressing need to innovate, an absolute restlessness, a capacity for thorough analysis of the issues at play in their art—and a high opinion of their own artistic and monetary worth. This commitment led Picasso to say, "Painting takes the upper hand. It makes me do whatever it wants," and Davis: "Music has always been like a curse with me because I have always felt driven to play it." Both artists cut across various trends and engaged in close dialogue with their public. Picasso had his Fauve, Rose, Blue, Cubist, Neoclassical and Surrealist periods; Davis moved through bebop, the cool, hard bop, modal jazz, electric, funk, pop jazz and hip hop. Both rebelled against academic training and had impeccable technique, an aesthetic cannibalism, a curiosity about other techniques or instruments, and an even surer instinct. Superstitious, they viewed their art as exorcism and mania (Picasso) or as therapy and obsession (Davis). Both were hard workers and had the same faith in "feeling" (Picasso said, "When you've worked a lot, forms come by themselves, paintings come by themselves"). Their exceptional personalities, egocentric and demanding, made them international stars, feared, criticized, adored; garnering celebrity, they lived a lifestyle unheard of in their respective realms. Images of the dark, irascible, magnetic look they shared in common received wide distribution, making them two icons of the twentieth century.

On closer consideration, there are differences. Picasso was a deeply individualistic artist who did not create a school except perhaps Cubism, with Braque, "a sort of research laboratory . . . without pretension or personal rivalry." An artist whose tremendous influence extended from Wifredo Lam to Jackson Pollock, Picasso nonetheless had no students—the great nineteenth-century studios were a thing of the past. His pantheon of painters included only dead artists, and Matisse. He showed little regard for his contemporaries, and as for the younger generation, abstraction was not worth much: "In the end, when people talk about abstract art, they always say it is music. . . . Everything becomes music. . . . I think that's why I don't like music." Picasso reigned alone as master, soliloquizing with Velázquez, Rembrandt, Manet and Cézanne, very prestigious and not very burdensome masters. "Picasso was a great artist, but now he is just a genius," as Braque once said. On the contrary, even though he always wanted to project a sound all his own—and despite the fact he could be difficult—Davis never concealed his admiration or his debt to mentors old and young, including Jimi Hendrix, James Brown and Prince, whom he admired openly to the point of envisioning future collaborations. Until late in life, Davis' constantly alert and unbiased mind enabled him to grasp what was interesting about the latest trends—breakdancing, hip hop, zouk and rap, as well as Stockhausen, Cage, Buckmaster: "I wanted to see what was going on in all of music. Knowledge is freedom and ignorance is slavery." With him, music escaped all categorization and the critics' ghettoization. And then, there was a veritable "Miles Davis University." The music director of a constantly shifting group, he was always on the lookout for young talent, with the infallible flair for which he was known. And he understood—sometimes bitterly—what it was like to be abandoned when sidemen left to form bands of their own, as he had previously done himself. No artist went to Picasso to ask his advice. The hermit communed with the mountain tops, declaring in 1945 that "the Americans are at the collective phase. In France, we are past that and onto the phase of individuality." Of course, the two professions are different, involving on the one hand solitary creation in front of the easel and, on the other, co-operation with other performers onstage. True, Davis did not gladly suffer another trumpet player onstage, and Picasso worked with production companies in the days of the Ballets Russes. All the same, there was no "Pablo Picasso University."

There is also the matter of financial success. A painter can just as easily lock himself into a style and survive the changing dictates of the marketplace to become a museum object, but music is subject to the caprices of fashion. Unlike art collectors and dealers, who consist of a fairly limited group of wealthy insiders, the growing record market depended on a constantly renewed base of young people. Davis, who understood these laws, did not want to become a museum piece (contrary to an artist, for whom it is the ultimate recognition). The market required him to evolve ceaselessly. In this era of speed, when change was the mark of youth, fashion regulated the laws of commerce. Davis was not ashamed of wanting financial success: "The real money was in getting to the mainstream." Nor was he ashamed of sincerely enjoying playing "the entertainer" for the widest possible audience: "As a musician and as an artist, I have always wanted to reach as many people as I could through my music. . . . Because I never thought that the music called 'jazz' was ever meant to reach just a small group of people, or become a museum thing." As an eternally hip artist, Davis always placed himself in the avant-garde, while Picasso wanted to be a classic. Above all, throughout Davis' entire career, his artistic choices were closely connected to the struggle against racism in the United States, and this is probably what made him the most vulnerable. He wanted to leave his mark as a great creator on an equal footing with the white classical musicians he liked—Stravinsky, Prokofiev and Rachmaninoff—contending that jazz was one of America's major contributions to twentieth-century culture. Miles Davis always defended the racial pride of an "unreconstructed black man" before a young audience, in contrast with the demeaning caricature of an Uncle Tom. Picasso was certainly haunted by a "pictorial and mental Hispanicity." Though a Spaniard in exile, a socially involved painter (Guernica, the Korean War) and a Communist sympathizer, he experienced nothing comparable to the contempt Davis was subject to because of the colour of his skin, "blacker than the blackest night." He was strongly opposed to the everyday reality of segregation, which explains his violence, paranoia, aggressiveness and fascination with boxing (and his black heroes Jack Johnson and Sugar Ray Robinson). Picasso was not self-destructive, unlike Davis, who was caught between the highs of drug use and the lows of depression: "I can see where I would be proud of my scars, because they show me that I didn't let this shit get me down." Far from complacent, without ever trying to please, his autobiography tells it like it is, explaining the point of view of an emblematic figure of the African-American conscience.

And what did Davis think of Picasso? An autodidact, he liked painting and, towards the end of his life, visited museums and generated copious amounts of paintings. In Paris in 1949, he had met the unforgettable Juliette Gréco, as well as Boris Vian, Sartre and Picasso: "In this century, in my opinion, you had Picasso, Dalí. . . . But Picasso, besides his Cubist work, had that African influence in his paintings, and I already knew what that was all about. So Dalí was just more interesting for me, taught me a new way of looking at things." Though Davis considered Picasso one of the "painters among great painters," the latter's borrowing from black art detracted from his originality, the way white rock music was clearly indebted to black music. Chosen for his record covers, the work of Mati Klarwein suited Davis' taste for Dalíesque phantasmagorias.

This presentation in Montreal is particularly significant, since, for more than thirty years, the city has been host to one of the largest and most prestigious jazz festivals, the Festival International de Jazz de Montréal, which featured a memorable Miles Davis several times. Hence, this first incursion into the realm of jazz on the part of the Montreal Museum of Fine Arts will have particular resonance. The exhibition continues the Museum's exploration of the connection between visual art and music that I recently initiated with the multimedia exhibitions *Warhol Live: Music and Dance in Andy Warhol's Work* and *Imagine: The Peace Ballad of John & Yoko*. My heartfelt gratitude to all our partners and colleagues, particularly the Musée de la Musique in Paris.

Quotations have been taken from *Picasso, Propos sur l'art* (Paris: Gallimard, 1998) and from Miles Davis and Quincy Troupe, *Miles: The Autobiography* (New York: Touchstone, 1990).

MILES IN MONTREAL
"WELCOME TO WINTER WONDERLAND"

ANDRÉ MÉNARD
VICE-PRESIDENT AND ARTISTIC DIRECTOR
FESTIVAL INTERNATIONAL DE JAZZ DE MONTRÉAL

From the very beginning, Miles Davis exerted an inescapable fascination. Over and above his constantly evolving music, his unique attitude and style set him apart, starting from his earliest creative period in the late 1940s. Throughout his life, he never ceased surprising and disconcerting us. There was no routine or backtracking for this artist who focused steadfastly on the future.

Miles Davis had appeared in Montreal's larger and smaller venues well before the existence of the Festival International de Jazz de Montréal [a.k.a. the Montreal International Jazz Festival], though only sporadically. He played at Place des Arts on two occasions ten years apart: the first in fall 1963; the second in 1973. In between, in 1964, he spent a week at the Casa Loma on Sainte-Catherine Street.

Soon after the Festival was founded, it forged a remarkable collaboration with Miles Davis. On Sunday, July 11, 1982, he closed the third edition—a pivotal year in the Festival's history—with an eagerly awaited concert. His self-imposed seven-year hiatus, begun in the mid-1970s, had ended a few months earlier. His absence had sparked the direst rumours about his health and his willingness to return to music and touring.

In a Théâtre Saint-Denis packed with anxious admirers, the trumpeter, wearing an elegant blue suit, stepped onstage at the head of a superlative band. His discreet and, it must be said, at times hesitant playing in no way impeded his magnetic hold over his sidemen and his audience. Fiery tempos followed muted, almost inaudible trumpet passages. At the end of the concert, the crowd exploded with joy, and Davis came backstage. This was my first contact with the man, and I sensed without a doubt that I was in the presence of a formidable but elusive figure. That meeting has left an indelible impression on me: I had never before been in the presence of such a powerful aura. I can attest to the fact that the famous mystique of the Prince of the Night [or Darkness] remained intact even at close range.

Davis gratified us with his presence at the Festival three more times. In 1983, his all-out performance proved he had regained full possession of his powers. Two numbers from this incredibly funky concert were included on his next record, *Decoy*. Everyone was proud that the Festival had become an integral part of his "documented" work.

Better yet, the next time he came, in 1985, Davis allowed his midnight concert on opening night to be filmed from every angle. Production got underway for what was to become a classic: it is still available in DVD format. Furthermore, the present exhibition provides the public with a chance to discover excerpts of that extraordinary evening. In it we hear and see a sombre, intense Miles Davis, who is also at times lighthearted, even playing hide-and-seek with the camera in the middle of a solo. High art!

Speaking of art, the 1988 Festival provided the opportunity for us to collaborate in another capacity with Davis. We asked Davis for a drawing to serve as the main visual theme of that summer's Festival. Instead, Davis invited us to inspect his whole portfolio, which Alain Simard and I spent an afternoon doing in a New York warehouse. After opening dozens of boxes and looking at hundreds of works in various formats that covered a wide range of subjects [quite a lot of women, though], bingo!—we hit upon a self-portrait on canvas. Davis immediately gave us permission to use it. In addition to the poster, the self-portrait appeared on all our stage backdrops in one guise or another. It was even featured in ads on the back of beer delivery trucks. Art in the streets . . . what could be better? The Place des Arts concert, his last for the Festival, was masterful.

The jazz great returned to Montreal one final time in February 1990 for a legendary series of three intimate performances at the Spectrum, his swan song in our city. He arrived at Dorval Airport [now Trudeau International Airport] decked out as always in all his finery and in an easy-going mood. He spent the entire ride from the airport to his hotel making jokes about the Canadian winter. Three outstanding evenings followed, each musically distinct. For the record, I recall the last one, when a magnificently bluesy tone permeated all his music, which for the space of an evening had once again become truly melancholy. Davis delivered over two hours of bewitching magic, then left directly for the airport. He travelled through the night to Los Angeles, where, the next day at the Grammy's, Ella Fitzgerald handed him a Lifetime Achievement Award.

A few months later, I ran into Davis in Paris at the entrance of a hotel where he was making a movie. He graciously offered me his hand and called me by my first name. Ouch . . . the powerful aura remained, but the man gave me a smile. Recalling these last exceptional moments in the presence of pure genius, I am still overcome with emotion twenty years later.

This exhibition is an opportune reminder of the extent of Davis' influence on all types of music. The unparalleled career of this free and uncompromising artist places him among the ranks of the greatest figures of the twentieth century. This fascination with Miles Davis is not about to fade. What was true in the past is true now and forever: WE WANT MILES!

Photo Festival International
de Jazz de Montréal, 1983.

View of Fifty-second Street, New York, 1947.
Photo William P. Gottlieb.

FROM ST. LOUIS TO FIFTY-SECOND STREET IN SEARCH OF BIRD

1926–1948

"One thing I do know is that the year after I was born, a bad tornado hit St. Louis and tore it all up. . . . Maybe that's why I have such a bad temper sometimes; that tornado left some of its violent creativity in me. Maybe it left some of its strong winds. You know, you need strong wind to play trumpet. I do believe in mystery, and the supernatural and a tornado sure enough is mysterious *and* supernatural."

There actually was a tornado on September 29, 1927. Even if it had been imaginary, what matters is the profession of belief it elicited. These lines from the opening of Miles Davis' autobiography reveal his fascination with the occult and with the fear it provoked; rather than shrinking from the dark side, he actively sought it out. He was not a religious man. The church experience has informed most musical careers in the African-American community. Davis, however, did not retain much of it, other than the decision he made while still a child to stop going to church, as he was tired of being treated like a sinner. In recalling his experience with Southern black music during visits with his grandfather in Arkansas, he remembered less of church itself, where he heard spirituals being sung, than of the road haunted by ghosts and hooting owls he took to get there on Saturday night. This was where he discovered the blues.

1

Cass, Vernon, John, Miles

2

3

Miles, Dorothy Mae, Vernon, Mrs.

4

Edna + Dorothy Mae

5

M.D. DAVIS

6

Son of a dental surgeon (bottom centre, in graduation attire), Miles Davis III (bottom right) grew up in a relatively well-off family in East St. Louis, Illinois. The middle of three children, he remained close to his older sister, Dorothy Mae (bottom left, on the right, Easter 1939), and his brother Vernon (top left, second from the left). His relationship with his mother, Cleota, known as "Mama Cleo," was more problematic (centre right, on the right). A year after Davis' birth, a tornado ravaged the city (top right), an event that left a strong impression on his imagination.

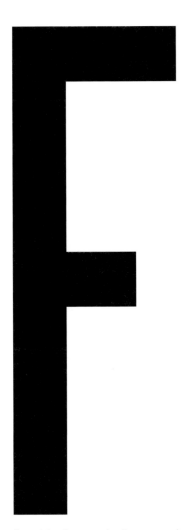

FROM FATHER TO SON. Although Christmas was important to Davis, it was less of a religious holiday and more of a family celebration. He was very attached to his family. One of his first indulgences, as soon as he signed with Columbia in 1955, was to spend every Christmas in Chicago with his sister. The head of the family was grandfather Miles Dewey Davis I, born six years after the abolition of slavery. In the time of slavery, the Davises were said to have been musicians in the service of white plantation owners. Miles I apparently forbade his children to play music to keep them out of barrelhouses, the only imaginable place for a black musician in white America. A native of Georgia, Miles I was married in Arkansas to Mary Frances; his second wife was Ivy, grandmother of Miles Davis III, the future trumpet player. Miles I moved to the countryside near Pine Bluff, south of Little Rock, Arkansas, where he purchased land. He worked as a bookkeeper for white farmers in the area, who ended up chasing him off his property, either because they took a dim view of this successful, self-made black man, or because they feared he might be indiscreet about their various schemes. He relocated to Noble Lake, southeast of Pine Bluff, where he began growing sugar cane, watermelons and corn, as well as specializing in fish farming.

Of his three daughters and six sons, we know only about Frank, Ferdinand and Miles II. Frank served as his bodyguard; Ferdinand studied at Harvard and then in Berlin. He went on to become editor-in-chief of *Color* magazine and regaled his young nephew, Miles III, with accounts of his life as a globetrotting ladies' man. Miles II, who was born in 1900, became a dentist after excelling as a student at Northwestern University's School of Dentistry. He married Cleota H. Henry, the only daughter of Leon and Hattie Henry, born in 1901. He opened a dental practice in Alton, Illinois, and Cleota bore him a daughter, Dorothy Mae, in 1924. Miles III was born May 26, 1926. The following year, "Doc Davis" moved to East St. Louis, where son Vernon was born in 1929. Shortly afterwards, the family moved to the corner of Seventeenth Street and Kansas Avenue, to a comfortable, thirteen-room white house with red awnings, a large garden and a garage for Doc Davis' Lincoln Zephyr. After a difficult start, with America in the throes of the Depression, the Davis family was embraced by the black elite of East St. Louis. They were active members of the Charleston Club and St. Paul's Baptist Church, and went to the Kiel Opera House to hear the St. Louis Symphony Orchestra conducted by Vladimir Golschmann (a former student of Schola Cantorum in Paris) and the leading soloists of the day, such as Rachmaninoff and Horowitz.

Mrs. Davis was a proud and elegant woman. Her son saw her as belonging to the segment of black society that aspired to racial integration through the positions of the National Association for the Advancement of Colored People (NAACP) and the National Urban League. On the other hand, he shared his father's ideas, which were based on the separatism

1

of Marcus Garvey, who advocated that African Americans return to Africa. Doc Davis, who had a flair for business, was exceedingly disdainful of poverty, which he found inexcusable. He asserted his racial pride and social standing in his political pursuits, in gambling—in which he lost considerable sums of money—and on the golf course, where young Miles would sometimes caddy for him. The two parents were increasingly at odds, especially over their children's future, which often led to heated arguments. Doc Davis trusted their choices as long as they succeeded, while Cleota Davis could not imagine any option other than following in the footsteps of their father and his brilliant academic achievements. When the couple divorced in 1944, Doc Davis moved to a colonial-style property he bought near Millstadt, eight miles south of East St. Louis, which he named "Mary Frances Manor" after his mother. There, he raised hogs, cows and horses. According to Davis' autobiography, his father became involved in local politics and even ran for office in the state legislature—albeit unsuccessfully.

The destiny of the young Miles Davis, who had his own horse on his father's farm, as he had on his grandfather's, is unique in the overwhelmingly populist world of jazz. At the age of thirteen, he was delivering the *Chicago Defender*, and it was not by chance that he chose black America's leading newspaper: it reflected the racial pride he owed to his father. Davis would say he had also inherited his father's independent spirit, which was what prompted him to earn his own pocket money, even though at various times in his life he was financially dependent on his father. Because of his short stature, Davis was nicknamed Little Davis or Little Doc Davis. He asserted himself by playing baseball and developed an interest in boxing, although he did not practise the sport. He spurned his mother's excessive affections, which he blamed for his brother Vernon's homosexuality. He hid his lifelong shyness behind a fierce arrogance. If he chose the trumpet, it was primarily because he was enthralled by the self-assurance of trumpet players. He probably realized the energy required to play the instrument and would incorporate this into his own on-stage persona.

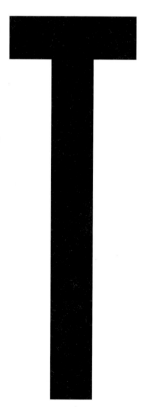

THE ST. LOUIS SOUND. Mrs. Davis would have preferred her son to take up the violin, which she herself played. She also played piano, and Davis would make a surprise discovery: she could play the blues. It was his mother who introduced him to jazz at home, with two recordings: one by Art Tatum and the other by Duke Ellington. In spite of this, she would later prove insensitive to her son's music. For Davis, the violin was a lost cause. St. Louis was a trumpet town, an obligatory stop for the riverboats going up and down the Mississippi, with cornettists and trumpeters from New Orleans who were spreading the gospel of jazz. A distinct school of trumpet playing first emerged in St. Louis around Charles Creath (1896–1951) and Dewey Jackson (1900–1963). These pioneers were followed by George Hudson, Walter "Crack" Stanley, R. Q. Dickerson, Irving "Mouse" Randolph, Bob Merrill, William "Sleepy" Tomlin, Joe Thomas, Louis Metcalf, Ed Allen, Bob Schoffner, Levi Madison, Elwood Buchanan, Harold "Shorty" Baker, Clark Terry and, later, Lester Bowie. British trumpeter Ian Carr describes the St. Louis sound as "a beautifully clear, round and singing brass sound that really projects and hangs on the air [with] an epigramma-

2

The city of St. Louis spawned a dynasty of trumpet players remarkable for their sound: Charlie Creath (opposite page, about 1922) and Dewey Jackson (above, at the Castle Ballroom in St. Louis, 1937) were its founding fathers; Walter "Crack" Stanley, pictured with Floyd Campbell's Singing Syncopators (below, third from right, 1929), one of its earliest descendants.

3

1

2

tic and witty melodic flair." Others have described it in contrast with the style of Louis Armstrong, the father of jazz trumpet, with its greater subtlety and delicacy, epitomized by St. Louis trumpeter Harold "Shorty" Baker (who played with Andy Kirk's and Duke Ellington's orchestras). To Ellington's wife, pianist Mary Lou Williams, Davis is said to have remarked, "Oh, if I could only play as sweet as Harold Baker!" He also had fond memories of Levi Madison. Clark Terry likened Madison's playing to angels singing, but lamented that madness would rob him of any chance at fame.

When did Davis first become aware of the local specialty? The timeline of his learning is unclear. It seems the vocation first surfaced when he was about nine, after a neighbour, Dr. John Eubanks, one of his father's friends, gave him a cornet. The young Davis took lessons with Dr. Eubanks' uncle, Horace Eubanks, a saxophonist and clarinettist. With the latter, he played only sustained notes, using a borrowed method that introduced him to the chromatic scale. He learned enough to be able to play the hits of the day. When he was twelve, he was assigned the task of playing reveille and taps at a Boy Scout summer camp. He listened to late-night jazz shows on the radio. Every morning, he was late for school because of the radio show "Harlem Rhythms." He was first interested in white trumpeter Harry James, a brilliant Louis Armstrong emulator who had a commercial bent and at times an outrageous playing style. However, this orientation was hindered by the lessons Davis took in elementary school and, later, in high school from Elwood Buchanan, his father's client and friend. Buchanan advised him to buy a trumpet to replace the cornet. It would be the elder Davis' gift to his son on his thirteenth birthday.

Elwood Buchanan belonged to the St. Louis school and had made a career playing on the riverboats. His recommended role models for his students were Shorty Baker, with whom he had played in Andy Kirk's orchestra, and the white trumpeter Bobby Hackett, a disciple of Bix Beiderbecke, whose subtle style contrasted with the bright, powerful sound of most trumpet players of the time. As well, by encouraging Davis to drop his Harry James-style vibrato, Buchanan anticipated a trend in modern jazz that involves slowing the vibrato, muting it or even suppressing it altogether, with just a slight ornamentation at the end of the note. Davis also took lessons with the principal trumpeter of the St. Louis Symphony Orchestra, Joseph Gustat, known as the "trumpet guru of the Midwest." They came from far and wide to consult him (Beiderbecke paid him a visit in 1926, followed by well-known players like Dizzy Gillespie and Buddy Childers, Stan Kenton's first trumpet). Many local trumpet players sought his advice, from Levi Madison to Clark Terry and Harold Baker. They all used his recommended mouthpiece, which had been designed for the manufacturer Frank Holton by Gustav Heim, Gustat's predecessor in the first-trumpet chair of the St. Louis Symphony Orchestra, in 1904–5. According to Clark Terry, this mouthpiece would contribute to defining the St. Louis style—and especially that of Miles Davis. It helped produce a full sound, but made playing in the upper register more of a challenge. Davis always carried his Heim mouthpiece with him, even when he did not have his trumpet, and had copies of it made throughout his life. While it caused him problems in the upper register at the beginning of his career, it was also responsible for the silky, singing sound for which he became famous.

FIRST STEPS. Davis saved his money to buy used records from jukeboxes. He did not avoid white musicians, whose big bands had been in vogue following Benny Goodman's success on the radio in 1935. He appreciated Buddy Rich (a virtuoso white drummer and big-band specialist whose meteoric rise began in 1938), Helen Forrest (a white singer who replaced Billie Holiday in Artie Shaw's big band in 1938, before joining Benny

Left to right: Harold "Shorty" Baker (standing, far right, 1932), with pianist Eddie Johnson's Crackerjacks; Levi Madison (second row, third from left, 1936), with the Original St. Louis Crackerjacks; bandleader George Hudson (standing, centre, in dark suit, about 1945) were among the most notable exponents of the St. Louis trumpet. Clark Terry (squatting, third from left) was one of the last proponents of the "St. Louis sound"; he was the teenaged Miles Davis' mentor.

Goodman). Of course, he also listened to black music, including the ubiquitous Louis Armstrong and bandleader Erskine Hawkins, learning the trumpet solo from his big hit of 1939, "Tuxedo Junction." He soon became interested in the musicians of the Midwest, primarily those from Kansas, Oklahoma and Missouri, precursors of the bebop revolution of the 1940s. The eldest was saxophonist Lester Young. His relaxed style, sense of space and attention to melody would have a decisive influence on Davis. He was also interested in Charlie Christian, who revolutionized the guitar while playing with Benny Goodman between 1939 and 1941. In 1938–39, Davis heard bassist Jimmy Blanton, who would take the jazz bass to a new level and who was quickly recruited by Duke Ellington during a stop in St. Louis.

In the early 1940s, Davis started hearing about the exploits of Charlie Parker, nicknamed "Bird," who was spearheading the bebop revolution. Two local musicians would figure in the young musician's development. In 1940, trumpeter Clark Terry became his advisor and chaperone, including him in jam sessions with the musical heavyweights of St. Louis. In 1942, Davis began spending time with pianist Emmanuel St. Claire Brooks, nicknamed "Duke" for his knowledge of Ellington's music. According to Davis, Brooks already played like Bud Powell, the future bebop star, but others said he also played like Art Tatum and Nat King Cole—the former, a forerunner of bebop piano, the latter foreshadowing the pianists with whom Davis would play in the 1950s. Brooks gave him piano and harmony lessons. With drummer Nick Haywood, Brooks and Davis formed a trio inspired by Benny Goodman's. When he was sixteen, Davis met Irene Cawthon, who would become his girlfriend. She believed in his talent and supported him, even if she disapproved of him playing with the bell of his instrument pointed downwards—a life-long habit he developed so he could hear himself better. She encouraged him to join the musicians' union and to apply to work with Eddie Randle's Blue Devils, St. Louis' premier orchestra and house band at the Rhumboogie. Jimmy Forrest, Jimmy Blanton, Clark Terry and Levi Madison had been members of the band. Count Basie's future arranger, Ernie Wilkins, had given them some of his earliest scores and, according to Davis, one of the saxophonists, Clyde Higgins, was already playing like Charlie Parker. It was his wife, Mabel Higgins, the piano player for the orchestra, who helped Davis develop his knowledge of harmony. As various touring bands came through St. Louis, he had the opportunity to jam with Lester Young and the pioneers of bebop: trumpeters Howard McGhee and Theodore "Fats" Navarro, saxophonist Sonny Stitt and even Charlie Parker himself. Davis' admiration for Parker worried Eddie Randle, who advised him not to sacrifice his beautiful tone for the virtuoso playing that typified the rising avant-garde. When Randle assigned him the responsibility of organizing rehearsals, Davis, at age sixteen, became the music director of one of the top bands in town. He drove to work in his father's car, wearing one of the ten suits he had bought at pawn shops, inspired by Fred Astaire and the Duke of Windsor. It was an elegant look, but not exactly in the latest style.

Sonny Stitt tried to lure Miles Davis away, but Mrs. Davis would not allow her son to quit school before graduation. She had hoped to send him off to Fisk University, the acclaimed black university in Nashville, where she had already registered her daughter, Dorothy, and which had a highly reputed music department. Davis had only one desire: to go to New York. His girlfriend, Irene Cawthon, who had been dancing since the age of seven, dreamed of joining the Katherine Dunham Dance Company, the leading African-American modern dance company. She urged Davis to look into enrolling at the celebrated Juilliard School of Music. However, the birth of Cheryl in June 1944 put an end to the young woman's aspirations. This time, it was Doc Davis who refused to grant his son legal authorization to marry a teenaged mother of lower social standing.

Eddie Randle's
RHUMBOOGIE
ORCHESTRA

Trumpeter Eddie Randle's (far right) Blue Devils was the house band at the Rhumboogie, located in the St. Louis Elks Club. Although he was the youngest member of the band, Davis (second row, far right) became its music director, responsible for organizing rehearsals.

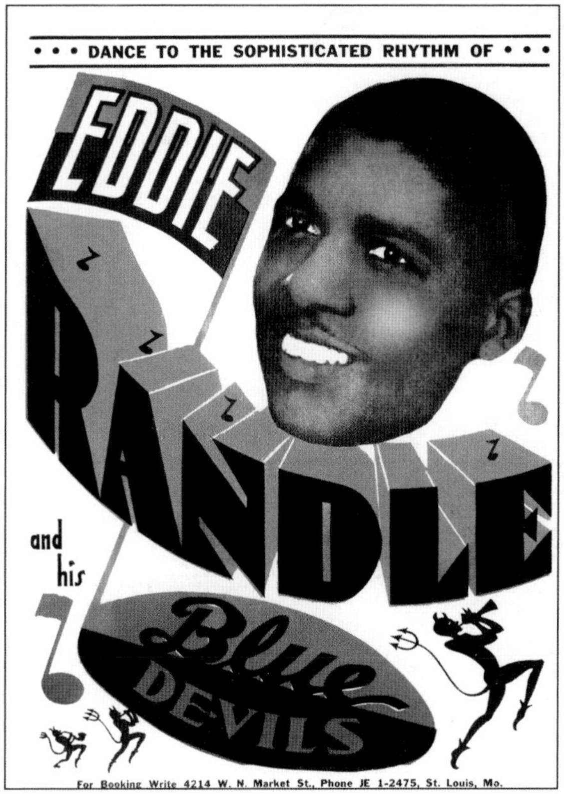
• • • DANCE TO THE SOPHISTICATED RHYTHM OF • • •
EDDIE
RANDLE
and his
Blue
DEVILS
For Booking Write 4214 W. N. Market St., Phone JE 1-2475, St. Louis, Mo.

BEBOP TAKES OFF. Early in the summer of 1944, eighteen-year-old Miles Davis left St. Louis for the first time with a band from New Orleans, Adam Lambert's Six Brown Cats. He was back in the city in July, just in time for the arrival of vocalist and trumpeter Billy Eckstine's big band, composed of the stars of the new bebop style: Dizzy Gillespie as music director, Charlie Parker, Lucky Thompson, Gene Ammons and Leo Parker in the saxophone section, Art Blakey on drums, and singer and pianist Sarah Vaughan. At the whites-only Club Plantation, the musicians in the band flouted the town's Jim Crow codes, and Billy Eckstine had to retreat to the town's black nightspot, the Riviera Club. It was there that Gillespie noticed Davis, who showed up to attend their rehearsals, trumpet case in hand. He suggested Davis replace Buddy Anderson, who had fallen ill, and the young man was barely adequate on trumpet. When the band left for Chicago, Dizzy Gillespie and Charlie Parker managed to convince Davis that his future was in New York. Although the first strains of bebop emerged in part in the large Midwest cities, it was in New York that the new style was flourishing.

Bebop emerged in a society preoccupied by complex issues, and the social context played a major role in the development of the style. The African-American community was preparing to take part in an armed conflict in the service of a nation that had failed to recognize its combat role on the front during World War I. In 1941, community leader Philip A. Randolph had to threaten the federal government with a march on Washington if blacks were excluded from the new jobs tied to the arms industry. In the climate of high racial tensions that led to riots in Detroit and Harlem in 1943, a new generation of African Americans was questioning its destiny and culture.

Featuring bebop's *crème de la crème*, singer Billy Eckstine's big band (below) played St. Louis in summer 1944. Initially booked at the Club Plantation, the band was forced to retreat to another nightclub, the Riviera, after some of the musicians provoked a series of incidents in defiance of the club's management, which enforced segregation, as witnessed by the racist illustrations on the menus. It was at the Riviera Club that Miles Davis met Dizzy Gillespie and Charlie Parker (top left, between Lucky Thompson and Billy Eckstine), the two leading lights of bebop, for whom he would continue to have a deep admiration. This feeling was echoed four decades later in *Horn Players* (1983), a triptych by painter Jean-Michel Basquiat (opposite page).

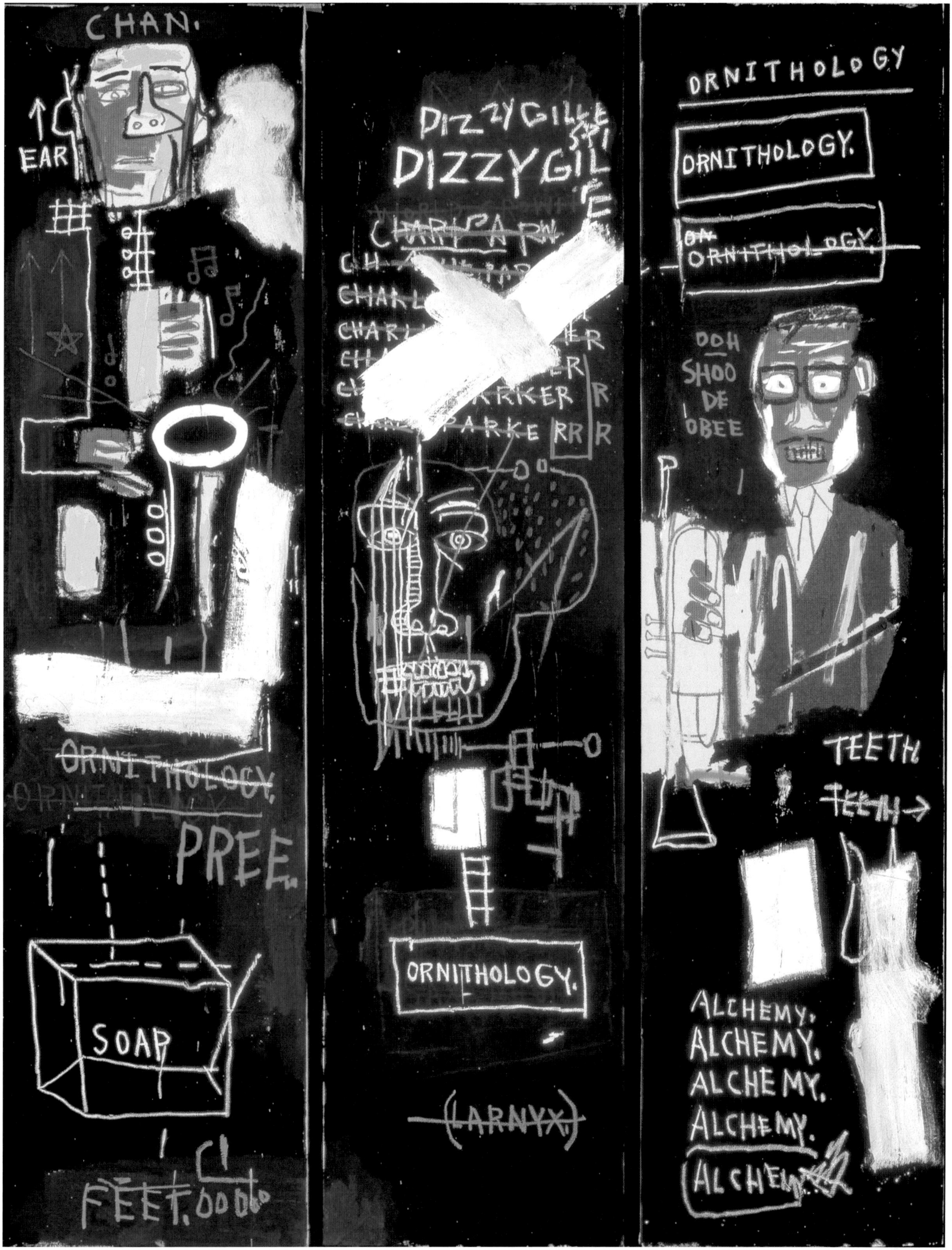
CHAN.
EAR
ORNITHOLOGY
PREE
SOAP
FEET.
DIZZYGILLE SPI
DIZZYGIL
PARKER
PARKE
ORNITHOLOGY.
(LARNYX)
ORNITHOLOGY
ORNITHOLOGY.
ORNITHOLOGY.
OOH
SHOO
DE
OBEE
TEETH.
TEETH
ALCHEMY.
ALCHEMY.
ALCHEMY.
ALCHEMY.
ALCHEM

When he arrived in New York in fall 1944, Miles Davis spent time with the main practitioners of bebop, whose virtuosity he admired, notably trumpeters like Howard McGhee (1947). Photo William P. Gottlieb.

Black musicians were tired of their role as white America's jesters. Some aspired to be considered as authentic artists and shunned the ranks of the large dance bands. Once their regular gigs were over, they preferred to frequent after-hours clubs, where they could experiment with new repertoire in which Broadway songs were distorted into abstract melodies. The harmonies, infused with tension and dissonance, invited improvisers to come up with angular, broken lines interwoven with the polyrhythmic accents of the drums. Along with harmonic and rhythmic virtuosity, there was dazzling instrumental technique, illustrated by the quick tempos, range of registers and bright sound. Compared to the sentimentalism of standard show tunes, bop was erratic, explosive and uncompromising. While America was discovering an artistic elite in New York—with John Cage, Jackson Pollock and Merce Cunningham—which finally distinguished it from Europe, in the clubs of Harlem and Manhattan (especially on Fifty-second Street), the boppers presented the black community with its first avant-garde, which was to transfix Miles Davis.

A MIDDLE-CLASS BOY IN NEW YORK. Miles Davis arrived in New York in late September 1944, with the support of his father, who paid his tuition at Juilliard. One of his first concerns was to find a place where he could go horseback riding. It is understandable that this young middle-class Midwesterner, landing in the bohemian circles of New York bebop, was often misunderstood. After spending a week at the Claremont Hotel recommended by the school, Davis moved to a studio on 149th Street his father had found for him, which was large enough to accommodate a rented piano. With a weekly forty-dollar allowance from his father, Davis had enough money for food and to get around town by taxi. Charlie Parker was soon taking advantage of the largesse of this privileged young man. In December, Cleota Davis agreed to look after Cheryl, and Davis and Irene Cawthon moved into an apartment on 147th Street rented by Bob Bell, a guitarist from St. Louis. Bell and his wife looked after the two lovebirds, inviting them to the restaurant they managed, driving them around, taking them to the races, offering Cawthon a job as a cashier. In 1947, Davis would dedicate "Sippin' at Bells" to them. Charlie Parker shared a room with drummer Stan Levey in the same building. Having developed a taste for Cawthon's cooking, he regularly got himself invited to dinner, while Davis tried to shield Cawthon from the boppers' lifestyle. After Cawthon went back to East St. Louis in the summer of 1945, Davis roomed with Stan Levey, who was puzzled by this young unemployed pedant who dressed in Brooks Brothers suits and whose father paid for tuition at a school he had never heard of.

Davis had nothing good to say about the instruction at Juilliard. He did, however, benefit from private lessons with William Vacchiano, principal trumpeter with the New York Philharmonic, whose students included Mercer Ellington, Duke's son, between 1938 and 1940, and, much later, Wynton Marsalis. In St. Louis, Davis had a habit of ordering scores, and instrumental method and music theory books. In New York, he borrowed Stravinsky, Berg and Prokofiev scores from the library, and when he attended classical music concerts, he would sometimes bring the score to follow along during the performance.

Disdainful of the lack of culture and curiosity in his black colleagues, Davis was keenly aware that black music was not getting the recognition it deserved at Juilliard. He kept his distance from white students. His grades steadily declined: at the end of his first year, he had to take make-up summer courses, but he later claimed to have skimmed through the program in a day (analyses of Mozart's *Requiem* and Hindemith's *Kleine Kammermusik* for wind quintet). When the academic year began in 1945, he went back to East St. Louis to explain to his father why he was dropping out of Juilliard.

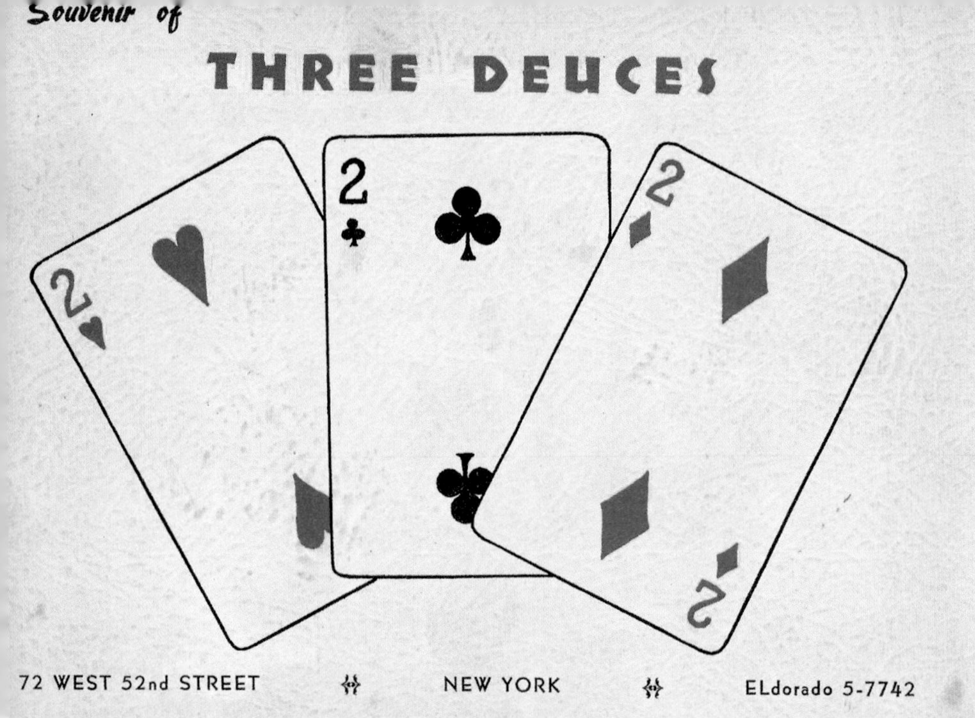

Once known as "Swing Street," West Fifty-second Street in Manhattan was home to the main jazz clubs outside Harlem in the mid-1940s. It was split between the "traditionalists" and the "modernists," but not everyone was inclined to welcome the boppers, for fear that their rough-edged music would drive away patrons who came primarily to eat, drink and be entertained.

The Onyx, Downbeat, Spotlite and Three Deuces were most receptive to the novelty of bebop. The Royal Roost, the self-proclaimed "Bopera House" (at the corner of Forty-seventh and Broadway), the self-explanatory Bop City (on Forty-ninth) and, beginning in 1949, Birdland (on Fifty-second), inspired by Charlie Parker's nickname, were the modern jazz hotspots where Miles Davis often played.

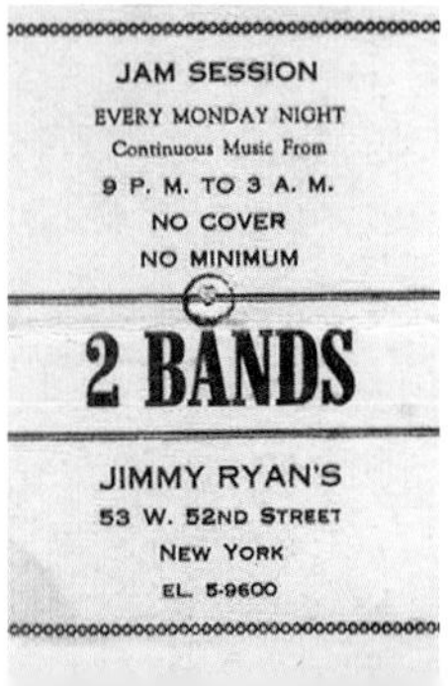

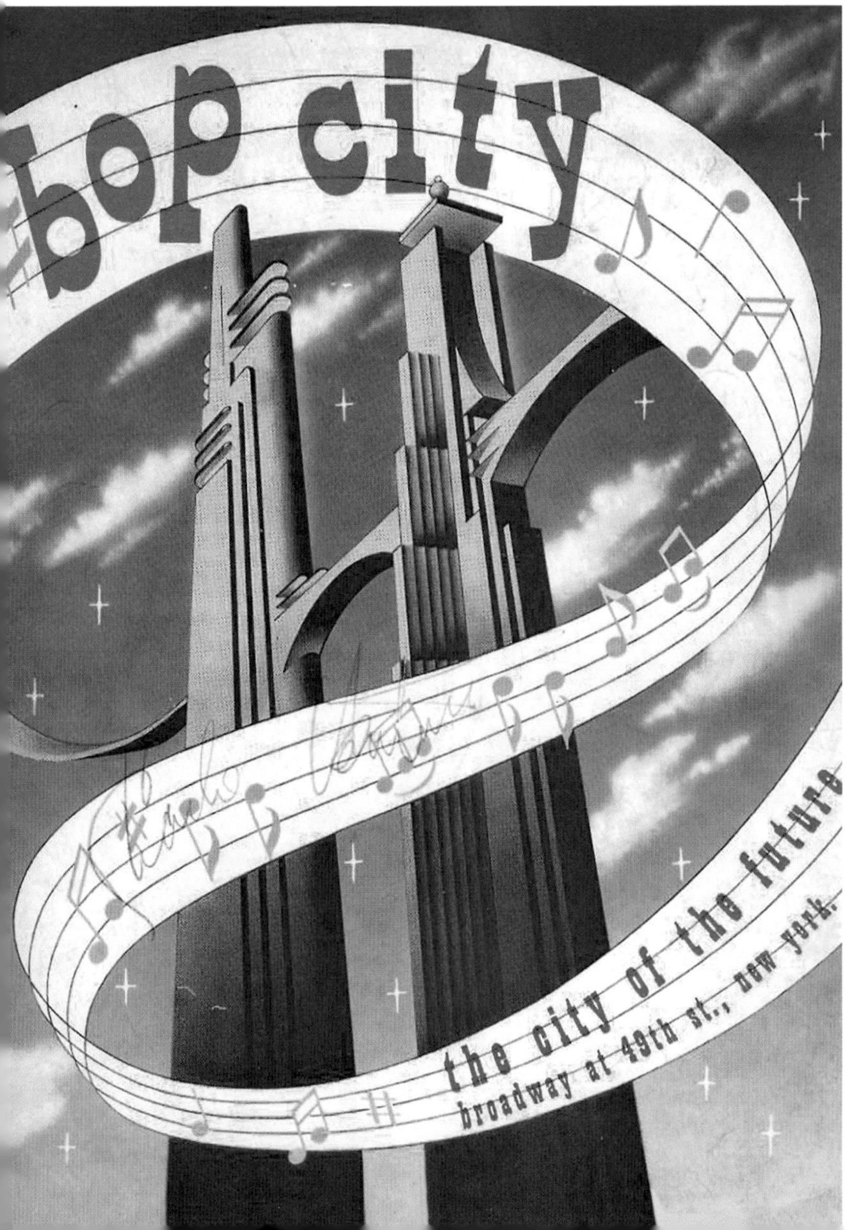

bop city
the city of the future
broadway at 49th st., new york

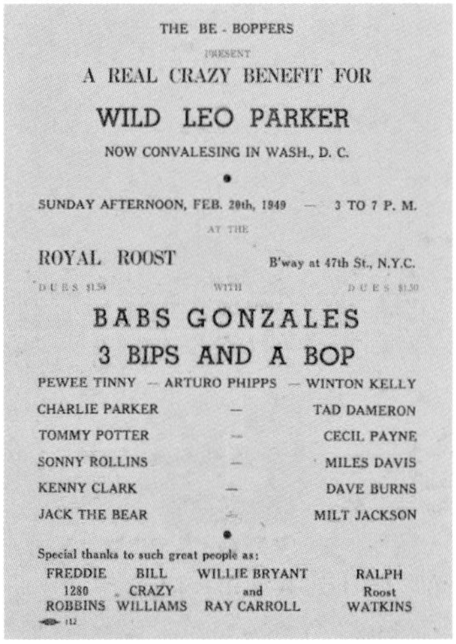
THE BE - BOPPERS

PRESENT

A REAL CRAZY BENEFIT FOR

WILD LEO PARKER

NOW CONVALESING IN WASH., D. C.

•

SUNDAY AFTERNOON, FEB. 20th, 1949 — 3 TO 7 P. M.

AT THE

ROYAL ROOST B'way at 47th St., N.Y.C.

DUES $1.50 WITH DUES $1.50

BABS GONZALES

3 BIPS AND A BOP

PEWEE TINNY — ARTURO PHIPPS — WINTON KELLY

CHARLIE PARKER — TAD DAMERON

TOMMY POTTER — CECIL PAYNE

SONNY ROLLINS — MILES DAVIS

KENNY CLARK — DAVE BURNS

JACK THE BEAR — MILT JACKSON

•

Special thanks to such great people as:

FREDDIE 1280 ROBBINS	BILL CRAZY WILLIAMS	WILLIE BRYANT and RAY CARROLL	RALPH Roost WATKINS

112

birdland
on broadway at 52nd street
... where the "bill" is always low!

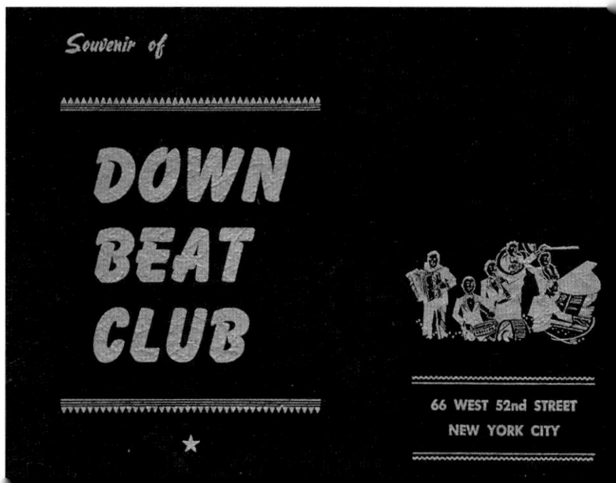

Miles Davis returned to the quintet formed by Charlie Parker (centre left) in 1947, after Parker's release from the psychiatric hospital in Camarillo, California, and his own return to New York. Pianist Duke Jordan (from the back), bassist Tommy Potter (left) and drummer Max Roach (hidden) made up the rhythm section of this group, which took up residence at the Three Deuces on Fifty-second Street.

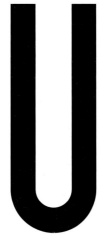

UNDER BIRD'S WING. After arriving in New York, Miles Davis roamed the city from Harlem to Fifty-second Street. He found Charlie Parker and Dizzy Gillespie and met Coleman Hawkins, who was accompanied by Thelonious Monk. He got along well with trumpeter Freddie Webster, who lived in the same apartment building and was ten years his senior. Webster played with the warm, mellow sound and relaxed phrasing of the St. Louis trumpeters transposed into the language of bebop. Davis shared what he had learned at Juilliard, and Webster recommended Davis as his replacement on a couple of occasions. From March 1945 on, they were always at the Three Deuces to hear Dizzy Gillespie and Charlie Parker, taking note of the chord progressions they heard. Sometimes a petrified Davis would even join his idols on stage.

While people were put off by his awkwardness, they were not indifferent, and on April 24, 1945, upon Dizzy and Bird's recommendation, he played his first recording session with the singer Rubberlegs Williams. He hid his nervousness behind his mute, far away from the microphone, avoiding solos, delivering a lovely, dreamy obbligato that hinted at something that was only just nascent. Its daring handful of Gillespie-style sixteenth notes was somehow out of place in this jump and bluesy context that foreshadowed rock and roll. That same spring, Davis rehearsed with Gillespie's big band, and sat in as needed for Joe Guy with Coleman Hawkins at the Downbeat. He got his first official New York job with saxophonist Eddie "Lockjaw" Davis at the Spotlite. In October, Charlie Parker hired him for his quintet, playing at the Three Deuces, the Spotlite and Minton's Playhouse. The group recorded for Savoy Records on November 26, 1945. In December, an all-star bebop team fronted by Dizzy Gillespie and Charlie Parker travelled to Los Angeles. Davis went to spend Christmas with his family in East St. Louis. When alto saxophonist Benny Carter came to town, Davis jumped at the opportunity to play with his big band, which was heading back to Los Angeles. Once there, he again teamed up with Charlie Parker and recorded with him for the Dial label. These tracks led to his being named a "New Star" in the 1947 *Esquire* critics' poll. Meanwhile, Parker was slipping deeper into drug addiction and was hospitalized in Camarillo, California, from July 1946 to February 1947. Davis next worked with tenor saxophonist Lucky Thompson, took part in some of Charles Mingus' early experimental big-band sessions and finally returned to the East Coast in the late fall with Billy Eckstine and His Orchestra. He saw Gregory, the son born to Irene Cawthon during his absence, for the first time.

After Eckstine's band broke up in February 1947, Davis joined Dizzy Gillespie's big band, where he played alongside Freddie Webster, Kenny Dorham and Fats Navarro, the high priests of bebop trumpet (Webster would be among the first to fall victim to the scourge of drugs that had begun to ravage the world of bebop). When Charlie Parker reappeared, Davis immediately agreed to his proposal to put together a quintet, becoming its music director. Max Roach was his main ally, while they were more or less pleased with Duke Jordan and bassist Tommy Potter. They managed to get Bud Powell to play piano in a second session for Savoy on May 8, 1947, to which Davis contributed "Donna Lee," his first recorded composition, erroneously credited to Charlie Parker. On August 14, Davis was back in the studio, for the first time under his own name, again with Charlie Parker and Max Roach, but this time with a pianist and bassist he had chosen himself, John Lewis and Nelson Boyd. He continued to play with the Charlie Parker Quintet until the end of 1948. In December, tired of the saxophonist's erratic behaviour, Davis, who had just put together his nonet, quit the group.

Among the "elders," saxophonist Coleman Hawkins was one of the rare few to look favourably on the young Turks of bebop and was therefore one of the first to hire Miles Davis. Here, at the Three Deuces in 1947. Photo William P. Gottlieb.

In 1947, Miles Davis (back row, second from left) played briefly in the trumpet section of his mentor Dizzy Gillespie's big band. Here, at the Downbeat Club in New York. Photo William P. Gottlieb.

Admitted to the bebop brotherhood, Miles Davis befriended the main proponents of the style. Charlie Parker, Miles Davis, Allen Eager and Kai Winding, at the Royal Roost, 1948. Photo Herman Leonard.

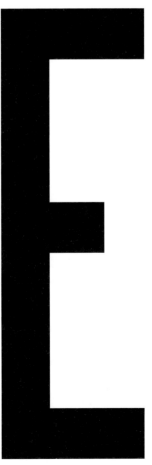

E**MERGENCE OF A STYLE.** For those who were surprised by the pairing of Miles Davis and Charlie Parker after Parker's association with Dizzy Gillespie, the Savoy session on November 26, 1945, provided some initial answers. On "Thriving on a Riff" (a characteristically bop theme that would be renamed "Anthropology"), Davis comes across as a Gillespie disciple, still insecure, using a mute to hide behind Parker in the theme statement. His articulation is somewhat awkward; he slows the tempo, repeats the same notes and struggles to order his phrases. There was something dogmatic about this young bopper, who had "his fingers glued in positions corresponding to diminished fifths," the dissonant sounds so dear to boppers. The effect of the Heim mouthpiece is evident in that it made it impossible for him to play high notes with any brightness; venturing beyond his range was extremely risky. Was it a technical limitation or a question of musical personality? "Why can't I play high like you?" Davis asked Dizzy one day, to which Dizzy replied, "Because you can't hear up there. You hear in the middle register." Davis' solos for the moderately tempoed blues tunes "Billie's Bounce" and "Now's the Time" provide additional insight.

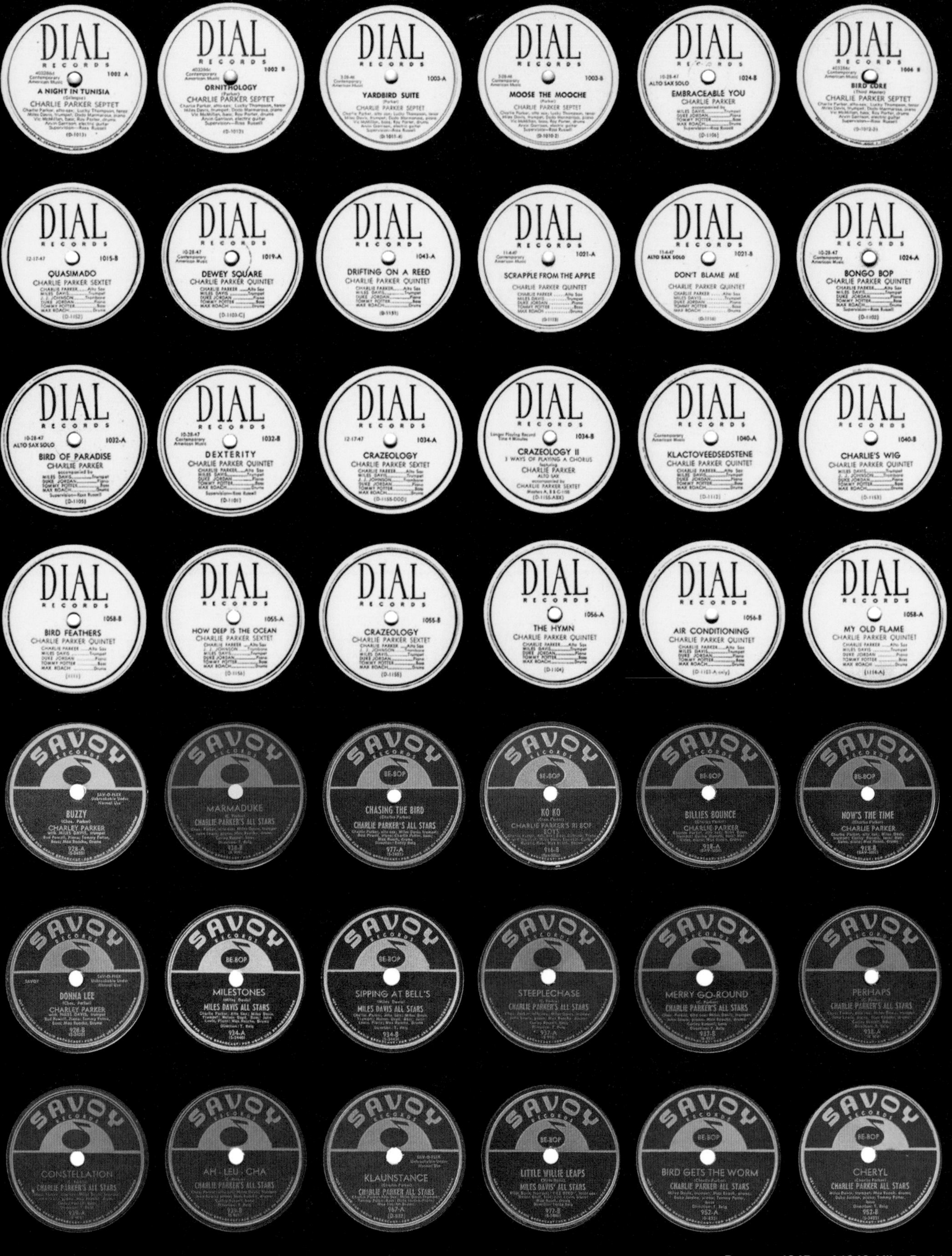

Between 1945 and 1948, Miles Davis took part in several recording sessions with Charlie Parker for the Dial and Savoy labels, which yielded a great many seventy-eights that have become collectors' items and—for painter Jean-Michel Basquiat—a source of fascination. Opposite page: *Bird of Paradise*, 1984.

"RELAXING AT CAMIRILLO" 1946©
DIAL RECORDS
BARONESS PANNONICA DE KOENIGSWATER©
"SWEDEN"
CHARLIE PARKER'S SAXOPHONE CAUSE
DIZZY
MILES DAVIS
BLUE DEVILS©
CHAN
BUD POWELL
FAT NAVARRO
MERCURY© MERCURY 1946 NOV 30
MERCURY
DIAL
RECORDS
SAX SOLO 1032-A
BIRD OF
PARADISE

Fats Navarro, Miles Davis and Kai Winding at the Clique Club (later Birdland) in January 1949. In the late 1940s, Miles Davis offered a distinct alternative to the bebop trumpet as played by Dizzy Gillespie and Fats Navarro.

The anonymous *Down Beat* columnist saw Davis' lack of taste and harmonic mistakes as symptomatic of the younger generation's exaggerated fascination with Gillespie's pyrotechnics. In contrast, Boris Vian wrote in *Jazz News* in May 1949, "One of the greatest moments in bop, in my opinion, is Miles Davis' chorus in 'Now's the Time.'" While Davis' orthodoxy is still discernible, the blues choruses seem the result of intensive premeditation leading to the extraordinary rhythmic construction on the fourth take of "Now's the Time" and the clarity of the ideas on the third take of "Billie's Bounce." These different attempts reveal an ambitious—if slightly arrogant—personality, determined to transcend the ordinary, not with flashiness, which his technical means prevented, but with the challenges he set himself by making difficult choices about the notes, their placement, as well as the Heim mouthpiece.

Davis' repertoire for his first session as leader shows the degree to which he dogmatically adhered to the boppers' harmonic views in music full of chromatics, but with an expressive restraint that contrasted with bop's aggressiveness. From November 1946 to the end of 1948, the ensuing recordings confirm Davis' two-faceted evolution as he gained growing mastery over the bop idiom in the fast tempos (such as "Bird Gets the Worm" from December 21, 1947, and "Constellation" from September 18, 1948), but with a tone and delicacy in the melodic and rhythmic constructions evident in the medium and slow tempos that heralded cool jazz ("All the Things You Are" and "Embraceable You" from October 28, 1947, and "Bluebird" from December 21, 1947). In the studio, the repeats from one take to the next betray the meticulous planning of each solo, while the Royal Roost concerts broadcast in December 1948 reveal the continuous interplay between Davis and Max Roach. In future, Davis' primary dialogue would be with the drummer of his band.

OUT OF THE COOL INVENTION AND SELF-LOATHING

1948–1955

In late 1947, Miles Davis met a beanpole of a man fourteen years his senior, who wanted permission to arrange "Donna Lee." Canadian-born Gil Evans was self-taught, having learned how to arrange by listening to seventy-eights of the big bands of the 1930s and 1940s. At the time of his first meeting with Davis, he was arranging music for the Claude Thornhill Orchestra. Thornhill was a white musician with very unusual ideas for the time. He eschewed vibrato and the brightness of the upper register in favour of soft orchestral layers, adding the flute, French horn and tuba to the usual big band sections (trumpets, trombones and saxophones). Davis agreed to Evans' request in exchange for the opportunity to consult his scores. The young trumpeter soon began spending time in Evans' one-room basement apartment, outfitted with a bed, desk, upright piano and phonograph. Day and night, people sat around the record player, listening to Charlie Parker and Lester Young, as well as Igor Stravinsky, Paul Hindemith, Maurice Ravel and Alban Berg. While he met up with a few of the boppers there—such as Max Roach, Charlie Parker and John Lewis—it was also an opportunity for Davis to reconcile his interest in classical music with his espousal of the jazz avant-garde in the company of arrangers like George Russell. With one of the most devoted regulars, baritone saxophonist Gerry Mulligan, Gil Evans had been

Other than a few concerts at the Royal Roost where the group made its debut in September 1948, the Birth of the Cool nonet existed only in the studio, recording for Capitol. Opposite page: the session on January 21, 1949. Photo Popsie Randolph.

toying with the possibility of assembling an experimental band to try out the ideas they came up with during their discussions. Davis took charge, organizing rehearsals to play arrangements by Evans, Mulligan, Johnny Carisi and John Lewis.

THE BIRTH OF THE COOL. The resulting nine-member ensemble broke with the orchestral logic of the big swing bands. The trumpet, trombone and saxophone sections were replaced by individual voices, divided among the instruments with sounds in the mellow middle and low registers (French horn, trombone, baritone saxophone and tuba). Although he was the natural choice for alto saxophone, Charlie Parker declined the offer. Gerry Mulligan convinced Miles Davis not to replace Parker with Sonny Stitt, who was closest to Parker aesthetically and who might have compromised their efforts to veer off the beaten path of bebop. In the end, it was white saxophonist Lee Konitz, a member of the Claude Thornhill Orchestra, who was assigned the alto saxophone chair, with his muted sound and relaxed articulation contrasting with bebop's erratic, rough sound. For Davis, it was the ideal setting in which the legacy of St. Louis, as he had begun to appropriate it through the language of bop, could blossom. It was also Davis who got the orchestra a two-week stint at the recently opened Royal Roost on Broadway, under the name of the Miles Davis Nonet. The poster at the club's entrance read, "Miles Davis Band, Arrangements by Gerry Mulligan, Gil Evans and John Lewis." This was revolutionary: arrangers' names were not normally advertised. However, nothing about the nonet's music qualified it as entertainment, and the audience, more accustomed to jazz they could dance to, was perplexed, even though Davis, slowing down the frenetic bop tempos, hoped to make the avant-garde compositions more accessible. While some black musicians accused him of betraying black music, Count Basie, who was on the same bill, had only praise: "Those slow things sounded strange and good. I didn't always know what they were doing, but I listened, and I liked it." Many musicians came to hear the orchestra, including arranger Pete Rugolo, who was working for a new record label recently established in Hollywood. On January 5, 1949, Miles Davis signed on with Capitol Records, and his nonet was soon in the studio for the first of three sessions.

In addition to its orchestral colours, expressive half tones, sophisticated harmonies and use of counterpoint—the strangeness culminating in Gil Evans' "Moon Dreams" with its almost suspended tempo—the nonet's repertoire is marked by the structural boldness of some of the arrangements, which completely break with the practices of the time: Gerry Mulligan's "Jeru," with its short passages in three-quarter time; "Boplicity," with a distension of the harmonic structure after the baritone solo that confuses the listener; "Deception," with similar distended stretches accentuated by suspensions of harmonic movement that foreshadow the modal jazz Davis would adopt at the end of the next decade. Far removed from the urgency of bop while greatly elevating the new jazz's harmonic concerns, Davis' playing conveyed a mixture of detachment and interiority, relaxation and intensity, natural and melodic angularity, through which an already utterly unique personality emerged.

Intended as a laboratory for composers, the nonet had only one arrangement by Miles Davis in its repertoire, an adaptation of "Conception" by George Shearing, which was recorded under the title "Deception" and credited to the trumpet player. Initially released as *Classics in Jazz* on Capitol, these recordings, designated the "origin of cool," were reissued on LP in the mid-1950s (below).

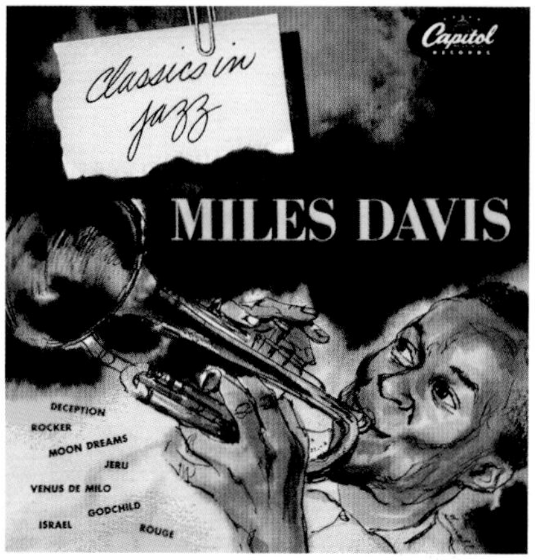

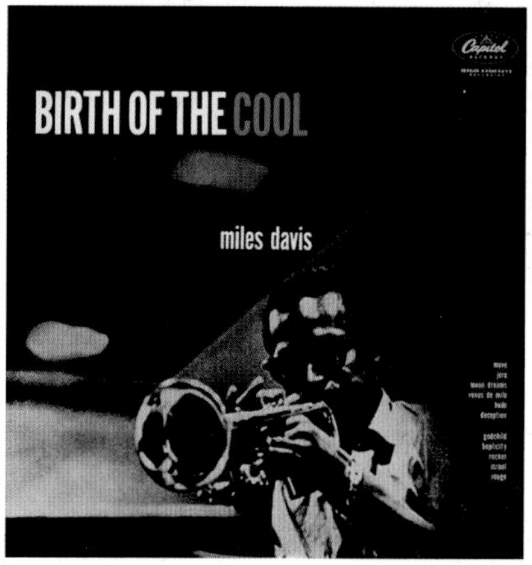

Alto saxophonist Lee Konitz (centre) and baritone saxophonist Gerry Mulligan (right), two of the main members of the Birth of the Cool nonet, went on to become major figures in cool jazz.

THIS WHITE GUY

In summer 1948, at the age of eighteen, I was in New York on vacation from the University of Miami, where I was majoring in sailing. No, actually sixteen of us were on scholarship to play dinner music in the student cafeteria, which was cantilevered over an artificial lake. When we played the way we wanted, we sounded like Stan Kenton. It was kind of like sailing at that.

In those days, I played my trombone like a kid skiing slalom, with more courage than finesse. The possibility of falling on my white face never occurred to me.

One night, I drove over the Triborough Bridge from my parents' house in Queens to Minton's Playhouse, in Harlem, where bebop was born. I parked on 108th Street, walked into the club with all the attitude I could muster, and played "Walkin'" with Art Blakey's band. Blakey was then known as Abdullah Buhaina.

Around 3 a.m., Miles, who had been in a dark corner—Miles always seemed to be in dark corners—came over as I packed up my horn. I slunk into a cool slouch; I used to practise cool slouches. We were both wearing dark shades, cool as can be.

"You got eyes to make a rehearsal tomorrow?" Miles asked me. "I guess so," I said, as though I didn't give one shit for his stupid rehearsal. "Nola's. Four." Miles made it absolutely clear that he could not care less if I showed up or not. Driving back over the bridge, I felt like a bat-boy who had just been offered a tryout with the team.

At 4 p.m., I found myself with Gerry Mulligan, Max Roach, John Lewis, Lee Konitz, Junior Collins, Bill Barber and Al McKibbon playing arrangements by Mulligan and Gil Evans. What we had in common was that we all played behind the beat with no vibrato, which was what made us "cool."

Miles was . . . cool. It was his first time as a leader, and he mostly relied on Gil to conduct the rehearsal. He must have picked up his famous salty act later, because he was a shy sweetheart back then.

About half of us were white, and I never thought twice about it. It did not seem historic or legendary. Who could have imagined that those two weeks with Miles in a Broadway jazz joint called the Royal Roost would give birth to an entire style? And that we'd still be talking about it sixty years later?

My seat on the bandstand was right next to Max Roach's high-hat cymbals. I missed several entrances listening to the complexity of his playing. The first week, we played opposite Count Basie, with Wardell Gray on saxophone. For the first time, Basie had a tenor player who could be considered in the same breath as my hero, Lester Young.

I was in love with music. She was my obsession. I could not see straight for love of her. But if music was, as Duke Ellington put it, my "mistress," we were to have a stormy affair. I cheated on her, lied to, neglected and beat on her. She was demanding. When she nagged, I left her, and when I neglected her she left me. I was to spend my life under too many hats.

Over the years, after I started to write words for a living, I interviewed Miles many times. He always greeted me with a hug. Once, when I asked him why he had hired me, he replied, "I liked your sound." It was the finest compliment I will ever receive.

In his autobiography, his description of our relationship went like this: "J. J. Johnson . . . was busy . . . so we settled on a white guy." Which is just about the way it was.

MIKE ZWERIN

JOURNALIST AND MUSICIAN MIKE ZWERIN HAS BEEN POP-MUSIC CRITIC FOR THE *INTERNATIONAL HERALD TRIBUNE* FOR MANY YEARS. HE IS AUTHOR OF *LA TRISTESSE DE SAINT LOUIS: SWING UNDER THE NAZIS* (QUARTET BOOKS, 1985). IN 1949, HE WAS BRIEFLY A MEMBER OF THE ORCHESTRA KNOWN AS BIRTH OF THE COOL.

*A previous version of this text appears in the liner notes of the CD *The Complete Birth of the Cool* (1998).

Although fleeting, the Parisian love affair between Juliette Gréco and Miles Davis, in spring 1949, deeply affected the musician and helped make him part of the legend of Saint-Germain-des-Prés. Photo Jean-Philippe Charbonnier.

SUCCESS IN PARIS. In addition to his final dates with Charlie Parker and his activities with the nonet, Miles Davis was diversifying, directing a quintet with Lee Konitz and the nonet's rhythm section, and playing with bassist Oscar Pettiford's orchestra. On January 3, 1949, he joined Dizzy Gillespie and Fats Navarro in the studio as part of an all-star ensemble put together by *Metronome* magazine. In the recording of this session, the respective styles of the three trumpeters can barely be distinguished. Davis also replaced Fats Navarro in pianist and arranger Tadd Dameron's big band. When Dameron was invited to put together a quintet to perform at the Paris Jazz Festival, he offered Davis the trumpet part. On May 8, at Salle Pleyel, Davis' bop was more flamboyant than ever. He dared to venture into sixteenth notes and the upper register, in addition to devising phrases very much his own, notably in the ballads ("Don't Blame Me"), in calm moments and in his use of silence ("Wah Hoo"), in the dramatization of the introductions ("Rifftide") and the codas ("Don't Blame Me," "Good Bait," "Lady Bird"), as well as the interplay with drummer Kenny Clarke ("Wah Hoo").

1

2

It was during this two-week stay that Davis met Juliette Gréco, a figure in post-war Saint-Germain-des-Prés, who had not yet embarked on her singing career. She spoke only a few words of English, he spoke not a word of French, but they fell for each other. Although it first went unnoticed, the affair progressively became part of the Davis legend. Its significance for Davis has to be placed against the dazzling backdrop of Paris. For the first time, he found himself dealing with international-star status, because his self-assurance in Tadd Dameron's group on stage at the Pleyel established him as the real leader of the band. He discovered that French audiences had an appreciation for jazz he had yet to see in the United States, and this appreciation found a voice in the writings of Boris Vian. Vian introduced him to the French intelligentsia, from Jean-Paul Sartre to Pablo Picasso, and guided him around Paris, a fascinating cultural capital for someone from the New World. In this city where the colour of his skin (and his physical beauty) elicited only curiosity, attraction and fascination, he discovered a freedom that had been hitherto denied him. It was embodied in the possibility of a relationship with a white woman, which, against the bohemian backdrop of Saint-Germain-des-Prés, met with no criticism. The wonder inspired by the woman he nicknamed his "Gypsy girl" cast a cruel shadow over his relationship with Irene Cawthon, which had been undermined by the clash of ordinary family life with his nocturnal world.

COOL RECEPTION. The return to the United States was brutal. The triumph in Paris was followed by the indifference of an America that had been plunged into the Cold War and the Communist witch hunts. In a country clinging desperately to its values, belonging to the black minority was not an advantage for anyone looking to follow the road less travelled. Black audiences turned away from bebop, which they felt was too complicated, in favour of music that was easier to dance to. The big-band leaders who had put the swing into the 1930s were disbanding their orchestras and scaling back to more economically viable formulas, to compete with jump bands, precursors of rock and roll, then in fashion. Moreover, the world of bebop found itself decimated by hard drug use. Falling victim to economic decline and unrelenting police scrutiny, the clubs on Fifty-second Street closed down one after another. Those on Central Avenue, that remarkable hotbed of black jazz in Los Angeles, met with the same fate. The only creative sector to survive was cool jazz, considered fresh by some, cold by others. Dominated by Charlie Parker's white successors, it was decidedly more relaxed than the edgy sound of New York bop. Followers of Lennie Tristano on the East Coast, and musicians from Woody Herman's and Stan Kenton's big bands on the West Coast, drew from the innovations of bebop to come up with erudite music with mellow sounds and soft angles, adopting their penchant for counterpoint and orchestral development from classical music, but with a relaxed feel inspired by Lester Young.

In some ways, Miles Davis was one of them. His trumpet style, although inspired by Charlie Parker and Dizzy Gillespie, was distinguished from theirs by the relaxed sound characteristic of Lester Young. He shared a common cause with Gil Evans (who would, nevertheless, fail to benefit from the golden age of cool jazz), Gerry Mulligan (who would soon spearhead California cool with Chet Baker) and Lee Konitz (a follower of Lennie Tristano and soloist with Stan Kenton). While it had a decisive influence on the band music flourishing on the West Coast with Shorty Rogers', Dave Pell's and Marty Paich's bands, Davis' nonet did not survive its initial gig at the Royal Roost, nor its three sessions for Capitol. Davis soon identified with the bitterness affecting the black jazz community, refusing to hide his anger when the group's recordings were issued in 1954 on an LP entitled *Birth of the Cool*.

Left to right: Invited in 1949 to take part in the first jazz festival presented in Paris after the war, the Miles Davis–Tadd Dameron Quintet (pictured at the right at Salle Pleyel) represented modern jazz in a program that also included trumpeter Hot Lips Page, trombonist Big Chief Russell Moore, clarinettist Sidney Bechet and the Charlie Parker Quintet (Idlewild Airport, New York, before departure). Boris Vian (below), one of Miles Davis' main champions in France, took great delight in introducing the trumpeter to existentialism and taking him to the nightclubs of Saint-Germain-des-Prés during his stay. Photo (right) Pierre Delord.

3

4

Beyond the music he performed, Miles Davis was the epitome of the cool jazz cat: a combination of nonchalance, detachment and elegance, immortalized backstage at the Shrine Auditorium, in Los Angeles, in 1950.
Photo Bob Willoughby.

1

2

3

Left to right, top to bottom: After the commercial failure of the nonet, Miles Davis renewed ties with the main exponents of bebop, such as bassist Oscar Pettiford, pianist Bud Powell, vibraphonist Milt Jackson and trombonist J. J. Johnson. In September 1950, Davis met up with some of them and their West Coast counterparts at Bop City, in San Francisco, while waiting for his court appearance for heroin possession after his arrest in Los Angeles (below, beside Dizzy Gillespie on the piano). Photo (top right) Marcel Fleiss.

DESCENT INTO HELL. Still, Miles Davis remained marked by the orchestra experience he sought to prolong. In summer 1949, he attempted—in vain—to put together a big band with Tadd Dameron. At Birdland, which had opened on Broadway, he headed a sextet with trombonist J. J. Johnson, saxophonists Stan Getz, Wardell Gray and Sonny Rollins, performing a repertoire that continued the ideas of the nonet and which gave J. J. Johnson an opportunity to try his hand at writing. Davis also recorded a handful of tracks with Sarah Vaughan for Columbia, on which his superb countermelodies can be heard. However, his life was following bop's slide. Since 1947, he had lived with Irene Cawthon and his two children in Jamaica, and then in St. Albans, both neighbourhoods in suburban Queens. Spending his nights in Harlem and Manhattan, where he had to put in a regular appearance so as not to slip into oblivion, he was pulled further away from suburban family life. He spiralled downwards into the nightmare of hard drugs. Cawthon was alarmed by his absences and increasing emotional distance. She made a futile attempt to get him to see a psychologist and alerted his father. To be closer to his work and drug supply, Davis moved his family to Manhattan, where the singer Betty Carter agreed to share her apartment (and the rent) and look after the children while Cawthon worked at the Brooklyn Jewish Hospital. In summer 1950, Davis sent his family to live with his mother, who had just bought a place in Chicago, where his sister, Dorothy, was teaching and his brother, Vernon, was studying music. It was there that Miles IV was born.

On September 15, 1950, while touring with Billy Eckstine's orchestra in Los Angeles, Davis and Art Blakey landed in jail for possession of heroin. Davis managed to convince the court of his innocence, but the affair went public when *Down Beat* magazine published an article on drugs and jazz that mentioned the Davis–Blakey case. In February 1951, *Ebony* addressed the subject in an article by singer Cab Calloway, entitled "Is Dope Killing Our Musicians?" Without naming names, Calloway cited the case of a young trumpeter recently arrested on the West Coast for possession of heroin. Even as *Metronome* magazine readers voted him top jazz trumpet player for 1950, rumours were flying: Miles Davis was not as good as he once was, Miles Davis had personal problems, Miles Davis could no longer be relied upon. The contracts virtually dried up.

THE BAD BOY AND THE WOMEN WHO SAVED HIM. To support his habit, Miles Davis would sometimes pawn his trumpet. He played on instruments he borrowed or rented, notably from Art Farmer. One day, Clark Terry found him sitting on the curb and took him back to his place. As Davis left unceremoniously, he took his friend's clothes, radio and trumpet, which he promptly pawned. In his autobiography, Davis intrigued many when he divulged he had resorted to pimping. While he never did so in the true sense of the word, he got into the habit of accepting money from women, whether or not they were prostitutes, who took an interest in him. With the exception of his father, it seems he accepted help only from women. They came to his rescue at critical moments in his life. This need for women and the power of attraction he exerted over them reveal an aspect of his personality. Although he does not disclose any surprises about Davis' power to attract and seduce, one of his biographers, John Szwed, stresses the fact that these women came from diametrically opposed segments of society.

In 1953, Miles Davis travelled with drummer Max Roach to Los Angeles, where Roach had been hired to play with the house band at the Lighthouse Café, a favourite haunt of West Coast musicians. While there, he met Chet Baker (left), who, while inspired by Davis' style, soon outranked him in popularity polls. Right: trumpeter Rolf Ericson. Photo Cecil Charles.

Sometimes, their social status was ambiguous, as in the case of Juliette Gréco, who represented both elite and bohemian Paris. Then there was another white woman from actor George Raft's circle, possibly a call girl, who came to Davis' rescue when he was going through tough economic times in Los Angeles, in spring 1946.

In the early 1950s, Davis took up with prostitutes who sought out his company and cared for him, but he also associated with women from good families, usually white. In St. Louis, in 1951, he met the daughter of one of the owners of Buster Brown Shoes. Although his parents objected to him going out with a white woman whose family spurned him, the relationship lasted until at least 1955. During this time, he also had an ongoing relationship in New York with a white call girl named Nancy, who sent him money to bring his quintet back from Quebec City, where they were stranded. He also saw Susan Garvin (comparing her to Kim Novak), who helped him during his years of depression and to whom he dedicated his piece "Lazy Susan" in 1954. He went out with Jean Bach, a rising radio personality he met in 1952. In Detroit, where he spent the winter of 1953–54, he let himself be supported by both a young designer (who had him make an appointment with a psychiatrist) and by a young woman whom he apparently abused so badly that he was threatened by one of the gangsters who controlled the Blue Bird Inn, where he was playing. He had to leave town.

Should this duality be seen as indicative of someone torn between his middle-class origins and the harsh music world of New York, between his interest in serious Western music and his desire to put down roots in the earthiness of the blues? Was his descent into a drug-fuelled hell the price he had to pay to be fully accepted by the New York musicians, who did not know what to make of his pedantry and his lifestyle? Was his neurotic use of African-American slang, like his admission of being a pimp, a way to erase the stigma of his social origins, or was it a way of disguising his shyness and lack of self-assurance?

RELAPSES. In any case, boxing was definitely part of Miles Davis' system of protection. It was drummer Stan Levey, a former professional, who introduced Davis to the sport in 1945 and began taking him to training gyms. In 1950, Davis met Johnny Bratton in Chicago, with whom he began boxing seriously. However, when he asked Bobby McQuillen to coach him, McQuillen made it clear he did not train drug addicts. Along with this rebuke, there was soon pressure from his father. The elder Davis had never stopped sending money, but one night in December 1951, he showed up at the Downbeat Club where his son was performing with Jackie McLean, to try to force him to kick his drug habit, bringing him first to his farm and then to East St. Louis, where he was placed under Mrs. Davis' supervision. When Davis began spending time at the Barrelhouse Club with saxophonist Jimmy Forrest, Davis relapsed and his father had him put in jail. Upon his release, the trumpeter agreed to be taken to the Federal Narcotics Hospital in Lexington, where many other jazzmen had been treated. However, when it came time to be admitted, he managed to convince his father that the two weeks he had spent in jail had been enough to break the habit.

Davis immediately fell off the wagon again. In 1953, Cawthon was back in New York and hunted him down in the clubs in the hope of extracting financial support for their children. Davis was spending less and less time on stage. In June, Max Roach humiliated him by slipping two hundred dollars into his pocket. It was too much. Davis called his father and asked him to send a train ticket. After spending some time on the family farm, Davis set out for California with Charles Mingus and Max Roach, but again had to call his father for help. He returned to his father's farm in November, where he sequestered himself, going cold turkey on his own, with no outside help. Although the episode has remained legendary in Davis' accounts of his final struggle against drugs, the reality was something else altogether: hired to play at the Blue Bird Inn in Detroit at the end of December, he fell back into his bad habits.

Heroin was common currency among young black jazzmen, and Miles Davis was not impervious to its influence. At the worst of his addiction, he no longer even owned his own trumpet and would sometimes fail to show up for recording sessions. Opposite page: in the studio for Blue Note, March 1954. Photo Francis Wolff.

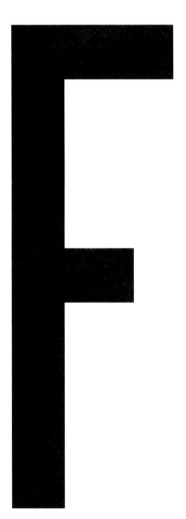

FRESH START. In the meantime, Miles Davis was troubled by two important events. The embodiment of cool jazz, a young white cat by the name of Chet Baker was named best trumpet player for 1953, and, while in Detroit, he heard the playing of Clifford Brown, the rising black trumpet star. In March 1954, Davis was back in New York, determined to make a comeback and telling anyone who would listen that he was making a fresh start. The future was uncertain, however, and once again his trumpet was in hock. He was playing Art Farmer's trumpet, and Farmer accompanied him to make sure his instrument did not vanish. Fortunately, Blue Note and Prestige immediately gave Davis an opportunity to prove himself.

This was not the first time Davis had recorded for a small jazz label. On January 17, 1951, he went from a session with the Charlie Parker Quintet for Verve to a session under his own name with a sextet (with Benny Green, Sonny Rollins, John Lewis, Percy Heath and Roy Haynes) for Prestige, a label he had signed with for one year. There were a few traces of the nonet, underscored by his solo on "Down," a few early indications of his rebirth in 1954, but also many signs of the fatigue that would characterize his recordings over the next three years. Of note are his short contribution to "Yesterdays," conducted by Lee Konitz (Prestige, March 8, 1951), and a long series of choruses on "Bluing" (Prestige, October 5, 1951) on LPs, a recent invention that made it possible to make longer recordings. "Yesterdays" and "Dear Old Stockholm" (Blue Note, May 9, 1952) were also important milestones, as was "Kelo" by J. J. Johnson, whose more dynamic compositions built on the nonet's legacy (Blue Note, April 20, 1953). Lastly, on May 19, 1953, for Prestige, "Tune Up" and "When Lights Are Low" exhibited a self-assured style that hinted at what was to come. In contrast, the Prestige session on January 30, 1953, with Charlie Parker on tenor saxophone, was not as memorable, as it all too clearly revealed Davis' and bebop's decline.

On March 6, 1954, Davis was back playing with a quartet at the Blue Note studios. As in previous sessions, bassist Percy Heath met the requirements of this modern jazz, which was known as hard bop, to distinguish it from earlier bebop. The two up-and-coming leaders in this new genre, Art Blakey and Horace Silver, played drums and piano respectively. Of Silver, Davis said, "I liked the way Horace played piano, because he had this funky shit that I liked a lot at that time. He put fire up under my playing and with Art on drums you couldn't be fucking around; you had to get on up and play." Silver and Davis were both living at the Arlington Hotel, and Davis often got together with his new friend to play his upright piano and share ideas: "I had Horace playing like Monk." How much truth is there in his claim? Without a doubt, Silver was very strongly influenced by Thelonious Monk during these years and, from this time on, Davis would always tell his pianists which chords, inversions and progressions he wanted to hear (as witnessed by photographs taken during these sessions). This prompted Jackie McLean to coin the expression "Miles Davis University."

MILES DAVIS IN THE STUDIO

Miles came back to town from Detroit at the start of 1951. I was working for Prestige Records and was in attendance at Apex Studios on January 17 when he did his first date for the label. In fact, I named a couple of the tunes recorded that night.

I didn't begin producing for Prestige until December 17, 1951, the eve of my twenty-third birthday, but it wasn't until 1953 that I would work with Miles in the studio. He hadn't recorded for Prestige since October 1951. This first session, on January 30, 1953, was going to be special, because Charlie Parker would be a member of the sextet led by Miles; however, instead of playing alto, Parker would be on tenor sax, as he was under contract to Norman Granz.

Prestige rarely held rehearsals, because the groups they recorded were usually working combos that were playing together in clubs and were completely familiar with their material. This date, however, was to include two new charts written for three horns, so I called a rehearsal a week before, to which I brought a rented tenor for Bird. He was the only one who showed. This necessitated running down the numbers on studio time.

The date was supposed to start at 2 p.m. Bird asked for some gin, so I ordered a fifth of Gordon's and twelve bottles of beer to be shared by the six musicians and myself. Miles, in his junkie period, was late for the date. Bird, trying to stay away from heroin, took advantage of the wait for Miles to take two long pulls on the Gordon's bottle and virtually empty it. He took a couple of short naps but mostly steamrollered on the tenor, sounding at times like a baritone. Miles finally showed up.

Doug Hawkins, the engineer I always worked with at WOR Studios, was not available that day, and I had only worked once before with his replacement, Bob Lee. It was taking the band a while to get comfortable with the arrangements. When we started taping, there were a number of breakdowns, some caused by Miles cracking notes. Time was moving along, and nothing was getting done. I don't remember exactly what motivated my next move, but I thought I might jolt him to generate some new energy. I walked out of the control room and told him, "Miles, you ain't playing shit."

The reaction I got was Miles moving towards his trumpet bag while saying to everyone else, "Cat says I'm not playing shit," and starting to pack up his horn. I saw my job walking out the door with him. In *Miles: The Autobiography*, he states that it was Bird who talked him out of leaving, but it was me, apologizing with "I really didn't mean that. I was just trying to make you really get into it."

I knew we didn't have enough minutes taped, and there were no more arrangements to be played. They tried to do Monk's "Well, You Needn't," but after several attempts broke down we abandoned it. I was thinking as fast as I could when, at 5 p.m., Bob Lee announced that he had to leave. Then the new engineer took over and shortly announced that the studio would close at 6 p.m. This was unprecedented. If you went overtime (more than three hours) you paid extra for it, but I had never heard of being shut down like this.

I came up with the idea to do "'Round Midnight." Its slow tempo would provide a long track. Bird and Miles intertwined when stating the theme at the beginning and end. Sonny Rollins played both of the bridges. After Bird's chorus, Miles soloed, leading into the standard Dizzy Gillespie ending that is part of Monk's classic. The performance is fraught with pain and beauty, speaking wordless volumes about that afternoon. The number ended as the second hand hit six o'clock.

Coming on the heels of the tribulations and triumph of January 30 was the date of February 19. Bob Weinstock, head of Prestige, wanted to do something out of the ordinary by asking John Lewis and Al Cohn to write two compositions each for an ensemble led by Miles that would include Lewis, Cohn and Zoot Sims.

We actually had two separate rehearsals, but Lewis wasn't pleased with the way his charts were being interpreted and suggested that Cohn bring in two more of his own compositions instead.

Trumpeter Jerry Lloyd (a.k.a. Jerry Hurwitz) was in attendance that day at Beltone Studios in mid-Manhattan, perhaps as Miles insurance. True to the form of his addiction years, Miles was late. By the time he walked in, I was ready to do a Cohn/Sims album in which Lloyd had at least one solo. Miles seemed to prefer

Photo Esmond Edwards.

Lloyd's trumpet to the one he had and asked if Jerry would lend it to him for the date, but Jerry was already out the door with some money I had given him for standing by.

Miles was the only soloist on "Tasty Pudding," catching the essential flavour of this lovely lament, connecting with it and sustaining its mood in his personal way. Evidence of his "chops" not being at their strongest appeared on "Willie the Wailer," when he didn't want to play two solo choruses in a row. I suggested that he and Al take turns within four choruses, and it worked out well.

In *Miles: The Autobiography*, he revealed that he and Zoot had gotten high together during the date, but neither showed any overt signs of this. Miles had praise for Al's compositions and arrangements.

On May 19, we were back at WOR. This session was the antithesis of January 30. Doug Hawkins was back at the controls, and anything that threatened to go wrong was immediately reversed by a seemingly built-in serendipity. The rhythm section for a Davis-led quartet was three quarters of the Modern Jazz Quartet: John Lewis, Percy Heath and Kenny Clarke.

Everyone was on time except for the usually reliable "Klook," as Kenny was known. We were unable to get in touch with him (I never found out why he hadn't shown), but just as the situation was veering towards hopelessness, who should walk in but Max Roach. By chance, he was visiting someone in another of the many studios of this major radio station and may have seen Miles' name on a listing of activities for the day. In the time it took for him to go home and return with his drums, Miles suggested that he and I should take a walk to the nearest pub. It was a gorgeous spring day. Upon arrival at the watering hole, he introduced me to the gin boilermaker: a shot-glass of gin in a mug of beer. We each had two, and, none the worse for wear, were in a comfortable state of elation. The session's four tunes went down in four takes. When John Lewis had to leave for a previously scheduled appointment (the original delay had made us go overtime), it just so happened that Charles Mingus was in the studio because Miles was recording Mingus' "Smooch"; its composer was therefore able to fill in on piano.

The last time I saw Miles was a chance meeting towards the end of the 1980s, when he came to visit someone in the building where I live. We hugged and he said, "How you doing, old buddy?"

IRA GITLER

IRA GITLER, A FORMER EDITOR OF *DOWN BEAT*, HAS BEEN WRITING ABOUT JAZZ SINCE 1951. IN THE EARLY 1950S, HE WORKED AS A PRODUCER ON MANY RECORDING SESSIONS FOR THE PRESTIGE LABEL, INCLUDING SOME WITH MILES DAVIS.

For his recordings in the early 1950s, Miles Davis teamed up with the leading practitioners of hard bop, including saxophonist Jackie McLean and trombonist J. J. Johnson, May 1952 (opposite page); brothers saxophonist Jimmy and bassist Percy Heath, and pianist Gil Coggins, April 1953. Photos Francis Wolff.

The most emblematic pianist of hard bop and an advocate for a return to gospel influences, with a decidedly funky style, Horace Silver recorded with Miles Davis on several occasions in 1954, for Prestige and for Blue Note (opposite page, March 6, 1954).
The two men even did a few concerts together (below). Photo Francis Wolff.

ON THE SIDELINES OF THE BLACK REVIVAL. On March 15, 1954, Miles Davis signed on with Prestige for three years, and the same quartet recorded a masterpiece entitled "Blue Haze," whose dramatic mood—exuding anguish—was created by dimming the studio lights after several failed attempts to capture the blues. On April 3, Davis replaced Art Blakey with Kenny Clarke, whose brush work he liked, because he wanted to use a mute (a cup mute, not the shrill-sounding Harmon mute he would later adopt). His recordings for Prestige included "Solar," a masterpiece of motivic improvisation (based on variations of melodic patterns). The key session that April took place on the 29th, with a sextet, the same rhythm section, trombonist J. J. Johnson and tenor saxophonist Lucky Thompson, his roommate in Los Angeles in 1946. This time, however, Davis arrived at the studio without a trumpet. Playing a dilapidated instrument borrowed from a Prestige employee, he recorded "Blue 'n' Boogie" and "Walkin'." In his autobiography, he explains, "I wanted to take the music back to the fire and improvisations of bebop, that kind of thing that Diz [Dizzy Gillespie] and Bird [Charlie Parker] had started. But also I wanted to take the music forwards into a more funky kind of blues, the kind of thing that Horace would take us to."

Just as "Blue Haze" hearkened back to the gloomy, bleak mood of the most primitive blues, "Walkin'" reconnected with the fundamentals of African-American culture, while superimposing a more positive mood on the blues form that evoked gospel and the churchy dimension that would be a constant in hard bop. Funky, churchy, hard bop: these were the new words associated with the new bop. Hard bop was a quintessentially black music, said to be in reaction to cool jazz. It was not far off, except that hard

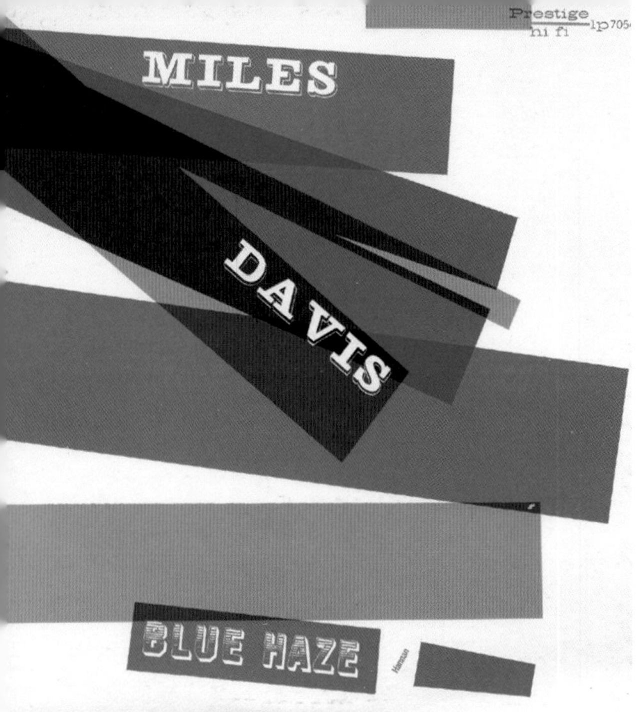

PRESTIGE LP 7025
miles davis and horns
featuring: al cohn zoot sims john lewis sonny rollins
compositions and arrangements by al cohn and john lewis

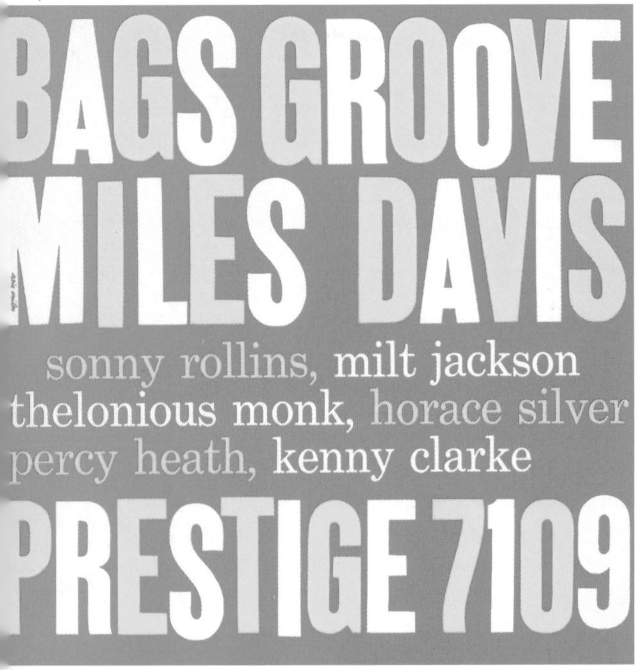

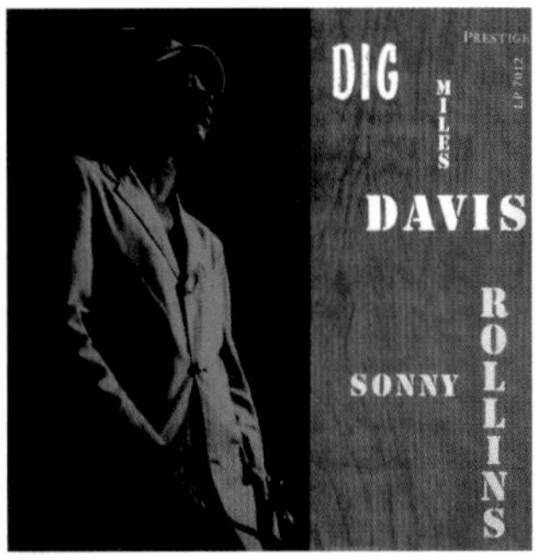

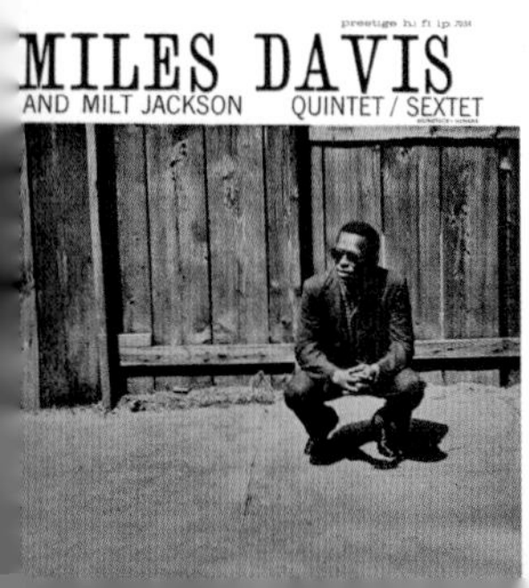

Along with the invention of the LP came the widespread use of the record cover, which gave rise to unprecedented graphic creativity. The independent labels often gave free rein to designers, who used the LP cover to experiment. Between 1951 and 1956, Miles Davis made many recordings, primarily for Prestige but also for Blue Note and Debut (founded by Charles Mingus), creating records that were sometimes just as famous for their cover illustrations as for the music.

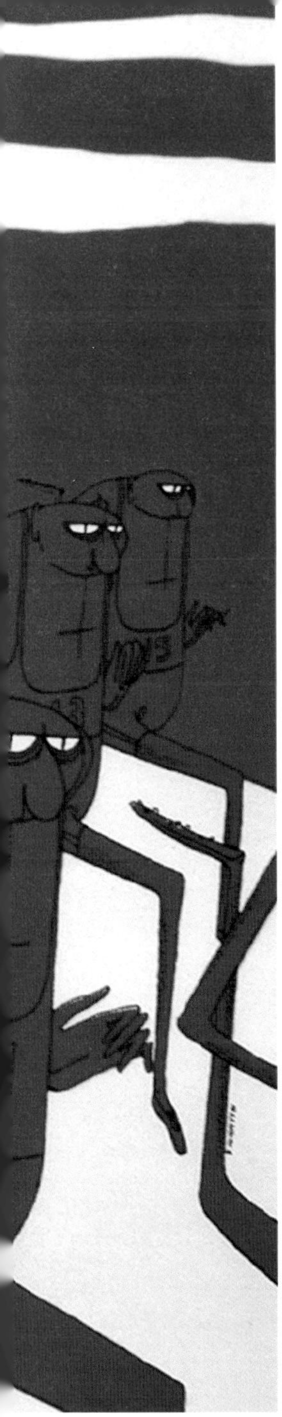

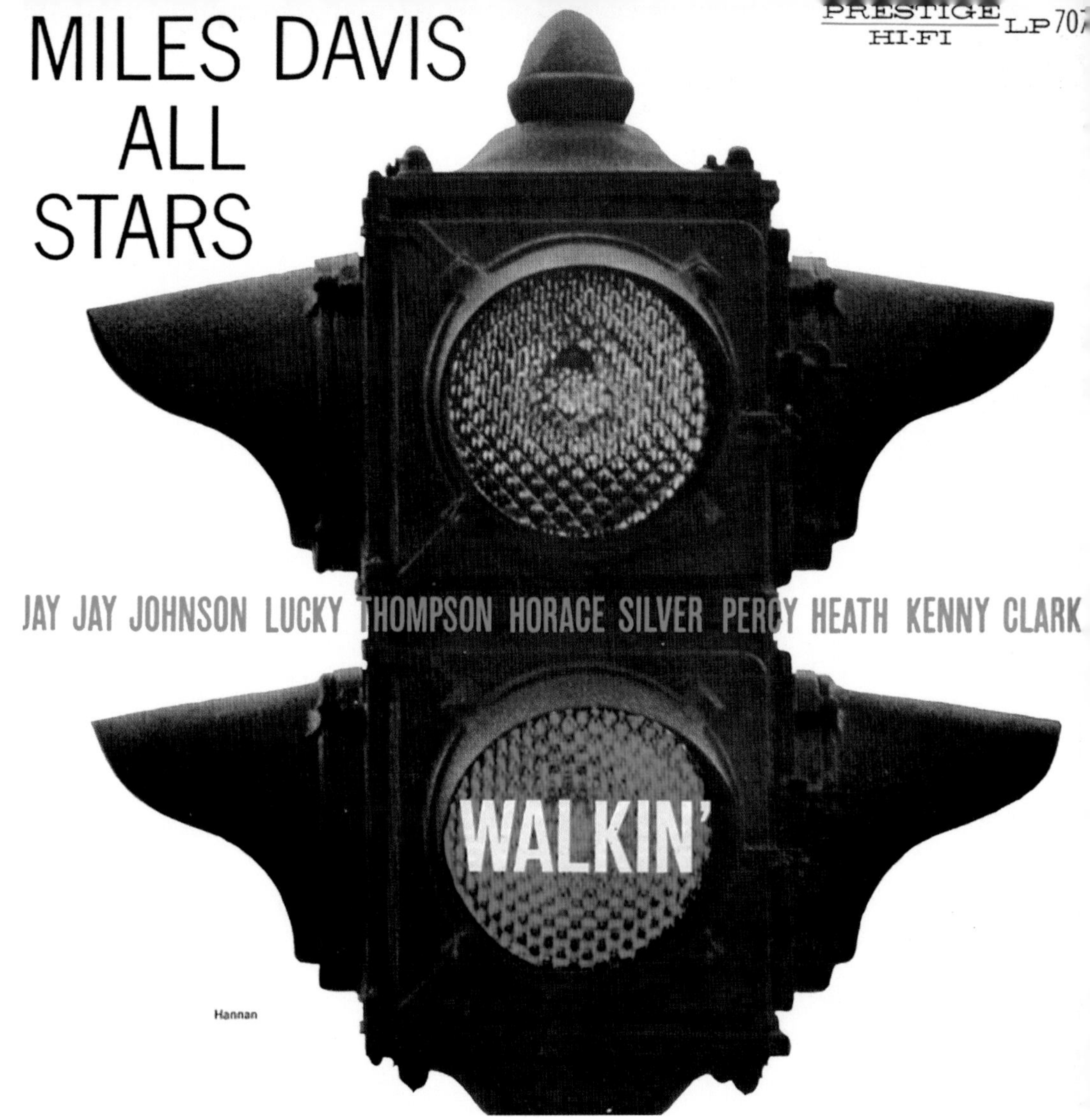

MILES DAVIS
ALL
STARS
PRESTIGE
HI-FI
LP 707
JAY JAY JOHNSON LUCKY THOMPSON HORACE SILVER PERCY HEATH KENNY CLARK
WALKIN'
Hannan

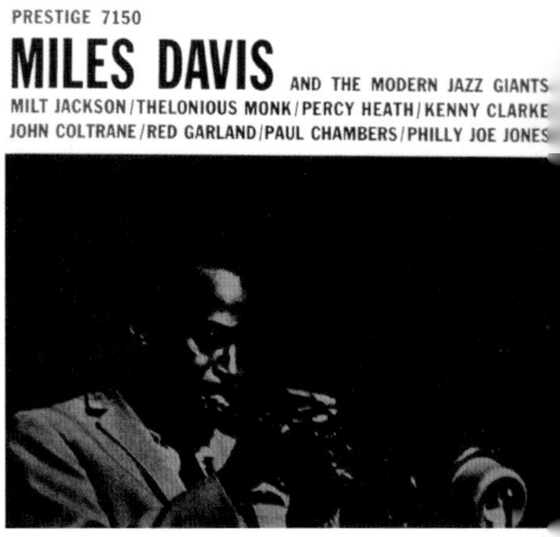

PRESTIGE 7150
MILES DAVIS AND THE MODERN JAZZ GIANTS
MILT JACKSON / THELONIOUS MONK / PERCY HEATH / KENNY CLARKE
JOHN COLTRANE / RED GARLAND / PAUL CHAMBERS / PHILLY JOE JONES

ILES DAVIS

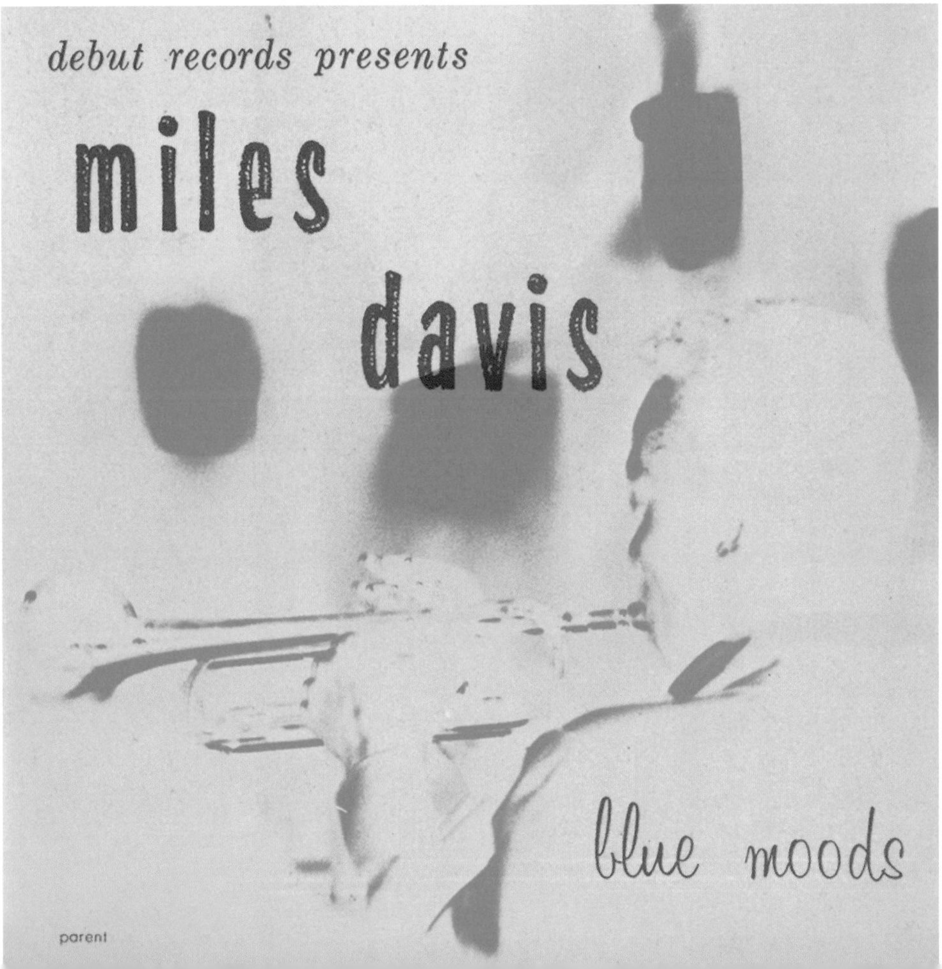

debut records presents
miles
davis
blue moods
parent

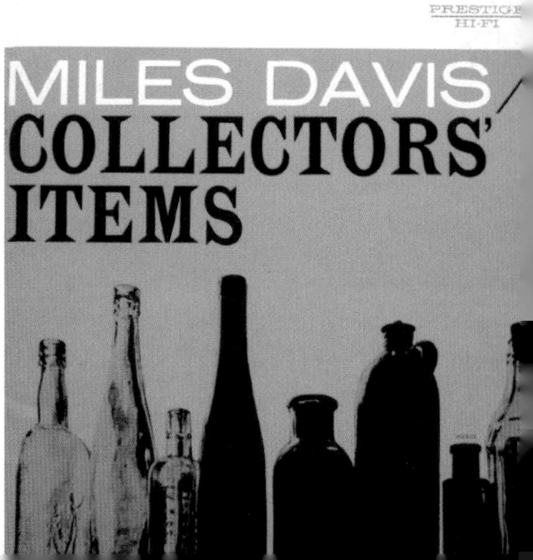

PRESTIGE
HI-FI
MILES DAVIS/
COLLECTORS'
ITEMS

ILES DAVIS

Miles Davis had specific ideas about the type of accompaniment he wanted to back his solos and had no qualms about demonstrating them himself at the keyboard, as pictured here with bassist Oscar Pettiford and pianist Gil Coggins at the Blue Note session on May 9, 1952. Photo Francis Wolff.

bop was intended as a response to bop itself, its harmonic acrobatics, unsingable melodies and undanceable rhythms that drove popular audiences, and especially black audiences, towards rhythm and blues.
The generation of trumpeter Clifford Brown (1930–1956) learned how to negotiate bop harmonies with an ease that made even its wildest melodies accessible. The stakes changed, and inventiveness was no longer driven by harmonic complexity. Before paving the way for the modal jazz Davis would espouse by the end of the decade, hard bop reconnected with the roots of black music: blues and gospel. It was funky, an African-American slang word for "strong-smelling," in reference to body odours. In other words, the harmonics of hard bop are stripped down and unadorned, sweating profusely in the trance of the swaying rhythms that combine the sensual message of rhythm and blues with gospel's sacred dimension. Davis' "Walkin'," with the heavy, insistent tempo laid down by the drums and dancing bass, is a melodic anthem that echoes the solemn, triumphant call to the black community to rise up, launched in unison by the nascent soul music and jazz of the time, by the voice of Ray Charles and by Art Blakey and Horace Silver's Jazz Messengers. The McCarthy years were drawing to a close, and the fight for black civil rights was set to resume. The movement would be galvanized the following year with the bus boycott in Montgomery, Alabama, initiated by Rosa Parks and endorsed by Martin Luther King.
Things are never simple, and not all hard bop was funky or churchy. Many of the musicians described as hard boppers remained true to the original spirit of bebop. Miles Davis, in particular, kept his distance. At each new stage in the history of jazz that he seemed to initiate (cool jazz, hard bop, modal, jazz-rock), he would stay on the edges of the fray. For now, he was in search of himself, while the members of his rhythm section were drawn towards other projects: Horace Silver and Art Blakey by the Jazz Messengers, Percy Heath and Kenny Clarke by the Modern Jazz Quartet. Davis teamed up with drummer Philly Joe Jones and travelled from city to city, where Jones would hire local musicians for Davis. From August 14 to October 2, 1954, Davis was back at the Blue Bird Inn in Detroit. The heroin there was of such poor quality that, during his stay, Davis was able to kick his addiction. He did, however, remain a more or less regular cocaine user.

MONK'S SILENCES. On December 24, 1954, Bob Weinstock, head of Prestige Records, assembled an all-star band around Miles Davis, consisting of Milt Jackson, Percy Heath and Kenny Clarke (three-quarters of the members of the Modern Jazz Quartet) along with Thelonious Monk. As soon as he set foot in the studio, Davis expressed his displeasure at having to play with Monk. He lost no time asking the pianist to refrain from playing during his solos. What was the reason for this behaviour? Ever since the sessions led by Charlie Parker, which were always chaotic, had he developed the taste for a tense atmosphere? This atmosphere was one he would continue to create in the studio throughout his career, sowing discomfort so that the musicians were literally beside themselves over some irritation or unfathomable suggestion.
In actual fact, Monk's accompaniment was so unpredictable that, by 1954, he had still not found sidemen who were performing at his level. Most other musicians considered it impossible to work with him. Davis had gotten into the habit of showing his pianists what he expected of them. Still, he was known to be shy and was a great admirer of Monk. As often happened when he was feeling vulnerable, he adopted the only defence he knew: aggression. The result was one of the most legendary sessions in the history of jazz and the famous episode when Monk "lay out." Monk stopped playing because he lost his place during his chorus, thrown off by the extent of his rhythmic lags during the second take of "The Man I Love." Davis intervened and prompted Monk with his trumpet, indicating where they were in the piece so that Monk could join in.

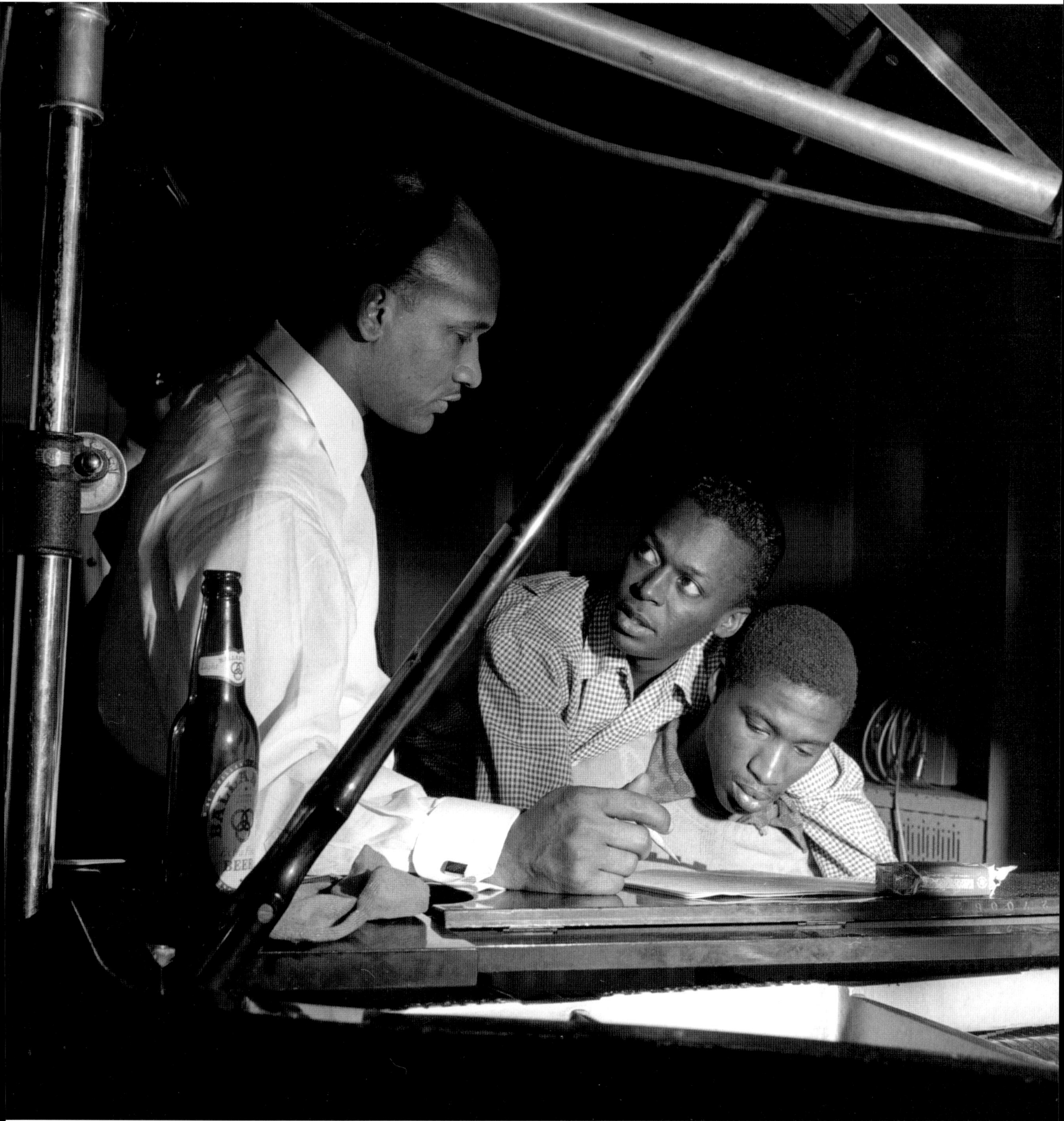

VOA

On July 17, 1955, Miles Davis' performance at the Newport Jazz Festival (opposite page, between Percy Heath and Gerry Mulligan) created a sensation and convinced producer George Avakian to sign him to Columbia. Photo Herman Leonard.

With an insistent interjection, Davis let Monk know that the joke had gone on long enough. Much has been written about this episode, and interpretations of it abound. Almost overlooked, though, were the essential characteristics of Davis' theme statement and improvised chorus: his maturity, his gorgeous sound (whether with an open instrument or the Harmon mute), his natural melodic expression, now totally free of the dogmatism of bop harmony, his sense of space, silence, mystery and drama. Initially, another piece was released, "Bags' Groove," with a solo by Thelonious Monk based on a blues tune whose abstract nature would also elicit much commentary.

A BIG FAT CONTRACT. Even though Miles Davis was back in favour with the experts (he tied with Dizzy Gillespie for first place in the 1955 *Down Beat* critics' poll), his financial situation was still precarious. In early 1955, after Irene Cawthon took steps to obtain alimony, he was arrested. While in prison, Davis learned of Charlie Parker's death from lawyer Harold Lovett, who managed to get him out three days later. Lovett would become both his trusted confidant and his business manager. He even convinced Charles Mingus and Max Roach to help Davis by having him record for their label, Debut. On July 9, 1955, Mingus called up trombonist Britt Woodman, vibraphonist Teddy Charles and drummer Elvin Jones for a session based on Mingus' own arrangements and those of Teddy Charles, a former Juilliard student. The resulting album, *Blue Moods*, was named by the *Metronome 1957 Yearbook* as one of the best jazz records of 1956. Somewhat forgotten today, it attests to the turbulent relationship between Mingus and Davis. In an interview with Nat Hentoff for *Down Beat* in November 1955, Davis criticized much of the contemporary jazz scene. He maligned the album he had just recorded for Debut and described as depressing the similarly avant-garde arrangements on which Teo Macero and Mingus had collaborated in 1953–54. Mingus was outraged by Davis' remarks and replied in a now-famous open letter.

A former Juilliard student who played regularly with Mingus, Teo Macero, of whom Davis was also critical, would later play a fundamental role in Davis' career as a producer. For that to happen, another figure had to make an appearance: George Avakian, a producer at Columbia. Founded in 1888, Columbia Records was one of three companies that controlled the record market until the many small labels emerged in the late 1910s. These small labels pioneered jazz recording, but Columbia soon became interested in the success of the "race records" intended for black audiences and took control of most of these independent labels. After the Depression, during which the label changed hands several times, Columbia shared the largest portion of the legacy of classic jazz recordings with RCA and MCA. In 1948, the company produced the first LP (or long-playing record). Compared to seventy-eights, longer recordings were now possible because of its 33 rpm speed and the microgrooves made possible with polyvinyl chloride. Still, it was the independent companies that captured the emergence and development of bebop. Until 1955, Davis' work was immortalized by the small labels: Savoy, Dial, Capitol, Prestige and Blue Note. Beginning in the 1950s, however, Columbia's new head of popular music had a vigorous policy to sign jazz players: Dave Brubeck in 1953, Louis Armstrong in 1955, Duke Ellington in 1956, Charles Mingus in 1959 and Thelonious Monk in 1962. On July 17, 1955, Avakian attended Davis' performance at the Newport Jazz Festival as part of an all-star band consisting of Gerry Mulligan, Zoot Sims, Thelonious Monk and the Modern Jazz Quartet's rhythm section. His rendition of "'Round Midnight" was a sensation, to the great surprise of Davis himself, who did not recall playing it any differently than he usually did. Nevertheless, two days later, on July 19, Davis, Harold Lovett and George Avakian dined together. The result: a contract with the most powerful jazz label of the time, a $2,000 advance on royalties and an agent, Jack Whittemore.

MILES AHEAD IN THE STUDIO FOR COLUMBIA 1955–1959

When Miles Davis signed with Columbia in summer 1955, he was still under contract to Prestige for two more years. Consequently, he convinced Prestige's founder, Bob Weinstock, of the advantage of letting him go over to Columbia: the records Davis made for Prestige would inevitably profit from the promotional support accompanying the first Columbia releases. The two companies came to an agreement: Columbia could begin recording Davis but would not release any records before the contract with Prestige ended in March 1957; in the meantime, Prestige could continue recording the trumpet player.

On June 7, 1955, Davis had already done a new session for Weinstock's label with Red Garland, Oscar Pettiford and Philly Joe Jones, released as *The Musings of Miles*. This was not the first time Davis had recorded with Oscar Pettiford, who was the first true bop bassist and would remain one of the most influential. Davis' interest in Pettiford, when he had just lost Percy Heath, demonstrates his exacting standards in his choice of bassists: he always had the best. In fact, he would always have the best rhythm section, surrounding himself with bassists who constantly proved useful for their depth of tone, rhythmic placement and harmonic expression, as well as drummers who could interact with the soloist.

The group Miles Davis formed with John Coltrane on tenor saxophone, Red Garland on piano (below), Paul Chambers on bass (left) and Philly Joe Jones on drums has come to be known as the "first quintet." It grew to a sextet in 1958 with the addition of Cannonball Adderley on alto saxophone (opposite page, between Davis and Coltrane). Photos Dennis Stock.

THE SEARCH FOR THE RIGHT RHYTHM SECTION. The space and silence at the heart of Miles Davis' solos actually make use of polyrhythms requiring constant dialogue with the drummer. This can be seen as the legacy of Charlie Parker. In 1954, composer-musicologist André Hodeir analyzed the saxophonist's playing from this standpoint in his book *Hommes et problèmes du jazz* [published in English as *Jazz: Its Evolution and Essence*, Grove Press, 1956]: "Since he plays a one-voice instrument, Parker can obviously only suggest this [polyrhythmical] aspect of his thought, and he does so by his accentuation. It is up to his partners to fill in the rest." It was by introducing silence, what jazz musicians call "space," by aerating his phrases, that Charlie Parker gave his drummer "the liberty . . . to develop [his] rhythmic counterpoint." In other words, Max Roach was not simply content to accompany Parker but integrated himself into a complex polyrhythmic architecture. Evidence of this is the striking interplay between Max Roach and Miles Davis during concerts by the Charlie Parker Quintet at the Royal Roost in fall 1948. Davis summed it up in his elliptical way: "We stop [as in earlier jazz forms], but we often let the drums lay out

altogether." In this regard, the choice of Philly Joe Jones was not a random one. One of the most outstanding successors of the bebop revolution instigated by Kenny Clarke in the 1940s, Jones emphasized the independence of the various components of the drum set. Furthermore, his concept of tempo coincided with Davis', which led the drummer to say, "I could never lose him, and he could never lose me. I always knew where he was. . . . I could get with Miles and go into *anything*, just like he does with me." Picking Red Garland was the result of Davis' interest in the music of Ahmad Jamal. He had first heard Jamal in 1953 over the telephone, when his sister called him from the phone booth at the Persian Lounge in Chicago, where the pianist was appearing with his trio. It was not yet the famous trio of 1958 with drummer Vernell Fournier, but a piano-bass-guitar combo of the type Nat King Cole had made popular in the early 1940s. Davis was immediately interested in the pianist: "He knocked me out with his concept of space, his lightness of touch, his understatement, and the way he phrased notes and chords and passages." A number of elements that characterized Jamal's music would become permanent preoccupations for Davis. In the first place, Jamal's chords and voicings tended to lighten up the harmony, in keeping with the art of insinuation and ambiguity then coming into style in jazz and which Davis championed. Jamal's concept of the band was so polyrhythmic that it challenged jazz's characterization as a simple succession of accompanied choruses, instead creating a collective feeling of groove, a rhythmic climate, a dramatic progression and a sense of suspense that kept the audience on the edge of their seats. It would be said of Jamal that he played the trio, not just the piano.

Beginning in 1955, the trumpet player's instructions to his new pianist, Red Garland, tended in this direction. In return, through his suggestions, Red Garland helped to expand Davis' repertoire, beyond directly borrowing from Ahmad Jamal's trio. Certain elements were taken from Jamal, such as the two-beat feel (the bass playing only the strong beats, as Paul Chambers would do in the first theme statement of "If I Were a Bell" and "All of You," and the snare-drum rimshot, which Philly Joe Jones liked to use to accent the fourth beat of the measure and which he said he borrowed from the guitarist of Jamal's trio, Ray Crawford (he provides an example during Red Garland's solo in "If I Were a Bell" on the album *Relaxin'*).

In late summer 1955, the young bassist Paul Chambers replaced Percy Heath. Like Heath, Chambers improved his left-hand grip on the strings, which lengthened the duration of the note, enabling him to bring out the melodic dimension of the walking bass and giving it exceptional drive. He also showed unusual virtuosity, not only in his solos (sometimes even using the bow), but also in his way of ornamenting the walk, even to the point of breaking it. Furthermore, his full sound augmented his impeccable timing perfectly in keeping with his partners in the new quintet.

JOHN COLTRANE, THE CUBIST. In his attempt to keep himself drug-free, Sonny Rollins stayed away from the New York scene. So Miles Davis turned to alto saxophonist Cannonball Adderley, who had created a sensation as the incontestable successor of Charlie Parker. Adderley, however, had to stay in Florida for a teaching engagement. After a tryout in Chicago with tenor saxophonist John Gilmore that went nowhere, Philly Joe Jones introduced Davis to John Coltrane. Davis had heard him play very convincingly opposite Sonny Rollins at a memorable jam session about March 1951. After waiting in vain for Sonny Rollins' return, Davis had Coltrane come to Baltimore for an

This superb red monochrome—taken by Marvin Koner, in 1956, at the Café Bohemia in New York and used on the cover of Miles Davis' first record for Columbia, *'Round about Midnight*—captures the musician's arrogant attitude, which was hidden more and more often behind dark glasses. Top right: onstage with the voluble Cannonball Adderley; bottom right: with the taciturn John Coltrane. Photos Marvin Koner; Carole Reiff (top right).

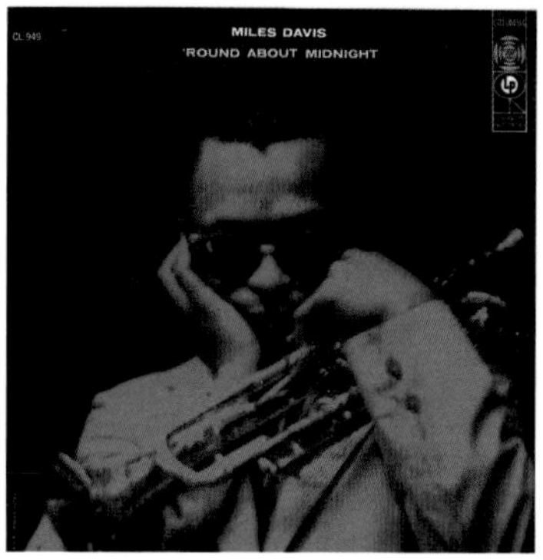

The Prestige LP *Miles*, also known as *The New Miles Davis Quintet*, was the recording debut of the first quintet, a group that shone in *'Round about Midnight*, Miles Davis' first record for Columbia.

engagement beginning on September 27, 1955. Soon, the New York clubs—Birdland, Café Bohemia, Basin Street—were fighting over the quintet, and on October 26, it recorded its first four titles for Columbia. However, not everyone liked Coltrane. Participation in Davis' quintet was an opportunity for this musician to come truly alive; though Coltrane's vocabulary was always expanding, up to that point he had been biding his time in rhythm-and-blues bands. The next year, his playing took off and he developed a language of bewildering intensity. Critic Ira Gitler describes this new style of improvisation as "sheets of sound." Coltrane launched an assault on bebop harmony by increasing its possibilities and angles so as to expose its ambiguities, just as the Cubist painters sought to reproduce an object by observing it from all sides at once. At first, the vibes between Coltrane and Davis were not good. Though the trumpet player had strong ideas, he was ill at ease expressing what he wanted and was disconcerted by this serious man who never stopped asking questions; he had trouble hiding his irritation. Still, Davis vaguely perceived the potential he would help develop: "I would show him a lot of shit. . . . I'd say, 'Trane, here are some chords, but don't play them like they are all the time, you know? Start in the middle sometimes and don't forget that you can play them up in thirds. So that means you got eighteen, nineteen different things to play in two bars.' . . . Trane was the only player who could play those chords I gave him without them sounding like chords."

THE QUINTET IN THE STUDIO. After a first session for Columbia, it was Prestige's turn to have a chance with the new quintet, on November 16, 1955. The record *The New Miles Davis Quintet* came out of this session. It was music without frills or special arrangements for the two wind instruments, where Miles Davis gave himself the majority of the theme statements, the rendition of the melody his only contribution to "There Is No Greater Love." This way of doing it, which became common for him, illustrates his interest in pop songs and their singers. He avowed great admiration for Frank Sinatra (who, as he himself admitted, influenced his phrasing) and Blossom Dearie (who impressed him with her way of demanding that her listeners stay silent). In 1961, he would insist that Shirley Horn share the bill with him at the Village Vanguard.

Beginning in the 1950s, popular songs held a special place in Davis' repertoire. He performed ballads with a Harmon, the most closed-sounding trumpet mute, which he held against the microphone to obtain a muffled, hoarse, nasal timbre, quite close to the sound of his own voice after he had polyps removed from his larynx in October 1955, and not very far either from the timbre of Billie Holiday's voice. One of his biographers, Jack Chambers, compares his interpretation of ballads to those sung by Billie Holiday: "It is sorrowing, and it is pained, but it is not self-pitying." Therein would appear to reside the main difference between the romanticism of Chet Baker and Davis' aloof approach, emphasized by his sense of silence, his ability to reshape a melody, deconstructing it into rarefied, incisive motifs verging on abstraction.

In just two sessions (May 11 and October 26, 1956), the quintet gave the Prestige label enough material for the four records Davis still owed them. The recordings took place in a state of urgency. Each time, a dozen titles were recorded, segueing from one to the next, as though the quintet were performing in a nightclub. The studio noises between pieces were left on the recording. Davis saying "Okay, all right" can be heard at the end of "When Lights Are Low," and "How was it, Bob?" at the end of "It Could Happen to You." Bob Weinstock asks for another take at the end of "Woody'n You," and Coltrane asks for the bottle-opener. The beginning of "You're My Everything" is interrupted by Davis telling Red Garland how to introduce the piece.

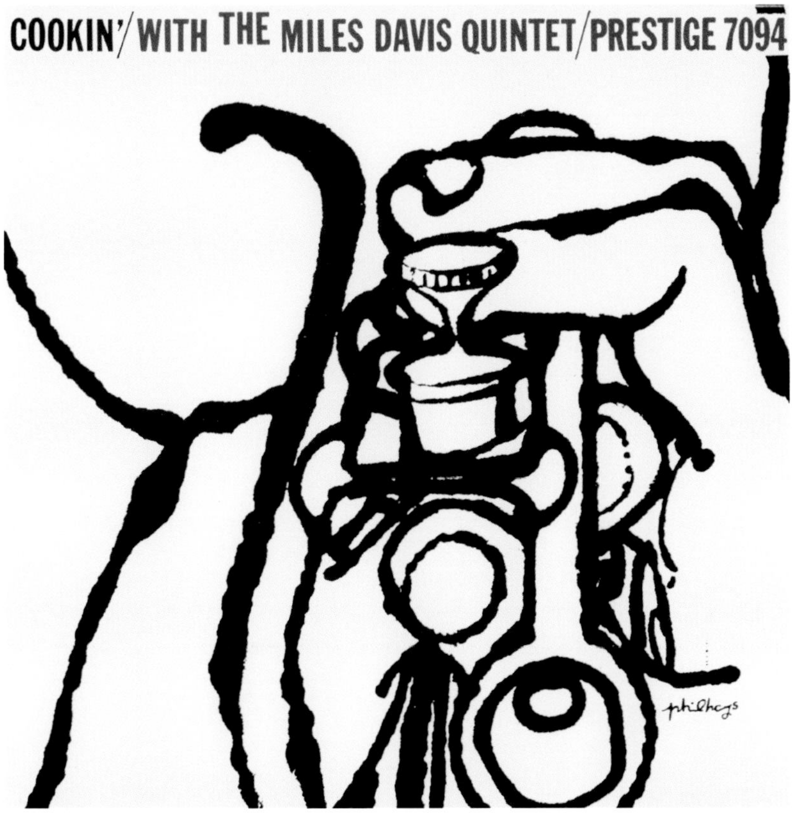

COOKIN'/WITH THE MILES DAVIS QUINTET/PRESTIGE 7094

In just two days in 1956, to fulfill his contract with the Prestige label, Miles Davis and his quintet recorded enough material for four albums, which were released with titles suggesting the "work in progress" atmosphere of these marathon sessions: *Cookin'*, *Relaxin'*, *Steamin'* and *Workin'*.

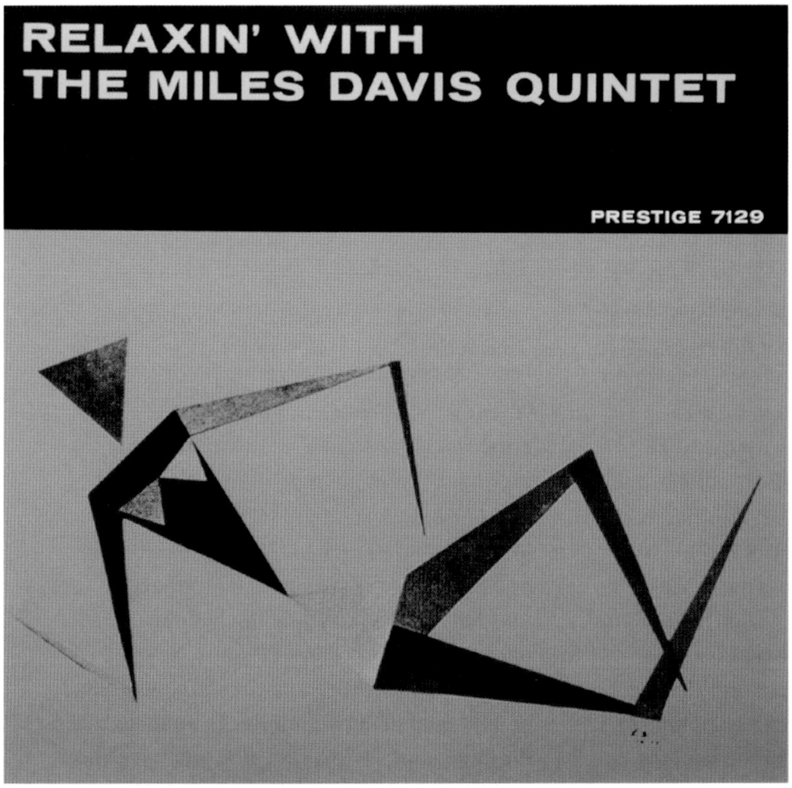

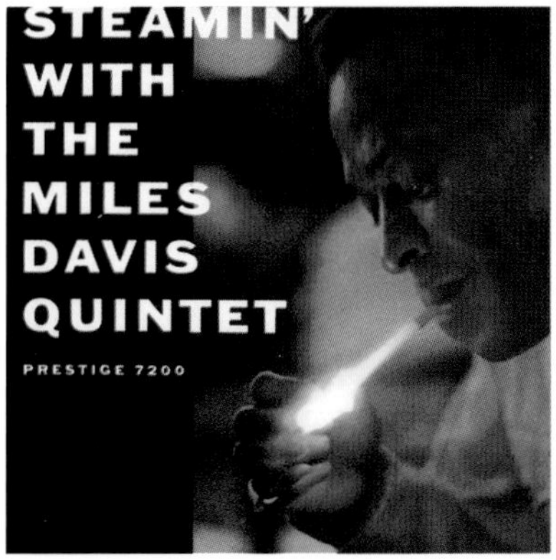

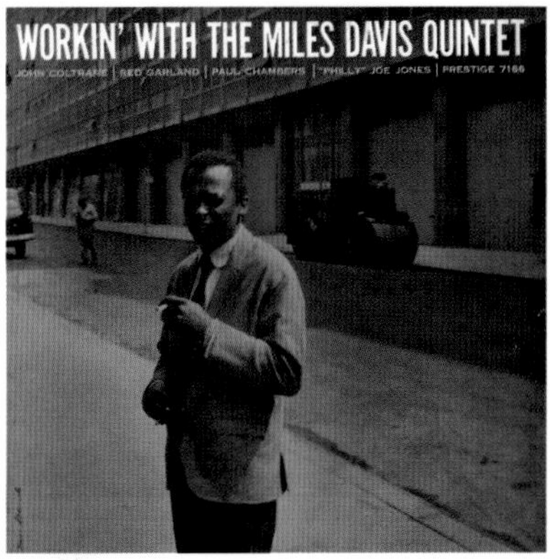

Miles Davis' voice would often be heard on his records, especially at the beginning and end of numbers on *Miles Smiles*, as well as in the middle of numbers during the electric years from 1969 to 1974, when he would direct his musicians, moving from one to the next to make suggestions. Back on December 24, 1954, when pianist Thelonious Monk made a slip at the beginning of the first take of "The Man I Love," eliciting complaints from his companions in a hurry to finish, Davis asked recording engineer Rudy Van Gelder to leave everything in. One must see this as a willingness to capture the sound of the studio, music in the process of being made. Davis' voice would even be electronically sampled at the end of his career and reinserted here and there in the music.

If the title of the first album derived from these sessions, *Cookin'*, refers to Davis' affinity for the kitchen, it also suggests the notion of a work in progress, which would be one of the musician's prime interests in the 1970s. His taste for urgency and risk in the studio may be compared to the Charlie Parker Quintet's lack of preparation for its sessions. However, Parker liked to record many takes, whereas Davis quickly tired of the exercise, often giving his best on the second or third take. During the 1956 sessions for Prestige, the first takes were run one after another. The spontaneous nature of these sessions has often been pointed out. In fact, the melodies are stated by Davis, alone or in unison with Coltrane. At the same time, the rhythm section's ways of playing, inspired by Ahmad Jamal, show a sensitivity to detail in the distribution of roles and the organization of scenarios. To be convinced, one need only listen to the piano's entrances and exits in "Woody'n You" and even more so in "Oleo."

However, an entirely different climate reigned at Columbia Records on June 5 and September 10, 1956 (*'Round about Midnight*). Every number was worked on in post-production to select the best solos from different takes and edit them together.

'ROUND (ABOUT) MIDNIGHT

Miles Davis and I became friends in 1946, soon after I returned from the war in the Pacific. Not only did his playing appeal to me, but I also found him to be a very pleasant, amiable young man and an interesting conversationalist. I followed his rising career, during which our friendship grew. But I was disappointed when, in 1949, Miles returned from Paris, where he had obviously taken up drugs. His playing had deteriorated, and he had become careless about his clothes and appearance—not the Miles I had known. I believe it was in 1951 that he became so unreliable about showing up for engagements that he was all but unemployed most of the year, even though he finished strongly as usual in the music magazine polls.

Soon after, Miles began suggesting that I should sign him to a record contract. Obviously, he had seen how I had signed rising talent such as Dave Brubeck and Erroll Garner, who had made an impression on smaller labels and quickly blossomed into major attractions on the jazz circuit thanks to Columbia's distribution and advertising strength. After checking with the musicians' union only to find out he had a contract with Prestige Records, which still had quite some time to run, I told him it was out of the question. (In any event, I had no desire to deal with an artist on drugs—I had had enough of such experiences already.)

A couple of years passed, and Miles asked me again. He had moved to a house a few blocks from my apartment in Manhattan, and from time to time would ask me to drop by—he was not well and feeling a bit lonely. In the winter of 1953–54, Miles started dropping in to play at the "open house" Monday nights at the original Birdland, on Broadway, essentially informal jam sessions that cost the management next to nothing to stay open on the traditional off-night for most clubs. I used to stop by to hear young talent. After a couple such Mondays, I realized that Miles was back to playing pretty well—which, I am sure, is why Miles was encouraged enough to make an unusual proposal. "Look, George," he said, "first of all, you've been coming to hear me play; you can tell I've kicked the drug habit. Why don't you call Bob Weinstock at Prestige and tell him you're going to sign me anyway when his contract ends, but meanwhile, if you can be recording me, you can release me on Columbia as soon as the Prestige contract expires. Bob will have the advantage of Columbia advertising me right away instead of waiting four or five months for a release. He'll have his whole catalogue of my LPs to sell at a time when you have only one Columbia LP to back up your advertising."

I had to admit that it was a novel and clever idea, but I was still reluctant to pursue it until my brother Aram and I went

Miles Davis and producer George Avakian in the studio at Columbia, 1956. Photo Carole Reiff.

to the 1955 Newport Jazz Festival where Miles came on as part of an unscheduled fill-in group consisting of Zoot Sims, Gerry Mulligan, Thelonious Monk, Percy Heath, Connie Kaye and himself. They played three tunes. At the end of the second (Monk's "'Round Midnight"), Aram turned to me and said, "You know Miles is straight, and after that performance there'll be people after him." We went backstage after the set, and I told Miles to come see me on Monday.

I outlined to Miles the plan I had started to formulate: Miles would organize and maintain a permanent sextet, which I would only release when the Prestige contract expired in early 1957. Apart from staying "clean," Miles would have to restore his standing as a reliable artist, which had badly deteriorated in recent years. The only booking agent who still had any faith in Miles was a good friend of mine, Jack Whittemore of Shaw Artists. I promised him that Miles and I would provide him with the musical product, live and on records, with advertising and promotion that would enable him to restore Miles' position on the jazz circuit. To my delight, Miles not only agreed but also said he had already started to organize a quintet consisting of Sonny Rollins, Red Garland, Paul Chambers and Philly Joe Jones. As soon as the group was ready, I said, I would schedule the recording of a first album, which would have *'Round Midnight* as its title, celebrating the performance at Newport that had pushed me to pursue Miles' unorthodox plan.

Jack lined up the first bookings, and things looked promising until Sonny Rollins was offered an opportunity to lead a group in Chicago. Miles soon found an excellent replacement in the up-and-coming Julian "Cannonball" Adderley, until Cannon was faced with a career decision—whether to give up his position as a tenured teacher in the Florida school system by taking a full-time job as a travelling musician. Caution won out and he chose security.

Meanwhile, Miles had begun auditioning replacements for the saxophone chair in his budding combo. "Take your time," I said to him. "The important thing is to have stable as well as solid personnel." In early September, Miles called and said, "I think I've got the man. Come down next week-end and listen to the group. If you like it, we can record in a couple of weeks when I come back to New York."

The saxophonist Miles had found was John Coltrane. Neither Miles nor Trane nor I could remember later whether I went to hear the new quintet in Philadelphia or Baltimore, but we all recalled that Trane blew a long solo on the last set that broke up the audience and eliminated any possible doubts about booking the group's first recording session. The first album was a success.

The next step was to decide how to present Miles in a new and exciting way that would propel his popularity beyond the familiar small-group format in which the public had known him ever since he had come on the scene. The first hint of what might come to pass came about quite unexpectedly.

My long-time colleague Gunther Schuller had begun developing a theory of music which he called "third stream"—the bringing together of classical music (the "first stream") and jazz (the "second stream") to form a new musical discipline. The vehicle for introducing this new synthesis was an orchestra made up of both kinds of musicians, assembled by Gunther in 1956 to perform a concert of his own contemporary classical compositions and the music of jazz composers John Lewis, J. J. Johnson and George Russell. Although the music had been prepared and rehearsed, the concert was cancelled when conductor Dimitri Mitropoulos scheduled the Schuller composition for a performance with the New York Philharmonic. Gunther promptly suggested that the carefully rehearsed concert orchestra record all four works for Columbia, with Mr. Mitropoulos (who was under contract to Columbia) conducting Schuller's *Symphony for Brass and Percussion* on one side of an LP, and Gunther conducting the other works on the reverse side. Our proposal accepted, the new musical concept was recorded efficiently and inexpensively in two afternoon sessions.

But how did Miles Davis become involved? The jazz compositions included three solos for solo trumpet or flugelhorn, which Gunther thought could be performed by Miles, who had just signed his contract with Columbia. Miles accepted my invitation and came to the first session, when the Schuller was recorded. Miles' participation in the second session, as a soloist with nineteen musicians under Gunther's baton, inspired my conception of Miles' second LP for Columbia. I thought of the sound as an enlargement of Miles' nonet for Capitol Records, which had been a commercial failure—but I loved the music. Miles would be the only soloist; the only possible arranger-conductor, I felt, would be either Gunther—who had also been the French hornist on the Capitol sessions—or Gil Evans. Miles, who had worked more closely with Gil, chose Evans—and the rest is history.

I had already decided on the album title—*Miles Ahead*, as in "Miles is forging ahead, miles ahead of everyone else." Art director Neil Fujita came up with a visualization of the title: a sailboat, presumably in a race but "miles ahead"—no competition in the background. Everything clicked. The album, following the success of Miles' first Columbia LP (*'Round about Midnight*—the publisher insisted on the exact copyrighted title of the lead composition), took off like a Frank Sinatra movie soundtrack.

Miles was unhappy with the "white chick" on the cover, sitting on the deck of the sailboat, and asked me to change it: "Put Frances on the cover." Frances Taylor was his girlfriend, who was dancing on Broadway in the hit show *West Side Story*. But I explained that if we stopped production, he would lose thousands of sales. *Miles Ahead* was being manufactured as part of our "express" shipping plan. Printing covers and liners in large quantities was relatively cheap, so we had manufactured tens of thousands of LP sleeves for it, and as the orders from the distributors came in, the factory would press an equivalent number of discs, which would be shipped within twenty-four hours. Moreover, I continued, the cover had caught on with dealers everywhere—but now, having established the concept of the album, a change of cover should make use of a photo of Miles to establish him as a personality. Miles agreed with the plan, chose the photo, and we used up the remaining original covers with no interruption of sales.

In Europe—especially in France—*Miles Ahead* was an equally huge hit. It established Miles permanently as the leading jazz artist for the rest of the twentieth century, continuing to this day—nearly two decades after his death.

GEORGE AVAKIAN

IN HIS WORK FOR A NUMBER OF DIFFERENT LABELS (COLUMBIA, WORLD PACIFIC, RCA VICTOR, WARNER BROS.), GEORGE AVAKIAN PRODUCED RECORDS BY SUCH GREATS AS LOUIS ARMSTRONG AND DUKE ELLINGTON. IN 1955, HE SIGNED MILES DAVIS TO COLUMBIA.

In 1956, during a Birdland All Stars tour, Miles Davis shared the stage with one of his boyhood idols, tenor saxophonist Lester Young. They played in a number of major European cities, including Amsterdam, pictured here. Photos Ed van der Elsken.

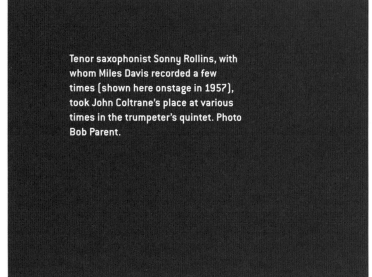

Tenor saxophonist Sonny Rollins, with whom Miles Davis recorded a few times (shown here onstage in 1957), took John Coltrane's place at various times in the trumpeter's quintet. Photo Bob Parent.

THE QUINTET'S UPS AND DOWNS. The Miles Davis Quintet became one of the leading bands on the contemporary scene, and the trumpeter took advantage of his success and the support of his lawyer, Harold Lovett, to become more and more demanding, reducing his appearances in nightclubs to three and then two sets a night, as opposed to the regulation five. In public, Davis' behaviour was unpredictable, high-handed, even arrogant. He arrived at the last minute, refused to announce his numbers, turned his back to the audience and left the stage as soon as he stopped playing, sometimes after only a few notes. Between sets, he avoided the audience and discouraged any attempt to approach him. He thus broke with the social interaction of nightclubs, as if trying to divest jazz of its function as entertainment. He turned his shyness into aggressiveness and proceeded by intimidation, hiding behind dark glasses and the unsociable attitudes of a bad boy. He wore expensive clothes, drove to the club at the wheel of his blue Mercedes 300 SL and lived in a spacious apartment at 881 Tenth Avenue. This is where he invited his children, who were living in Brooklyn with Irene Cawthon, on weekends and where he threw parties, often doing the cooking himself.

Miles Davis pursued his affair with the brilliant Jean Bach, whom he cautioned against his own musicians, hardly the sort of people with whom one would socialize. In fact, while he seemed to have escaped from the abyss, things were quite different for the members of his quintet, who faced serious addiction problems. John Coltrane often fell asleep onstage and neglected his appearance, in contrast with Davis' elegance. Davis constantly had to keep Philly Joe Jones away from the bar. Paul Chambers and Red Garland sometimes disappeared just before going onstage. At the Café Bohemia, in October 1956, Davis called on Sonny Rollins to fill in for John Coltrane, who had walked off-stage. In November, the trumpet player temporarily disbanded his group to take part in the Birdland All Stars' European tour. In addition to Miles Davis, the line-up included the Modern Jazz Quartet, Bud Powell solo and Lester Young. Powell, Young and Davis were each accompanied by the French rhythm section of pianist René Urtreger, bassist Pierre Michelot and drummer Christian Garros.

Back from France, Davis re-formed the quintet but soon announced his intention of leaving the stage. He said he had had enough of the business, was tired of jazz, and mentioned offers he had received to become the music director of a record company and teach at Howard University, in Washington, D.C. Almost permanently in residence at the Café Bohemia, the members of his quintet played a round of musical chairs that, in late summer 1957, saw even the great drummer Art Taylor leave in the middle of a concert, exasperated by Davis' criticisms. After replacing John Coltrane, Sonny Rollins left in turn to put his own group together. He was replaced by Belgian Bobby Jaspar until Cannonball Adderley accepted Davis' offer.

REUNION WITH GIL EVANS. While the quintet was on the rocks, a new project took shape, set in the context of an emerging current that favoured a blend of jazz and classical music. It was spearheaded by two former members of Miles Davis' nonet, pianist-arranger John Lewis, co-founder of the Modern Jazz Quartet, and French-horn player, composer and theoretician Gunther Schuller. Even before Schuller named this trend the "third stream" in 1957, it was given substance in a 1956 Columbia recording of a series of ambitious pieces, notably "Three Little Feelings" by John Lewis and "Poem for Brass" by J. J. Johnson, in which Miles Davis played solos on the flugelhorn, a new instrument for his audience. These compositions gave producer George Avakian the idea for a new project of the same orchestral scope for Davis, providing an opportunity for him to get back together with Gil Evans.

George Avakian gave the two carte blanche on the condition that the recording include a piece with the title he had chosen for the record: *Miles Ahead*. Davis proposed "The Duke" by Dave Brubeck, a new star in the Columbia catalogue, and Ahmad Jamal's "New Rhumba." Gil Evans brought the song "I Don't Wanna Be Kissed" (made famous by Doris Day and already covered by Ahmad Jamal), "Springsville" by Johnny Carisi (who had written for the nonet) and "My Ship" by Kurt Weill. "The Meaning of the Blues" and "Lament," run together, were by Bobby Troup and J. J. Johnson respectively; "The Maids of Cadiz" was derived from Léo Delibes, and "Blues for Pablo" was inspired by Manuel de Falla's *Three-cornered Hat* and popular Mexican folk music. To take advantage of the length of a twelve-inch LP, Gil Evans decided to link the pieces together with short aural transitions to make one long suite. Aside from the flugelhorn solos, which Davis would re-record afterwards, the orchestra was inspired by Claude Thornhill's instrumentation with French horns, tuba and only one saxophone among the winds (clarinets, flute, oboe). The rhythm section had no piano. The bass and drums—Paul Chambers and Art Taylor—were from the Miles Davis Quintet, and one finds the sense of detail that characterizes his small groups, combined with the orchestral textures developed by Gil Evans.

In 1957, Miles Davis (at right) chose Gil Evans (left) to arrange and direct a large ensemble recording Columbia had decided to make. It was released as *Miles Ahead*. When Davis learned that a photo of a young white woman was to illustrate the cover, he demanded that it be changed (below, left). Photo Don Hunstein (right).

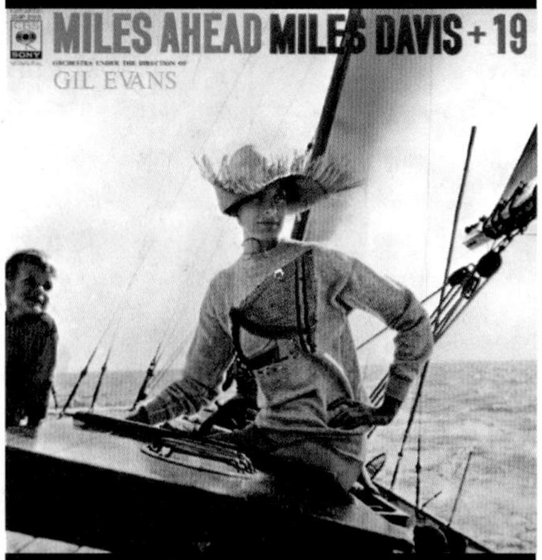

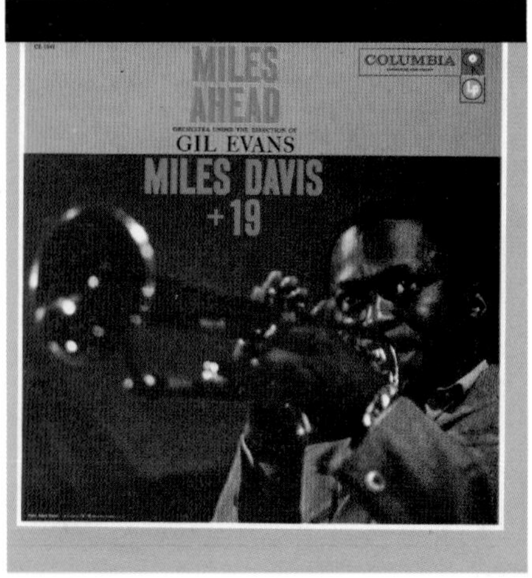

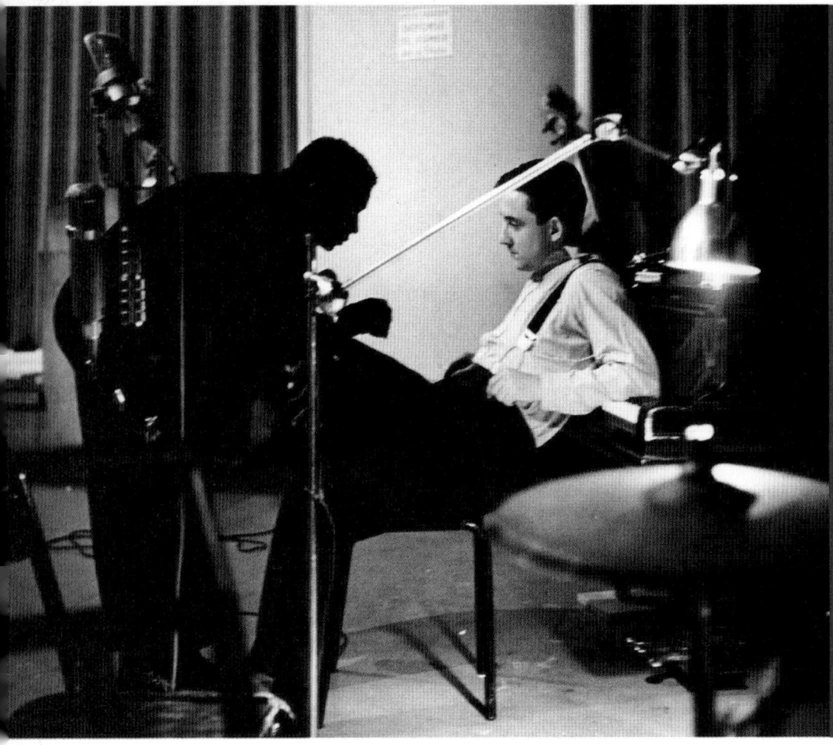

ASCENSEUR POUR L'ÉCHAFAUD. At Birdland in 1957, Miles Davis met Beverly Bentley, an actress who had just finished filming *A Face in the Crowd* for Elia Kazan. Through her, he became interested in the theatre and the movies, and he gave her records by Aram Khachaturian, Ernest Bloch, Claude Debussy and Maurice Ravel. She recommended him to compose the music for Carrie Bliss' *The Big Knife*, but he declined. It was another woman who would persuade him to lend his trumpet to the movies, Jeanne de Mirbeck, sister of pianist René Urtreger. He had met her in November 1956, the evening of the Birdland All Stars' first concert at Salle Pleyel in Paris, and they had an affair. When, in fall 1957, producer Marcel Romano proposed another European tour to Davis in a quintet including René Urtreger's trio, the prospect of seeing De Mirbeck again, combined perhaps with the lassitude he felt in the face of his own quintet's misadventures, motivated him to accept. This time, Davis' old accomplice Kenny Clarke was on drums, and Romano added his young protégé, saxophonist Barney Wilen, to the quartet. However, the tour did not meet with the expected success, beyond a few large concerts in the great halls of Europe (Amsterdam, Stuttgart, Brussels and Paris, at the Olympia and Salle Gaveau).

In Paris, with no other responsibility than showing up evenings at the Club Saint-Germain, where he was engaged with his French quintet, Davis found himself on vacation, far from the cares of his New York life. The Club Saint-Germain was then frequented by Alain Cavalier and François Leterrier, two assistants of Louis Malle, who had just filmed *Ascenseur pour l'échafaud* [released in North America as *Frantic*], which was in need of a musical score. Marcel Romano, who was toying with the idea of producing a documentary of the tour filmed by François Reichenbach, had not been able to find the funding. The idea took shape to ask the trumpeter to write the music for Malle's film. Failing to convince him, Romano and Malle asked De Mirbeck to intercede, and she succeeded in dragging her lover to a screening, about which Davis made no comment. Later in the day, getting out of the shower in his room at the Windsor, he asked his young companion to pass him the cornet that had just been given to him by the firm of Couesnon, and he began playing the famous bass line that accompanies Jeanne Moreau's frantic wanderings throughout the film. The night of December 4–5, Davis dragged his French quintet to Le Poste Parisien Studio and, starting from the experimental fragments he had begun to devise on the piano with his musicians at the Club Saint-Germain, he improvised the music for *Ascenseur pour l'échafaud*, which would contribute to the success of a still somewhat awkward first film.

The year after that, Louis Malle asked Davis to write the music for *Les Amants* [*The Lovers*], but the budget could not accommodate the trumpet player's conditions, which included recording in New York with a twenty-piece orchestra.

Recorded in a single night, the background music for *Ascenseur pour l'échafaud* [a.k.a. *Frantic*] made a success of the film by Louis Malle (opposite page, left), starring Jeanne Moreau (opposite page, right). Miles Davis and his musicians improvised most of the music live in the studio while watching a projection of the film. Photos Vincent Rossell (opposite page); Gérard Landau (above).

As one of the best modern jazz groups, the sextet with John Coltrane and Cannonball Adderley headlined all the major American festivals in 1958. Photo Bob Parent.

THE SEXTET. Leaving Paris for New York on December 20, 1956, Miles Davis found a new wife and a new band. In 1953, during a stay in Los Angeles, he had been introduced to Frances Taylor, a member of the Katherine Dunham Dance Company. He saw her again in New York, where she was dancing in *Mr. Wonderful*, the show Sammy Davis, Jr. presented on Broadway in 1956. In the process of getting a divorce from dancer Jean-Pierre Durand, with whom she had a young son also named Jean-Pierre, she was in the cast of *West Side Story*. Davis attended the show's premiere at the Winter Garden in September 1957 and returned to see it often. He soon settled her in his apartment on Tenth Avenue and, a sign of growing jealousy, asked her to leave the show and devote herself entirely to him, even forbidding her to dance in the movie version of *West Side Story*, despite the insistence of the choreographer, Jerome Robbins.

As soon as he was back in the United States, Miles Davis got his old quintet together again and added Cannonball Adderley. John Coltrane had stopped using drugs since he was fired from the Café Bohemia in April 1957. Thelonious Monk, who had seen Davis hit Coltrane backstage and was upset by it, offered to hire the saxophonist. The two recorded together several days after the incident and played at the Five Spot several weeks in a row, pursuing their collaboration until the end of the year. Alongside the pianist—or in his absence when Monk abandoned the stage, leaving him alone with the bass and drums—Coltrane found new solutions for his kaleidoscopic approach to bebop harmony. Davis, who often came to listen, began to miss Coltrane. When the sextet

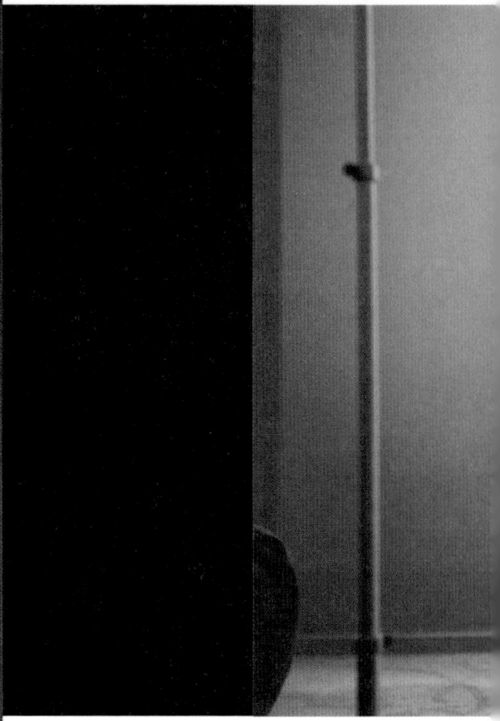

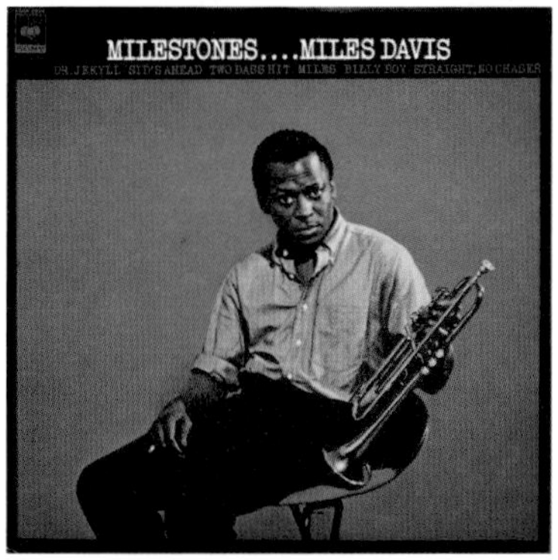

Columbia used photographers Roy De Carava and Dennis Stock for the covers of the recordings *Porgy and Bess* and *Milestones* (above). Opposite page: images from the session for the album *Milestones*. Photos Dennis Stock (opposite page).

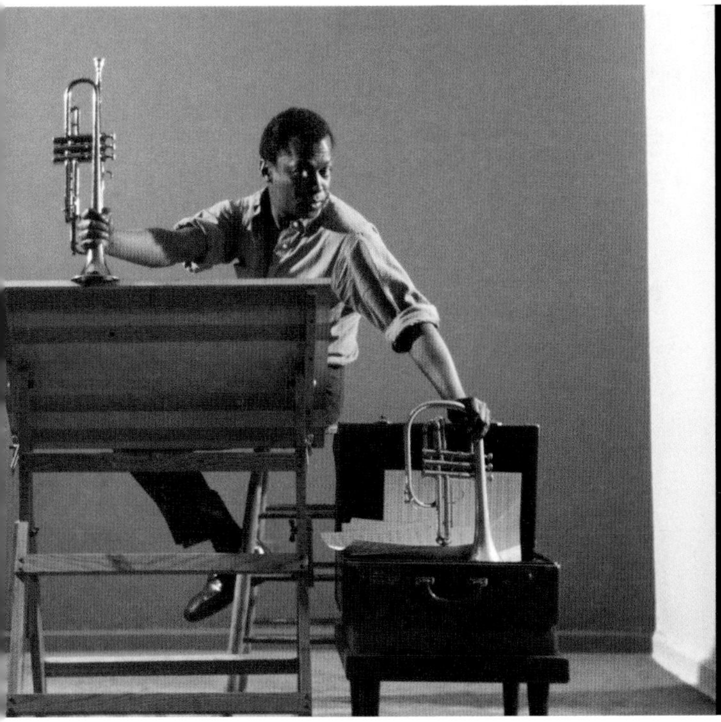

was formed, some people were surprised to see Coltrane, this avant-garde figure, associated with Cannonball Adderley, then considered the heir to Charlie Parker and thus the keeper of the flame. Davis responded simply that this combination framed his music perfectly. Miles Davis' fascination with Coltrane was inseparable from his interest in Cannonball Adderley's roots in the bop/blues tradition, and at times he enjoyed holding one up as an example to the other and vice versa. His predilection for Adderley at the time was so great that he agreed to take part in his Blue Note recording of *Somethin' Else*, in fact serving as artistic director and contributing, besides his trumpet playing, an arrangement of "Autumn Leaves" that was obviously inspired by Ahmad Jamal's trio. However, in early 1958, it was his own sextet's sessions for Columbia that caused a stir. They captured quintessential Davis at the head of a group reconnecting with the power of "Walkin'," of which "Sid's Ahead" is an updated version. At the peak of his technique, the trumpeter ventured into the upper register with ease. While the sound is full, it does not lack the dramatic effects of timbre. In the extreme tempo of "Dr. Jackle," rapid figures alternate with remarkably clean attacks and sustained notes gliding over the surge of the rhythm section. In the incredibly effective arrangements of the first theme statements, the band produces a massive sound that drops back in the heat of the solos, in keeping with the contrast between Coltrane's incantatory flight and Adderley's wild zigzags. Evident is Davis' total confidence in his bassist, instilling the group with an unfailing groove while constantly taking liberties. The bass is given a solo in most of the pieces. The exchanges with the drums in "Sid's Ahead" and Miles Davis' hand-off to Philly Joe Jones in "Dr. Jackle" likewise demonstrate the interaction between the two men. On the other hand, Red Garland stormed out during the recording of the last piece, "Sid's Ahead," irritated by the lack of piano solos and the silences periodically imposed on him while others were playing.

WITH AND WITHOUT PIANO. Miles Davis had already asked Thelonious Monk to hang back during his trumpet solos at the session on December 24, 1954. However, what might appear like a strategy to shield himself from Monk's strange accompaniments was actually normal for Davis. In the final solo of "Solar" on April 3, 1954 (*Walkin'*), he had Horace Silver stay quiet. In "Oleo" the same year, he let the piano accompany only the bridge. In the 1956 version, it seems that Red Garland was told to refrain from using his left hand during his own solo. These withdrawals of the piano and single-note solos with no left hand were at first the subject of specific instructions. As drummer Jimmy Cobb would explain, "Piano players, when they first got with the band, they were always confused, because he would tell them when to play and when not to play, so they got so they wouldn't know when to play." Later, Wynton Kelly and Herbie Hancock would adopt the habit and "lay out" (stop playing) on their own initiative. The first experiments in playing without piano date back to 1947, in the first two trumpet choruses of "The Hymn" with Charlie Parker, and 1949, with "Moon Dreams" by Gil Evans. Evans later abstained from using the piano in his collaborations with Davis, who became aware of the effectiveness of the formula in 1952 (at the very time when Chet Baker and Gerry Mulligan were experimenting with the pianoless quartet on the West Coast). Miles Davis then took part in a tour with a band without piano made up of Milt Jackson, Percy Heath and Kenny Clarke. As Davis himself explained, "When somebody *did* want a piano, either I or one of the other guys played piano behind whoever wanted it. . . . If nobody wanted piano, then whoever was playing could just stroll, which meant playing whatever you wanted with only drum and bass behind you and that empty spot where the piano ordinarily would be. It was like walking down the street on a bright, sunny day without

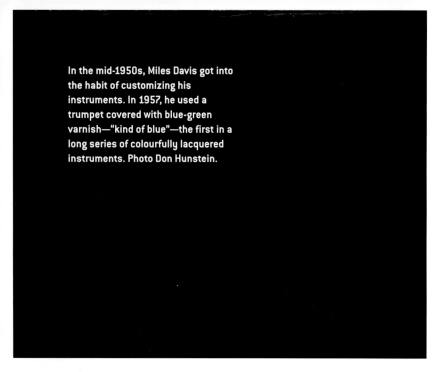

In the mid-1950s, Miles Davis got into the habit of customizing his instruments. In 1957, he used a trumpet covered with blue-green varnish—"kind of blue"—the first in a long series of colourfully lacquered instruments. Photo Don Hunstein.

nobody or anything being in your way. That's what I meant by strolling; also, using your own imagination. Playing without the piano freed up the music. I found out on this tour that sometimes a piano got in the way."

MODAL MUSIC. Miles Davis developed a mistrust of the harmonic constraints imposed by the piano, which led him to an interest in modal music. Simply put, a mode is a melodic scale that one might think of as a ladder, where the number of rungs, or degrees, and the spacing between them are determined by the nature of each individual mode. There is a wide variety of musical scales throughout the world: heptatonic (seven degrees, like the Western major scale), hexatonic (six degrees) and pentatonic (five degrees). In some forms of folk music, pieces generally rest on a single mode, employing a static harmony sustained by a held or repeated note (a drone) or a continually repeated pattern (an ostinato). Although Western classical music uses only a restricted number of modes—the well-known major scale and its related minors—it relies on two types of movement. The first type, embodied in the cadence, is based on principles of functional harmony according to which a melody is developed by initially focusing on some degrees of the scale, then on others. The effect is one of stability leading to instability when dissonances are encountered, followed by a return to stability. The other type of movement, or harmonic progression, is embodied in the concept of modulation, which involves capitalizing on a moment of instability to pass from one scale to another, generally identical, with its first degree higher or lower than that of the previous scale.

Based on this harmonic system, bop carried the principle of movement to the extreme. The accompaniment (piano and bass) issued more and more instructions, requiring soloists to accelerate cadential movement and harmonic progression, even taking shortcuts. At first, Davis was enthusiastic about such gymnastics, which he brought to a peak at the first recording session under his name on August 14, 1947, with tunes like "Little Willie Leaps" and "Sippin' at Bells." Consequently, he achieved a natural melodic style ill suited to those acrobatic backgrounds, and he got into the habit of recasting harmonies and pieces to please himself. From the late 1940s on, he was often drawn to static harmony. In his arrangement of George Shearing's "Conception," renamed "Deception" for the nonet, he stretched out the original chart and introduced moments of harmonic suspension.

These suspensions became more frequent during the 1950s, taking the form of interludes, particularly in "Dear Old Stockholm" [a traditional Swedish theme whose folkloric nature is germane to this discussion], "The Leap," "Take Off," "In Your Own Sweet Way," among others. Elsewhere, he looped cadential fragments, as at the end of the solos in "If I Were a Bell." In the arrangement of "Autumn Leaves" for Cannonball Adderley's album *Somethin' Else*, he borrowed an ostinato from Ahmad Jamal, spinning out an endless coda whose harmonic stasis recalls the contemplative character of Asian music. The sequences improvised while viewing *Ascenseur pour l'échafaud* adopted this monochromatic aesthetic to convey mood more radically still, and when, the next year, Davis took part in recording *Legrand Jazz*, he deplored Michel Legrand's overly dense orchestrations.

While a first "Milestones," composed in 1947, saddled the soloists with a convoluted chord progression, the "Milestones" from the album of the same name, recorded by the sextet in 1958, was a milestone indeed. Retitled "Miles" for the second pressing to avoid any confusion between these two unrelated themes, its only directive to the soloist was to play in one mode and then another. The same approach recurs in Gil Evans' adaptation of the opera *Porgy and Bess* for Davis, as Davis explained to journalist Nat Hentoff in December 1958: "When Gil wrote the arrangement of 'I Loves You, Porgy,' he only wrote a scale for me to play. . . . You don't have to worry about [chord] changes and you can do more with the [melodic] line. It becomes a challenge to see how melodically inventive you are."

BILL EVANS AND THE CLASSICAL INFLUENCE. At the decade's close, the air was filled with the modal concept, as theorized by composer George Russell in his *Lydian Chromatic Concept of Tonal Organization*. It was Russell who advised Davis to hire pianist Bill Evans to replace Red Garland in the sextet. The new arrival introduced the trumpeter to Ravel's String Quartet in F Major and his Piano Concerto in G Major, recently recorded by Arturo Benedetti Michelangeli. Together they listened to Rachmaninoff and Khachaturian, interested in how composers at the beginning of the century used modes to revitalize classical music's harmonic habits and open new pathways of harmonic progression.

While drummer Jimmy Cobb replaced Philly Joe Jones, Bill Evans' delicate touch, more abstract harmonizing and exquisitely subtle improvisation deeply affected Davis' music during the session of May 26, 1958, dominated by ballads played with a mute at moderate tempos. However, the live tracks of the records attest to music of an entirely different nature, where Bill Evans' vigorous punctuation and articulation keep the new sextet's flame alive. Nonetheless, the group's harmonic horizons were considerably broader. Uncustomarily, Davis intervenes but rarely to indicate his expectations to the pianist. On the other hand, he was very critical of Cannonball Adderley's playing, which he considered passé: "Cannonball, you don't have to play *all* those notes." Nevertheless, at the end of an engagement at the Village Vanguard in November 1958, Bill Evans left the group.

Photo Don Hunstein.

MY MAN'S GONE NOW
PRAYER

Pianist Bill Evans shared his classical background with Miles Davis' group, which helped to expand the band's harmonic horizons and had a decisive influence on the development of the use of modes. Photo Chuck Stewart.

The only white man in one of black music's foremost ensembles, Bill Evans must have had to endure a lot of criticism, and Miles Davis himself, despite his deep admiration for Evans, did not spare him, nicknaming him "Whitey." It is also true that the time had come for Bill Evans to look after his own career with his trio.

WHAT KIND OF BLUE? Early in 1959, Miles Davis was proud of his new pianist, Wynton Kelly, whom he saw as a combination of Red Garland and Bill Evans. He especially appreciated Kelly's ability to anticipate the soloists' ideas. On March 2, 1959, the pianist was in the studio with the sextet to record "Freddie Freeloader" for the upcoming album *Kind of Blue*. However, when they started on the second track, "So What," which takes up the bimodal principle of "Milestones," Bill Evans was invited to sit down at the keyboard. Evans' presence dominates the whole record—finished at a second session on April 22—almost stealing the limelight in what remains one of Davis' greatest masterpieces. At the outset, *Kind of Blue* was to be a double homage in Davis' image: to the origins of blues and gospel on one hand and to Africa on the other. Davis had come into contact with the blues at his grandfather's place in Arkansas, a hundred kilometres west of the cradle of the genre, the Mississippi Delta (a narrow triangle south of Memphis, not to be confused with the mouth of the great river). He had not lost sight of this music, and John Lee Hooker remembered seeing Miles Davis in the audience during his stint in Detroit in winter 1953–54. Gospel, on the other hand, was only a faint memory for Davis, who had always steered clear of any form of religion: "I also remember how the music used to sound down there in Arkansas, when I was visiting my grandfather, especially at the Saturday night church. . . . I guess I was about six or seven. We'd be walking on these dark country roads at night and all of a sudden, this music would seem to come out of nowhere, out of them spooky-looking trees that everybody said ghosts lived in. Anyway, we'd be on the side of the road—whoever I was with, one of my uncles or my cousin James—and I remember somebody would be playing on guitar the way B. B. King plays. And I remember a man and a woman singing and talking about getting *down*! . . . But I think that *kind* of stuff stayed with me, you know what I mean? That kind of sound in music, that blues, church, back-road funk kind of thing, that Southern, Midwestern, rural sound and rhythm. I think it started getting into my blood on them spook-filled Arkansas back roads after dark when the owls came out hooting." Like Art Blakey's "Moanin'" and Horace Silver's "The Preacher," "So What" and "All Blues" are built upon a game of call-and-response between the front-line horns and the rhythm section. However, like Gil Evans' arrangement for "Prayer" on *Porgy and Bess*, Miles Davis stood apart from the razzle-dazzle and fervour of "churchy" music then in fashion, the eerie introduction to "So What" and the piano tremolos in "All Blues" tending to evoke his fantastical memories of the little country roads at dusk.

THE WRONG ROAD TO AFRICA. Miles Davis said he discovered Africa at a performance by the Ballet africain de Guinée, which he saw with Frances Taylor. He came away strongly impressed by the musical and choreographic polyrhythms: "I didn't write out the music for *Kind of Blue*, but brought in sketches for what everybody was supposed to play because I wanted a lot of spontaneity in the playing, just like I thought was in the interplay between those dancers and those drummers and that finger piano player with the Ballet Africaine

Kind of Blue was recorded in New York in 1959 at Columbia's Thirtieth-street studio. Pianist Bill Evans (above), who had left the group, returned for the occasion. The group's regular pianist, Wynton Kelly, was asked to play on just one track. John Coltrane's and Cannonball Adderley's solos contributed to the success of this record, which half a century later is recognized as the most famous jazz record in history. Photos Don Hunstein.

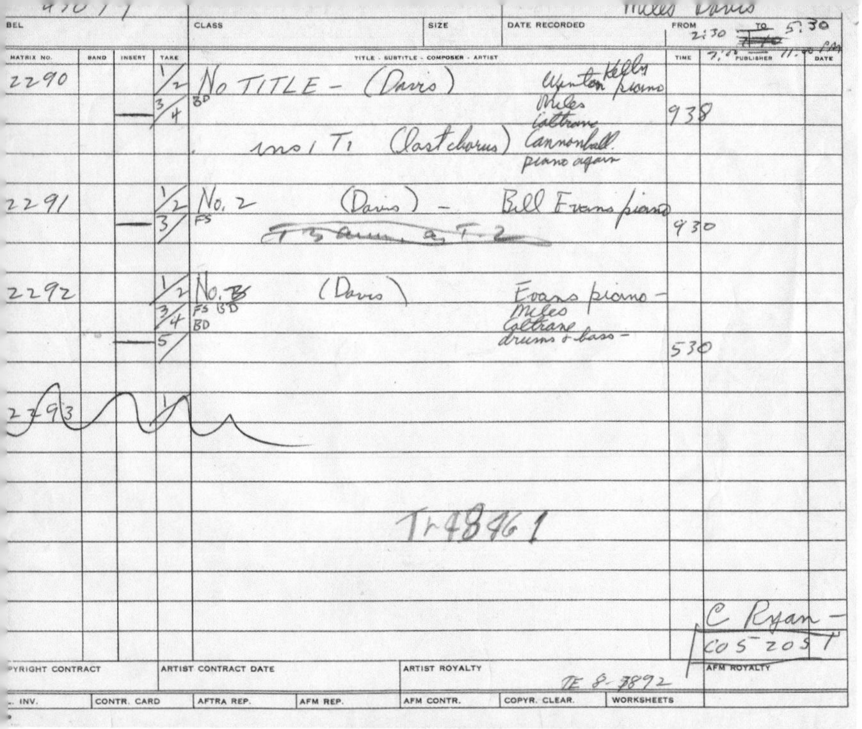
BEL | CLASS | SIZE | DATE RECORDED | Miles Davis | FROM 2:30 TO 5:30, 7:00 to 11:00

MATRIX NO.	BAND	INSERT	TAKE	TITLE - SUBTITLE - COMPOSER - ARTIST		TIME	PUBLISHER	DATE
2290		—	1/2, 3/4 BD	NO TITLE – (Davis) ins / T1 (last chorus)	Wynton Kelly piano, Miles, Coltrane, Cannonball, piano again	9:38		
2291		—	1/2 FS, 3/	No. 2 (Davis) – ~~[struck through]~~	Bill Evans piano	9:30		
2292		—	1/2, 3/4 FS BD, BD, 5/	No. 3 (Davis)	Evans piano – Miles, Coltrane, drums & bass –	5:30		
2293			1					

TR 48461

C Ryan – CO5 2051

TE 8-3892

COPYRIGHT CONTRACT | ARTIST CONTRACT DATE | ARTIST ROYALTY | AFM ROYALTY

INV. | CONTR. CARD | AFTRA REP. | AFM REP. | AFM CONTR. | COPYR. CLEAR. | WORKSHEETS

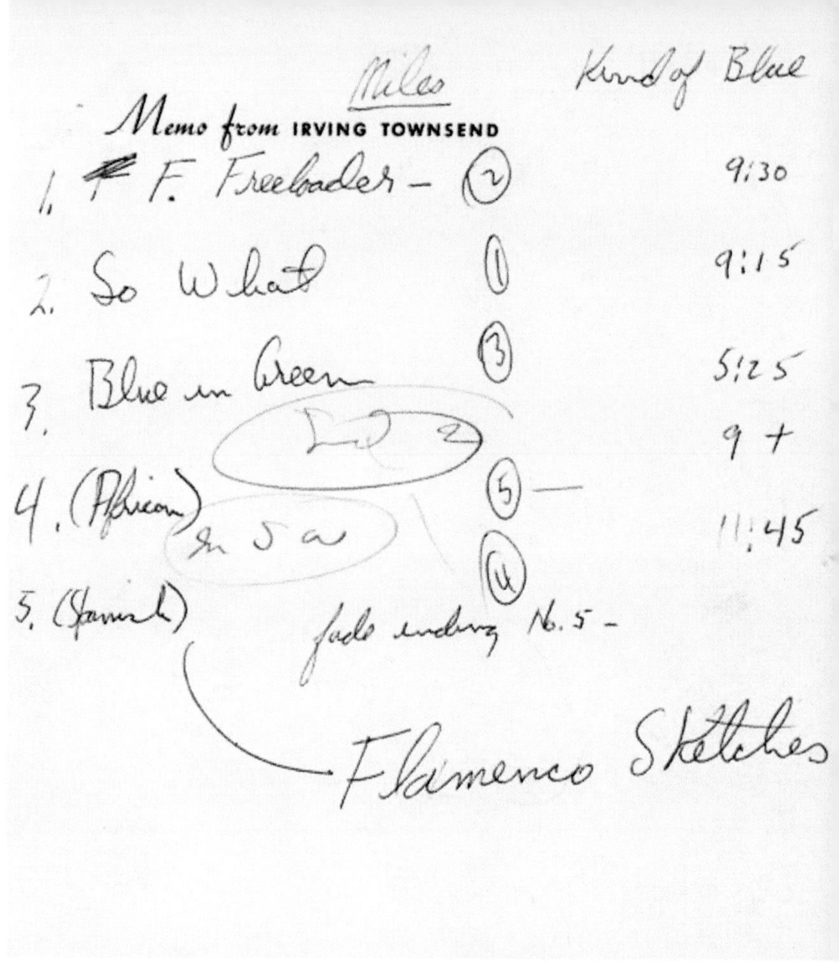
Miles — Kind of Blue

Memo from IRVING TOWNSEND

1. F. Freeloader – (2) 9:30
2. So What (1) 9:15
3. Blue in Green (3) 5:25
(circled: [illegible] 2) 9 +
4. (African) (5) – 11:45
(circled: In 5 [illegible])
5. (Spanish) (4)

fade ending No. 5 –

Flamenco Sketches

Written by pianist Bill Evans, the liner notes for *Kind of Blue* (below) sought to enlighten the listener on the nature of jazz improvisation and described the structure of the various pieces. Its didactic intention helped acquaint many jazz musicians with the idea of using modes.

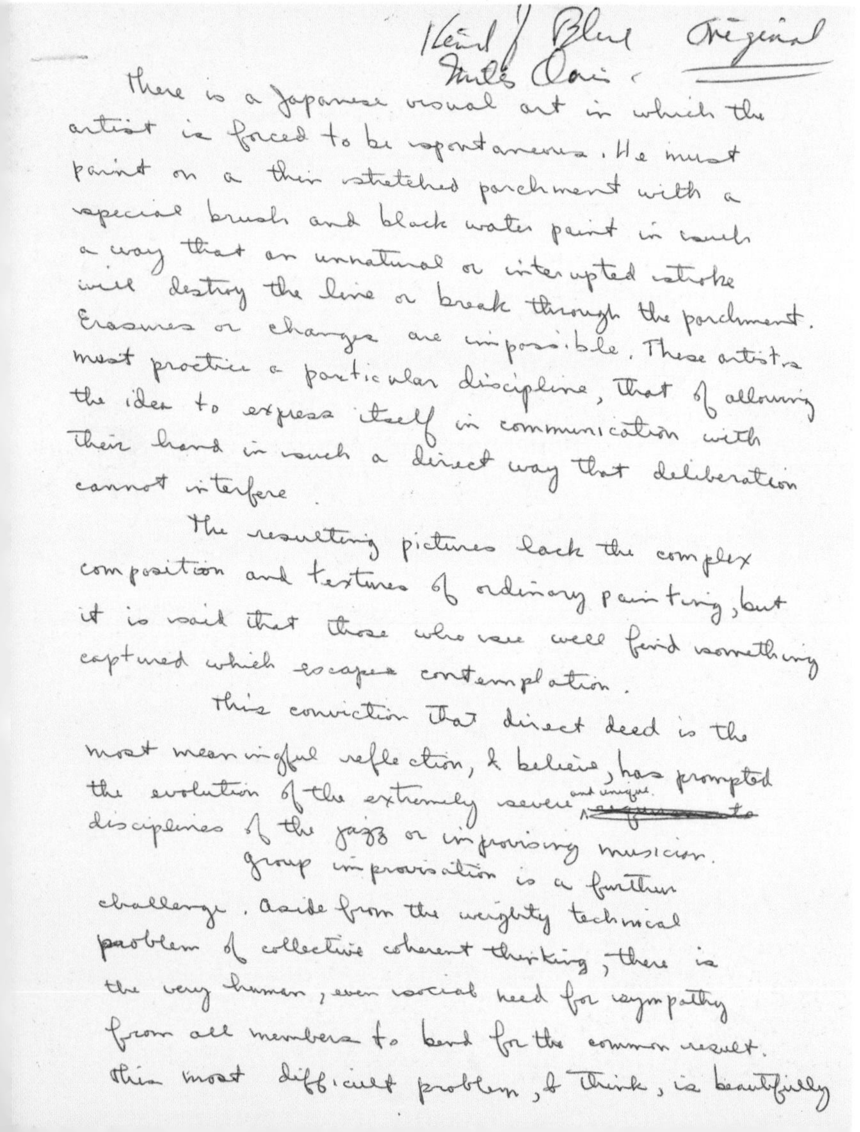
Kind of Blue — Original
Miles Davis

There is a Japanese visual art in which the artist is forced to be spontaneous. He must paint on a thin stretched parchment with a special brush and black water paint in such a way that an unnatural or interrupted stroke will destroy the line or break through the parchment. Erasures or changes are impossible. These artists must practice a particular discipline, that of allowing the idea to express itself in communication with their hand in such a direct way that deliberation cannot interfere

The resulting pictures lack the complex composition and textures of ordinary painting, but it is said that those who see well find something captured which escapes contemplation.

This conviction that direct deed is the most meaningful reflection, I believe, has prompted the evolution of the extremely severe and unique ~~[struck through]~~ disciplines of the jazz or improvising musician.

Group improvisation is a further challenge. Aside from the weighty technical problem of collective coherent thinking, there is the very human, even social need for sympathy from all members to bend for the common result. This most difficult problem, I think, is beautifully

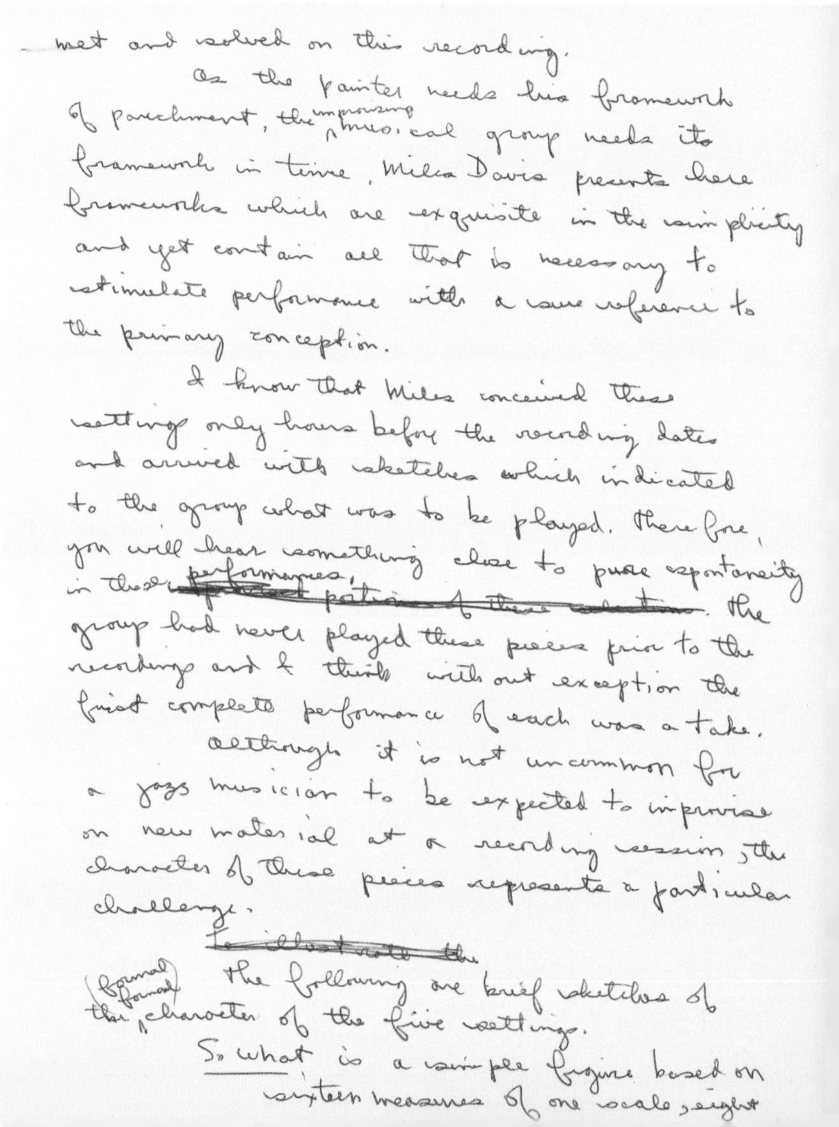
met and solved on this recording.

As the painter needs his framework of parchment, the improvising musical group needs its framework in time. Miles Davis presents here frameworks which are exquisite in their simplicity and yet contain all that is necessary to stimulate performance with a sure reference to the primary conception.

I know that Miles conceived these settings only hours before the recording dates and arrived with sketches which indicated to the group what was to be played. Therefore, you will hear something close to pure spontaneity in these performances, ~~[struck through]~~. The group had never played these pieces prior to the recordings and I think without exception the first complete performance of each was a take.

Although it is not uncommon for a jazz musician to be expected to improvise on new material at a recording session, the character of these pieces represents a particular challenge.

~~To illustrate the~~

The following are brief sketches of the (formal) character of the five settings.

So What is a simple figure based on sixteen measures of one scale, eight

Miles M I

Memo from IRVING TOWNSEND

Side I
1. 62291 — T3 — So What 9:15
2. 62290 — T4 — F Freeloader 9:30
3. 62292 — T5 — Blue in Green 5:25

II
62293 T1 — Flamenco Sketches
62294 T2 — ~~(No TITLE)~~ All Blues

Ya

of another and eight more of the first following a piano bass introduction in free rhythmic style.

Blue in Green is a ten measure circular form played by the soloists in various augmentation and diminution of time values.

All Blue is a series of five scales, each to be played as long as the soloist wishes until he has completed the series.

F. Sketches is a six-eight, twelve measure blues form that produces another mood through its few modal changes and Miles Davis' free melodic conception.

F. Freeloader is another twelve measure blues form given new personality by effective melodic and rhythmic simplicity.

Perhaps those who hear well will find something captured which escapes contemplation

Bill Evans.

Kind of Blue was completed in two sessions, March 22 and April 2, 1959 (opposite page, session sheet). Producer Irving Townsend's handwritten annotations (top centre) reveal that some of the pieces had no titles when they were recorded—"Flamenco Sketches" and "All Blues" are designated as "Spanish" and "African" respectively, adjectives that indicate the trumpeter's sources of inspiration. An error in these annotations resulted in titles being misattributed on the first pressing of the album. Photo Don Hunstein.

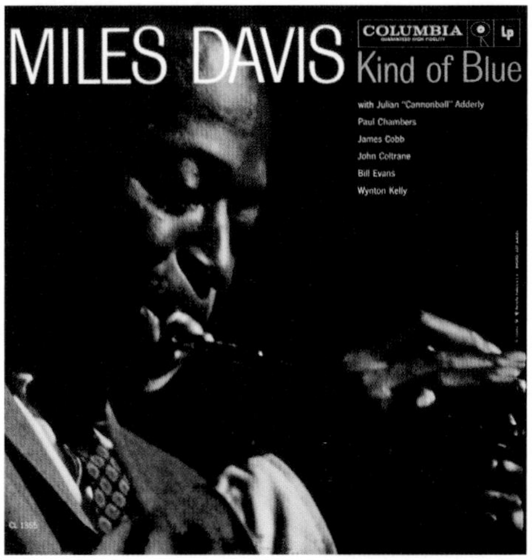

Photo : Vernon Smith.

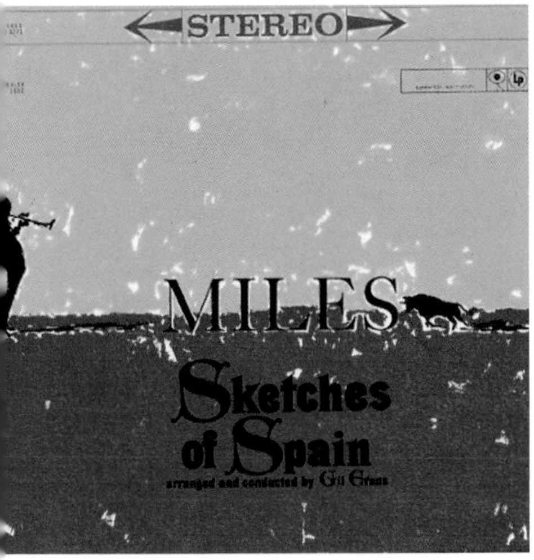

The third joint record created by Miles Davis and Gil Evans (opposite page, during the sessions in November 1959), oriented towards Spain and flamenco, *Sketches of Spain* contains the famous adaptation of Joaquín Rodrigo's *Concierto de Aranjuez*. Photo Vernon Smith.

[sic]." What is left of Africa in *Kind of Blue*? Perhaps the rhythm of the sanza (the African thumb piano) in the 6/8 meter adopted at the last minute for "All Blues," originally written in 4/4.

In the absence of a title, the record's producer, Irving Townsend, wrote "African" in his session notes. However, it must be admitted that the African influence is not obvious, and Davis says as much in his autobiography: "We were into Ravel (especially his 'Concerto for the Left Hand and Orchestra') and Rachmaninoff ('Concerto No. 4')." He probably did not yet have the musicians capable of meeting such a challenge, and he would have to wait until the 1970s to achieve his goal.

Bill Evans recalls going to Davis' apartment at his request: "He thought I would know how to give precise instructions to the musicians in order to realize the concept for this music." Bill Evans composed "Blue in Green" based on a chord suggested by Davis; "Flamenco Sketches" developed out of one of the pianist's pieces, "Peace Piece," recorded as a solo a few months earlier for the record *Everybody Digs Bill Evans*. While the left hand tirelessly repeats the same harmonic figure in the manner of Indian music improvised over the drone of a held note, the right hand explores a single mode. Davis proposed that Evans start from this mode and develop a script. They both sat down at the piano to try out different possibilities. They decided to add four more modes to the first and give them to the soloists of the quintet. None of the pieces was written out except for the five modes and the order in which each solo would explore them. One of these modes, over which each of the solos tended to linger, was the Phrygian mode, characteristic of flamenco. The resulting piece was called "Flamenco Sketches."

FLAMENCO. This was not Miles Davis' first encounter with Spanish music. Spain was already present on *Miles Ahead* in "The Maids of Cadiz," after Léo Delibes, and "Blues for Pablo," inspired by Manuel de Falla and unidentified Mexican folk material. Flamenco had provided a stimulating field of exploration for composers of the late nineteenth and early twentieth centuries, when European classical music was permeated by a double current oriented towards regional expression and modal language. Thanks to George Avakian, however, Gil Evans had discovered flamenco at the source. The producer was in charge of the publication of a collection of folk music undertaken by ethnomusicologist Alan Lomax, and he intended to have Gil Evans work along these lines. In 1958, Beverly Bentley had given Davis a three-record box set entitled *Antologia del cante flamenco*, which had been influential in the spread of the genre. On the way home from a flamenco show Frances Taylor had dragged him to, Davis stopped at a record store to buy everything that had anything to do with the style. When he introduced Gil Evans to Joaquín Rodrigo's *Concierto de Aranjuez* in early 1959, Evans decided to adapt the slow movement for trumpet and orchestra. He also composed "Will o' the Wisp" (after Manuel de Falla's *El Amor Brujo*), "The Pan Piper" (after a panpipe solo collected by Alan Lomax in 1952 in the Spanish province of Galicia), "Saeta" (after a traditional *saeta* sung by Lolita Triana and Ramón Montoya in *Antologia del cante flamenco*) and "Solea," a monumental extrapolation of Andalusian *cante jondo*.

However, the *Concierto de Aranjuez* still provokes debate among some jazz connoisseurs today. Gil Evans' adaptation did not meet with universal approval, any more than the rest of this Spanish program. It was certainly not the first time the arranger had teetered on the edge of kitsch, but he always managed to keep his precarious balance without falling over, thanks to the iconoclastic grace of his harmonies and the safeguard provided by his enigmatic orchestrations. More than anything, Miles Davis' poise, extreme concision and natural reserve resistant to any pathos were the strongest possible guarantees against the kitsch Gil Evans liked to court. Except for "Song of Our Country," after Heitor Villa-Lobos, which was not released until 1981, all the pieces came out in 1960 under the title *Sketches of Spain*. By the time the record came out, John Coltrane had left Davis' group.

MILES DAVIS GIL EVANS

Eddie Lang–Joe Venuti; Django Reinhardt–Stéphane Grappelli; Duke Ellington–Billy Strayhorn; Charlie Parker–Dizzy Gillespie; Bill Evans–Scott LaFaro. . . . The history of jazz has no shortage of mythic collaborations. Without a doubt, the collaboration between Miles Davis and Gil Evans belongs in this pantheon of legends.

It has to be said, however, that the success of this partnership was certainly not a foregone conclusion, given the differences in their ages (fourteen years), the colour of their skin and their individual musical brilliance and personalities. A lot has been said about Gil Evans' famous one-room basement apartment on Fifty-fifth Street, where, in 1948, everybody assembled night and day. Miles Davis was part of the scene, but he was not necessarily a regular at these casual gatherings. In terms of their relationship, the experience of *Birth of the Cool* served as a tryout. Gil Evans was credited for only two arrangements, "Boplicity" (a Miles Davis composition) and "Moon Dreams" (a third, "Why Do I Love You?" came out only later). Looking back, it is easy to see that, as polished and innovative as these pieces seemed at the time, they were only an indication of what was to come.

As Davis commented, "I liked the way Gil wrote music and he liked the way I played." And Evans: "We had this thing, this sound, in common. Not necessarily the details; the first thing you hear when someone plays or writes, or even talks, is the sound, the shape of the wave. And having that in common is what makes collaboration possible."

Even so, their budding partnership was prematurely aborted due to disappointed expectations, and the paths of their lives diverged. Miles Davis began the long descent into the hell of heroin, from which he would not emerge for some years. Meanwhile, Gil Evans entered the tunnel he would revisit periodically during his career. Evans was one of those artists who, like an eclipse, drops out of sight then reappears—in his case, with a certain regularity. How he survived is hard to say, but these absences from the public eye gave him time to complete his apprenticeship, to let his evolving style mature.

Even if the two musicians never really lost sight of each other, they only reunited in 1956. This was the year that Gil Evans worked for singer Helen Merrill, who recommended Evans to Davis. On the recording of "'Round Midnight," Evans arranged at least three transitional bars between the trumpet's statement of the theme and John Coltrane's solo (and possibly the rest). This same year, Davis got his first Columbia contract, which presented new means for developing his music and his visibility. The approach featured the trumpeter's quintet with Coltrane, but also included the idea of recording with a large orchestra. Though the names of many arrangers were bandied about, Gil Evans got the job. *Miles Ahead*, recorded in 1957, was the first of a miraculous series of four albums released under Davis' name that would include *Porgy and Bess* (1958), *Sketches of Spain* (1959–1960) and *Quiet Nights* (1962).These four records form a whole in terms of their exceptional consistency, despite their varied themes. They might even be considered as concept albums before their time.

Gil Evans and Miles Davis never again lost touch, but they also never again collaborated on an entire record, though projects were often announced, always hoped for. A number of proposals were considered—the music for a play, *Time of the Barracudas*, a *Tosca*, but none would ever see the light of day.

In 1968, "Falling Waters" was recorded, though it would only be released in 1996. This piece serves as a hint of the work that could have been. A new project was proposed to Gil Evans on numerous occasions, right up until the end of his life, to which he always replied while turning to speak to someone else, "Tell [Davis] to join the club."

Nevertheless, an echo of Gil Evans reappears in the recordings of Miles Davis, as Evans attended many sessions, pencil in hand: for example, in the introduction of "So What" on *Kind of Blue* (only learned of long after its release); in the composition of "Petits Machins" on *Filles de Kilimanjaro* (which Gil Evans recorded under its original title, "Eleven"), perhaps even on the whole record; possibly on "Circle in the Round" with guitarist Joe Beck; in some melodic fragments on *We Want Miles*, on *Star People* . . . and most likely through many other contributions, which were never properly credited.

What then passed between these two? Something unique, something that goes beyond the perfect setting an inspired arranger provides an exceptional soloist, the skills and talents of each complementing and enhancing the other, that intangible, inexpressible *je ne sais quoi* of which French philosopher Vladimir Jankélévitch speaks (and which perhaps occurs in similar cases in other contexts). Perhaps it is best explained in Miles Davis' autobiography, when he describes his reaction to Evans' death:

"A week after he died, I was talking to him and we had a conversation that went something like this. I was in my apartment in New York, sitting on my bed looking at the picture I have of him on the table across from my bed, by the window. The lights were dancing in through my window. All of a sudden, a question came into my head for Gil, and I asked him, 'Gil, why did you die like you did, you know, down in Mexico?' And then he said, 'That's the only way I could do it, Miles. I had to go down to Mexico to do it.' I knew it was him because I could tell his voice anywhere. It was his spirit coming down to talk to me."

Everything is there: the photograph on the table, the lights dancing through the window, the conversation between the living and the dead, those things we just have to do, the voice we would recognize anywhere, the spirit that speaks—all the ingredients necessary for music that will never die.

LAURENT CUGNY

FRENCH COMPOSER AND BANDLEADER LAURENT CUGNY FOUNDED THE BIG BAND LUMIÈRE AND WAS MUSIC DIRECTOR OF THE ORCHESTRE NATIONAL DE JAZZ. HE AUTHORED *LAS VEGAS TANGO* (P.O.L., 1990), A BIOGRAPHY OF GIL EVANS, WITH WHOM HE COLLABORATED CLOSELY IN 1987.

Photo Vernon Smith.

Miles Davis smiles again: the young musicians who accompanied him in the mid-1960s, like saxophonist Wayne Shorter, contributed to re-awakening his interest in music and getting him out of his rut. Here, in Berlin, in September 1964. Photo Jan Persson.

MILES SMILES CONTROLLED FREEDOM

1960–1967

In 1960, Miles Davis seemed to be a man who had everything. Back from hell, he had just produced four of the greatest masterpieces in the history of jazz, one after another: *Miles Ahead*, *Milestones*, *Porgy and Bess* and *Kind of Blue*. His collaboration with Gil Evans allowed him to broaden his audience beyond the world of jazz. *Life* magazine presented him as a model of success in the black community. In 1962, he was interviewed at length in *Playboy*. His New York concerts were attended by celebrities like Marlon Brando, Ava Gardner, Richard Burton, Elizabeth Taylor and Paul Newman, whose lifestyle he shared. His Mercedes was replaced by a Jaguar, then by the first in a long series of Ferraris. He bought and remodelled an old five-storey Russian Orthodox church at 312 West Seventy-seventh Street in Manhattan. Ten rooms were rented or reserved for Davis' children (Cheryl, Gregory and Miles IV) and Jean-Pierre, Frances Taylor's son. Davis and his new girlfriend moved into this luxuriously appointed duplex, outfitted with an intercom system with loudspeakers hidden in the walls. Upstairs, there was a music room with a piano incorporated into the furniture, and in the basement, a gym.

"It Was Police Brutality"

'BEAT MY HEAD LIKE TOM-TOM'

Miles Davis Protests N.Y. Cop-Beating

'They Beat On My Head Like A Tom - Tom'

Judges Clear Miles Davis

Jazz Star, 2 Cops, in Battle That Blocks Traffic on B'way

← THIS IS WHAT THEY DID TO MILES DAVIS

THE battered, bleeding figure on the left is trumpeter Miles Davis, one of the great names of modern jazz and the idol of a million disc collectors and fans.

This dramatic picture, flown to the MELODY MAKER from New York, shows Davis, still bleeding from head wounds, being marched into the city's West 54th Street Police Station House by Patrolman Gerald Kilduff.

BEATEN

A few minutes earlier he had been taking a breather between sessions at the world-famous jazz-haunt, Birdland, when he was told to move on by Kilduff.

NEXT: MILES DAVIS TO FIGHT NEW YORK

Jazzman Miles Davis Battles Two Cops Outside Birdland

Miles Davis Jailed For Disturbance

Jazzman Davis Bopped In Scuffle With Cops

Outside Birdland on August 26, 1959, Miles Davis was the victim of a violent incident with the police that made front-page news and reminded him that his success did not protect him from the latent racism of an America still subject to segregation laws. Left: just after his encounter; right: Davis' lawyer Harold Lovett and a police officer. Photos Bild Ullstein (left); Fred Klein (right).

BLOWS AND WOUNDS. As a couple, Miles Davis and Frances Taylor invested a lot of effort into setting up their home. Davis was madly in love with his girlfriend, to the point of becoming violently jealous, while he continued to see Beverly Bentley regularly, even proposing marriage to her when she grew distant. He married Frances Taylor in December 1960 but only stopped seeing Bentley when she married the writer Norman Mailer in late 1963. Despite the complexity of his relationships, Davis could be sociable. His humour was appreciated, though it could take an aggressive turn when he was not feeling confident. He was known for a tendency to melancholy and even depression that made him turn in on himself. Race relations were a subject of constant concern, which was aggravated by a painful incident.

On the evening of August 26, 1959, the sextet had just finished a set at Birdland that was recorded by the Armed Forces Radio Service. Davis was smoking a cigarette at the break when a police officer asked the crowd lingering at the entrance of the club to keep moving so as not to block the sidewalk. He addressed Davis, who replied that he had no reason to move along because he worked there. Tension mounted quickly, until three officers gave Davis a severe beating. He arrived at the police station covered in blood, and a doctor had to give him five stitches. Charged with disorderly conduct and assaulting an officer, he had his temporary cabaret card revoked, without which he was forbidden to play in New York.

The next day, when Davis was released on bail, the incident made the front page of the newspapers. After two hearings, the charges against him were dropped and his arrest deemed illegal, but he was deeply marked by this episode, convinced that the officer's aggressiveness was due to the fact that he had seen him accompany a white woman to her taxi just prior to the incident. Furthermore, at a time when the African-American community was fighting for civil rights in a climate of extreme violence, Davis was conscious that his acquittal was due to his fame, contacts and wealth. Therefore, one can understand his distress when, during a benefit concert for the African Research Foundation on May 19, 1961, with the Gil Evans Orchestra at Carnegie Hall, his old friend Max Roach burst in with a group of protesters to denounce the foundation's colonialist attitude. To make matters worse, Davis, who had been suffering increasing pains in his left hip and leg for several years, learned that he had a hereditary illness, sickle-cell anemia, a disease of the red blood cells that can cause heart attacks, anemia, joint pain, cardiopulmonary disorders, infections and ailments of every kind, including pneumonia.

HOW TO REPLACE COLTRANE? Miles Davis' companions deserted the sextet, which had been very active musically throughout 1959. After Bill Evans, Cannonball Adderley defected in early fall. John Coltrane gave notice that he would leave the group as soon as it returned to the United States from a major European tour. From March 21 to April 10, 1960, the quintet played in twenty major European cities. The recordings made during the tour reveal a Davis at times on the edge of abstraction in the theme statement of a ballad, often distorting the timbre, intonation, articulation and melodic for-

Miles Davis married dancer Frances Taylor on December 21, 1960 (opposite page, in London in September of the same year). A few months later, he insisted that Columbia Records put the portrait of this "black beauty" on the cover of the record *Someday My Prince Will Come*, rather than the usual white playmate.

mulation. In the up tempos, he favoured dialogue with drummer Jimmy Cobb, playing around with space, distending and interjecting terse formulas, while the piano made an increasing number of impromptu entrances and exits. However, it was Coltrane who caused a sensation. Despite the strong negative reactions to these long stretches in some venues, particularly the Olympia in Paris, Coltrane attacked pieces like "So What," massaging the phrases, saturating them with colliding ideas, with an impetuosity that presaged his future evolution.

In spring 1959, Coltrane put an end to his exploration of bebop harmony with the record *Giant Steps*. From then on, he took the lead in an exploitation of modes that Miles Davis, the initiator, would be unable to follow, where, abandoned by Bill Evans and "Trane," he knew he could not venture alone. Wayne Shorter could help him get over this hurdle. When Coltrane tried to have himself replaced by Shorter on the 1960 European tour, Davis vehemently rejected the idea. Now that Coltrane was gone, Davis regretted his decision, but it was too late. Shorter was now well ensconced in the Jazz Messengers. Eventually, Coltrane was succeeded by Sonny Stitt, a bopper from the very beginning, and when the new quintet appeared at the Olympia in the fall, the contrast was striking. In early 1961, Davis hired Hank Mobley, a calm hard bopper who had earned recognition with the Jazz Messengers. On March 7, 1961, Davis undertook, with Mobley, the recording of a new album during which he alternatively attempted to prolong and renounce *Kind of Blue*. "Drad-Dog" is an extension of "Blue in Green" but has neither its formal daring nor magic. On the other hand, "Pfrancing" (also known as "No Blues") is a typically churchy blues riff in the hard-bop tradition. This puzzling title is a play on words (prancing, dancing, frantic) in honour of Frances Taylor, whose face is on the record cover of *Someday My Prince Will Come*.

SOMEDAY MY PRINCE WILL COME. The record took its title from the well-known song from Walt Disney's *Snow White*. As Miles Davis explains in his autobiography, "It was on *Someday My Prince Will Come* that I started demanding that Columbia use black women on my album covers. . . . I mean, it was my album and I was Frances' prince." The song was recorded on March 20, 1961. After the trumpet, saxophone and piano solos, Davis was restating the theme like a crooner when John Coltrane suddenly appeared in the studio, tenor saxophone in hand. All at once, it was as if the sun had risen on a misty morning. Sight-reading the chords in the score, Coltrane launched into a solo with a stunningly relaxed feel, inventiveness and construction. In just two choruses, everything is expressed in a tremendous rhetorical arc, and Davis restates the theme yet again before letting the piano turn on a bass pedal for a long time, as if commanding time to suspend its flight. Although Coltrane was only passing through, he returned the next day for one last time and took Hank Mobley's place in "Teo" (entitled "Neo" in public), a sort of waltz version of "Flamenco Sketches." Coltrane's solo shows the range of his vocabulary in the area of modal jazz and the distance he had already put between himself and his companions. Was Davis ready to set out on the path that would lead Trane to free jazz? His experience of what was still called the "new thing" (hearing the Ornette Coleman Quartet at the Five Spot in November 1960) only elicited his sarcasm.

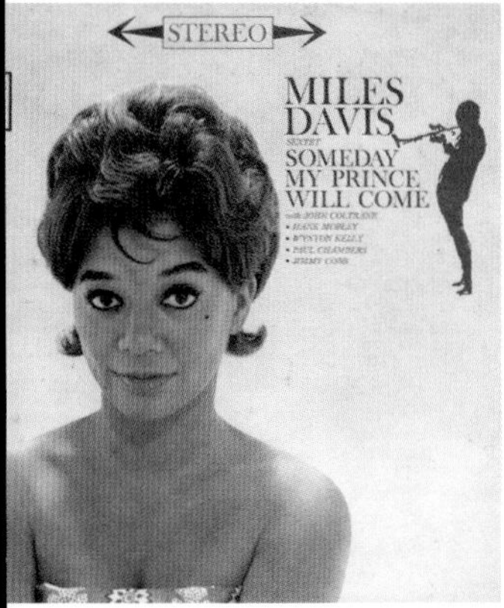
STEREO
MILES DAVIS
SOMEDAY MY PRINCE WILL COME

THE MAN

Miles Davis said that he had changed jazz five or six times, and that was true enough. But he was also a master of stagecraft, of *mise en scène*, and he changed the way jazz and race were seen. Davis turned his bandstand into a new kind of stage, changing its expressive and dramatic potential. He refused to acknowledge applause or speak to the audience, often turning away from them like Stanislavsky-trained Method actors Marlon Brando, James Dean or Montgomery Clift. All of these actors broke with theatrical practice and embraced an intimate and emotionally charged form of acting, more real for being improvised. Their personae—brooding, rude and inarticulate—were understood to be part of their rebellion, their unease part of their incomplete commitment to existing society. And behind a mask that seemed incapable of expressing anything, one sensed an intelligence impossible to put into words. Their gestures, inarticulateness and detachment merged with elements of cool, a West-African aesthetic in which beauty and character unite in self-possession, while at the same time resonating with Baudelaire's conception of the dandy as an aristocratic bohemian whose coldness is rooted in opposition and revolt.

Miles Davis never played the entertainer, never let himself be seen as just a black musician. He might present himself with the hauteur of royalty; he might appear as the artist of principled violence; or he might wilt an audience with a look, a gesture, the calculated understatement of a mime. He was jazz's Marcel Marceau.

In the 1950s, America was becoming aware of shifts in social and gender roles. Sociologists were talking about the age of conformity, the weakening of the superego, the other-directed person. It was feared that a new economy was creating a society in which people were too well adjusted and externally motivated. Apparently, men were becoming soft and emotional, i.e., more like women, resulting in what was perceived as a crisis of masculinity.

Into the heightened anxiety and exaggerated claims for male selfdom walked Miles: authentic and inner-directed to a fault, with the material aspirations of a *Playboy* man and the Beats' drive for self-expression. Some saw him as a natural existentialist, alienated because of his colour, but still out there every night, seeking freedom, risking everything in his solos. He was the avatar of hip.

Miles' bands were discussed with the passion of sports fans, the changes in his music dissected like great movements in painting, his every action read for meaning. A discourse developed around him, one that bore weight in matters of race—stories about his demons, his pain and his ambition. Whenever he took one of his respites from work and disappeared, stories spread: he was injured, sick or dead; he was unable to play; he was coming back with some innovation that was more than his fans could bear.

He was the man.

JOHN SZWED

PROFESSOR OF MUSIC AND JAZZ STUDIES AT COLUMBIA UNIVERSITY AND PROFESSOR EMERITUS OF ANTHROPOLOGY AT YALE UNIVERSITY, JOHN SZWED IS THE AUTHOR OF A BOOK ABOUT SUN RA, *SPACE IS THE PLACE: THE LIVES AND TIMES OF SUN RA* (DA CAPO PRESS, 1998), AS WELL AS THE MOST RECENT BIOGRAPHY OF MILES DAVIS, *SO WHAT* (SIMON & SCHUSTER, 2002).

Photo Leigh Wiener.

In April 1961, Columbia took advantage of a two-week engagement at the Black Hawk in San Francisco to record Miles Davis and his group live. A two-volume album was made of these performances. Photo Leigh Wiener (right).

NOW
MILES
DAVIS
The
BLACK HAWK
400
TURK
CLUB
COCKTAILS
CLUB
YOUNG ADULTS
UNDER 21
PLEASE USE 216 HYDE
ENTRANCE
No Persons
Under 21
Allowed

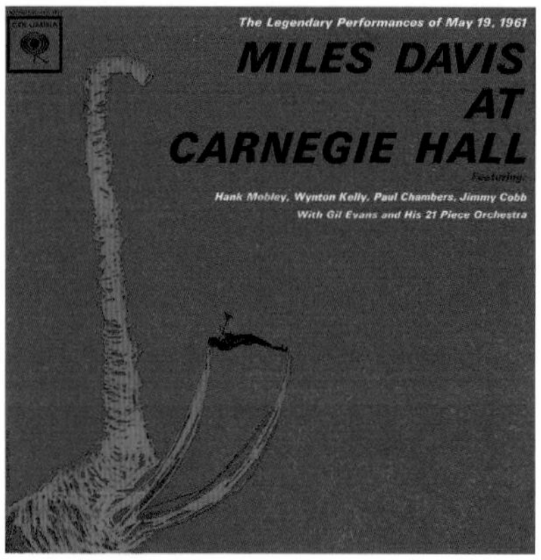

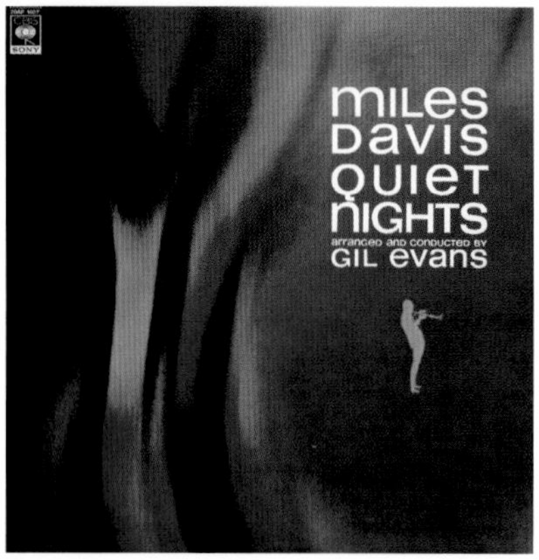

Miles Davis' large orchestra projects with Gil Evans ran out of steam in the early 1960s. The performance in May 1961 at Carnegie Hall in New York, almost the only example of their collaboration in concert, was made into a record (Davis' saxophonist was then Hank Mobley—lower left). The following year, producer Teo Macero finished the album *Quiet Nights* as best he could from a montage of tapes the two men had left incomplete (opposite page, during the sessions in August 1962). Photos Vernon Smith (left); Don Hunstein (right).

Davis would not have the same opinion of Coltrane's evolution, but the comparison affected him. He evidenced a growing animosity listening to Hank Mobley, and weariness gradually overcame him: "Playing with Hank just wasn't fun for me; he didn't stimulate my imagination." Performing at the Black Hawk in San Francisco in April 1961, Davis was recorded on the 21st and 22nd for the release of two volumes with identical jackets (Frances Taylor appears at his side), entitled *Miles Davis in Person at the Blackhawk, San Francisco* and subtitled *Friday Night* and *Saturday Night* respectively. On the recordings, he is in top form, supported by a luxurious rhythm section that purrs like a powerful limousine engine, but one gets the impression that the creator he had always been until *Kind of Blue* has given up and is no longer anything but a tremendous stylist destined to repeat himself concert after concert. At the end of the year, Hank Mobley was replaced by Rocky Boyd, an obscure disciple of John Coltrane with a short-lived career. Then, in 1962, Davis hired Sonny Rollins and J. J. Johnson, reconstituting the sextet he had led in the wake of the nonet in the early 1950s.

AT A STANDSTILL. At the same time, Miles Davis was working on a new project with Gil Evans (which would be called *Quiet Nights*) apparently borne by the new rage for Brazilian music. It seems that Evans had become familiar with Brazilian music before 1962 through the international section of the Columbia catalogue. He even seems to have sent some recordings of Antonio Carlos (Tom) Jobim and João Gilberto to producer Creed Taylor before Taylor produced the famous *Jazz Samba* with Stan Getz and Charlie Byrd, which ignited "bossamania." Nevertheless, the recording of his new record with Davis dragged on. Tom Jobim's "Corcovado" and "Aos pes da Cruz" by

In spring 1963, Miles Davis surrounded himself with a new rhythm section—pianist Herbie Hancock, bassist Ron Carter and the young drummer Tony Williams—which first appeared on the record *Seven Steps to Heaven*. Opposite page: in Berlin, September 1964. Photos Jan Persson.

Pinto and José Gonçalves were recorded July 27, 1962; "Song No. 1" (co-written by Davis and Evans, but inspired by composer-guitarist Francisco Tarrega's "Adelita") and "Wait till You See Her" by Richard Rodgers are from August 13; and "La Valse des lilas" ("Once upon a Summertime") by Michel Legrand and "Song No. 2" (based on a Mexican folksong) were recorded on November 6, 1962. In the meantime, Columbia prepared a Christmas album entitled *Jingle Bell Jazz*, bringing together several jazz artists from the catalogue. "What the fuck am I supposed to play for them? 'White Christmas'?" Davis asked singer Bob Dorough. With Dorough, he recorded "Blue Xmas."

By the end of 1962, the sessions with Gil Evans were at a standstill. Sonny Rollins had left the quintet and was occasionally replaced by Jimmy Heath. Then Wynton Kelly and Paul Chambers withdrew, obliging Davis to pay compensation to the organizers who had hired the group for the beginning of 1963. In May 1962, following his father's death, he discovered a letter he had neglected in which his father announced that he was dying. Davis' morale deteriorated, and he felt the effects of the sickle-cell anemia, which often prevented him from working. Alcohol and cocaine, which he had never completely stopped using, now played a large role in the medical arsenal meant to give him relief, but they drove him ever more inwards.

SEVEN STEPS TO HEAVEN AND AN OUTBURST. In April 1963, wanting to put a new quintet together for a series of concerts on the West Coast, Miles Davis tried out some young musicians from Memphis and chose George Coleman, a tenor saxophonist recommended by John Coltrane. On bass, he hired Ron Carter, originally from Detroit like Paul Chambers, and very much in demand on the New York scene. From Jackie McLean, he finally borrowed a seventeen-year-old drum prodigy, Tony Williams. Williams rehearsed with the sextet in New York but was not available for California. On April 16, when Davis went to the studio for two days of recording in Los Angeles, he entrusted the drumsticks to Frank Butler, an influential African-American drummer from the West Coast, and filled out the quintet with Victor Feldman, a young British-born pianist living in California. Davis had already cited Feldman as an example of a good non-American jazz player and had great confidence in him. He chose Feldman's composition "Joshua," co-wrote another with him ("Seven Steps to Heaven") and took his suggestion for a piece by two British fellow citizens ("So Near, So Far"). The rest were ballads played as a quartet without saxophone. The choice of the ballads "Summer Night" and "I Fall in Love Too Easily" may well have been influenced by Shirley Horn, with whom Davis had shared the bill at the Village Vanguard the year before. "Baby, Won't You Please Come Home" and "Basin Street Blues" were borrowed from the traditional pre-swing jazz repertoire.

Well connected at the Hollywood studios, Feldman declined the offer to follow Davis. Back in New York, Davis contacted Herbie Hancock, then twenty-three years old, inviting him, George Coleman, Ron Carter and Tony Williams to rehearse in his music room. For two days, Davis simply listened to them over the intercom in his apartment. The third day, he appeared briefly and made a date for the next day, May 14, 1963, at the Columbia studios. They got back to work on "Seven Steps to Heaven," "So Near, So Far" and "Joshua," which gained in ease and would replace the Los Angeles versions on the record to be released as *Seven Steps to Heaven*. Ornamented with a counter-melody that strongly recalls the melodic habits of George Coleman, "So Near, So Far" went from 4/4 to 6/8 time, with the original meter showing through at times, in an interplay of illusions that would now be the quintet's daily bread. The record was finished in July and included these three titles, plus three others chosen from among those recorded in Los Angeles the month before.

STEREO
"360 SOUND"
MILES
DAVIS
SEVEN
STEPS
TO
HEAVEN

Stimulated by the young players who accompanied him, Miles Davis questioned his old habits and forged an intimate connection with his new sidemen, which became obvious on stage. Pictured here in Berlin with Herbie Hancock, September 1964. Photo Jan Persson.

Although not selected, "Summer Night" appeared a few months later, in December 1963, filling out the last "Brazilian" recordings with Gil Evans that producer Teo Macero had taken the initiative to release, provoking Davis' fury. A saxophonist, Teo Macero had studied composition and worked with electroacoustic music at Juilliard from 1948 to 1953. He then worked with Charles Mingus and contributed ambitious scores to the advent of "third stream." Hired by Columbia in 1957, when the company was a pioneer in sound engineering and editing, he took part in the post-production of *Porgy and Bess* and then succeeded Irving Townsend during the production of *Kind of Blue*. His name is credited for the first time on the back of *Someday My Prince Will Come*, which he boldly edited. When *Quiet Nights* appeared, Gil Evans and Miles Davis felt betrayed, as their recordings from 1962 remained incomplete. In their view, Macero's manipulations were not enough to make them suitable for release. Davis turned his back on Columbia Studios.

NEW RHYTHMS. Miles Davis focused his attention on his new quintet and asked his agent to book them more dates. The age of the musicians he had just recruited is worth noting. The youngest, Tony Williams, was nearly twenty years younger than he. A great admirer of Philly Joe Jones and the 1958 sextet, Williams demonstrated a galvanizing enthusiasm. He encouraged Davis to revisit his repertoire of standards from the 1950s. Curious by nature, he listened to free jazz and convinced Herbie Hancock to play with Eric Dolphy. Later, Williams' interest in rock would contribute to the group's navigation towards new rhythm concepts in jazz. In classic jazz (1930s–1950s), the players

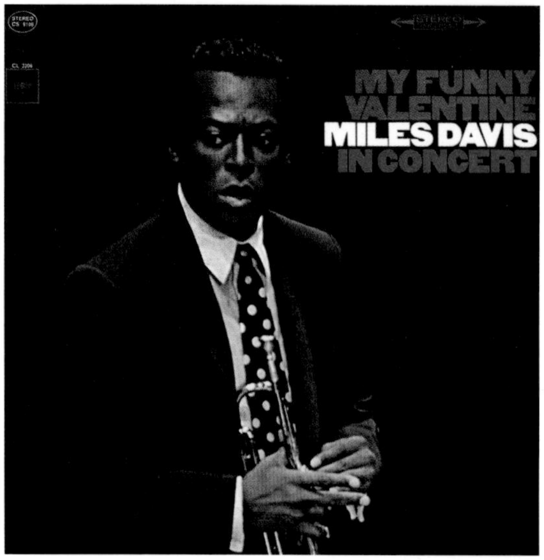

developed their phrasing according to what was called "swing feel" or "jazz feel." In a phrase of eighth notes, they played uneven eighths ("swing eighths"). Though the division of the beat mostly depends on such factors as the tempo of the piece and the musician's personality, the first eighth notes are usually twice as long as the second eighths (i.e. "da-a ba – da-a ba," etc.). This arithmetic can also be heard in the archetypal pattern maintained by the drummer on the ride cymbal, spelling out "ding-a ding" where "ding-a" is the uneven eighths and "ding" a quarter note (i.e. "di-ing a di-i-ing"). In the1950s, bop drummers tended to break this pattern down in a virtuoso arithmetic of triplets (three even eighths), which, since the start of the decade, Elvin Jones had systematized and distributed to all the components of the drum set. Tony Williams likewise practised this form of distribution but tended to break the beat into two even eighth notes or four sixteenth notes. If he contributed to the rapprochement of jazz and the popular music of the 1960s (rock, soul), which favoured these even eighths, he played with the ambiguity of the two rhythmic modes, juxtaposing and combining them with a sense of colour that contributed to the greatness of what is known as the "second" Miles Davis Quintet. As Davis explains in his autobiography, Tony Williams "made me play so much that I forgot about all the pain in my joints, which had been bothering me a lot."

TAKING RISKS. Herbie Hancock was a young piano prodigy who assimilated an advanced level of classical literature for the instrument at an early age, as well as the funky style of Horace Silver, injecting both into the music of his first regular employer, trumpet player Donald Byrd. To Miles Davis' band he brought the piquant flavours of black music and the delicacy brought to jazz by Bill Evans. In particular, he was of a generation that, following Evans, had familiarized itself with a modal vocabulary, thus reinventing the language of harmonic progression, which suddenly seemed to attain the fourth dimension. A stabilizing factor, Ron Carter was heir to Paul Chambers, not only in terms of timing (the quality of his inner tempo) but also imagination, range of vocabulary and virtuosity. If he represented the persistence of tradition by his anchoring in the tempo, the new forms of logic developed by his two accomplices held no secrets for him. Thus, he happily got involved in the play of illusions and traps the pianist and drummer engaged in behind George Coleman's solos once Davis' back was turned. The saxophonist did not fully engage in the risk-taking that sometimes went wild. Under the guise of great elegance, he resisted the pranks of his cohorts, who transposed onto the terrain of free and interactive initiative the exact scenarios Davis formerly dictated to his rhythm section. While they spent their nights in hotel rooms talking about what they had just played and imagining other hïjinks for the next day, the saxophonist worked tirelessly on his future solos. Davis himself would reproach him: "I pay you to practise *on* the bandstand." On the other hand, he would soon ask his rhythm section to accompany his solos with the same intensity as those of Coleman. No sooner said than done, as Herbie Hancock remembers it: "And then one day, Miles said, 'Why don't you play like that behind me?' I remember when that happened, we were in Detroit . . . some club there, and we were playing all kinds of crazy things behind George and behind Miles we played really straight. Anyway, that's when Tony and I started playing our little musical games behind Miles in a way, because we were developing this thing. . . . After four days, it turned around and he was leading it. Not only was he in it, but he really established that thing. And his playing was different after that. It was a most uncannily rapid adaptation to this other sound that I could ever imagine. . . . That's what Miles does. He feeds off everybody else and kind of puts it together."

On February 12, 1964, Miles Davis gave a concert at Philharmonic Hall in New York (opposite page), the recording of which was released in two volumes. The renditions of "My Funny Valentine" and "Stella by Starlight" have come to serve as benchmarks. However, the proportion of standards in the repertoire gradually decreased when George Coleman (right) was replaced by Wayne Shorter in September of that year.
Photos Vernon Smith.

A PHENOMENAL STRIPTEASE. Since Miles Davis stayed away from the studios after his rift with Teo Macero, we have to rely on live recordings to take the measure of this band, especially the concert at Philharmonic Hall in New York on February 12, 1964 (released in two volumes: *My Funny Valentine* and *Four & More*). When Davis announced, as the musicians went onstage, that their fee would be handed over to the ongoing campaign to register black voters in the Southern States, a heated dispute erupted backstage. In Davis' opinion, the resulting tension contributed to the outstanding performance that evening. Listening to "Stella by Starlight" gives an idea of the extravagant liberties taken by the band. After an introduction by Herbie Hancock reminiscent of Bill Evans, Davis sets out the first two notes of the melody, which hints at a medium tempo (about 120 quarter notes per minute, or 120 to the quarter note), then continues to play a rubato (elastic tempo; literally "stolen time") duo with the pianist. When the bass enters, it briefly plays the tempo, and the attentive listener has one measure to grasp that the tempo is half as fast as the one suggested (i.e. 60 to the quarter note). After which, the bass no longer states the tempo but ornaments the beat, while Davis puts the melody through all sorts of variations, compressions and distensions that mislead the listener. The melody's shape is revealed in successive fragments and by transparency, as if in a phenomenal striptease. The eroticism of the situation peaks; there is an ecstatic yell from the audience when, responding to Davis' impulse, Herbie Hancock sets the beat at 120, an illusion that Tony Williams upholds as the harmonies continue to unfold at 60, with many suspensions and other rhythmic and harmonic feints that toy with the listener's expectations. George Coleman's isolation and the rhythm section's complaints about him led to his departure. Miles Davis was still thinking about Wayne Shorter, who remained attached to the Jazz Messengers. Tony Williams lobbied for Eric Dolphy, but this ambiguous avant-garde figure had just drawn unflattering criticism from Davis: "The next time I see him, I'm going to step on his foot." The trumpeter eventually let his drummer convince him to hire saxophonist Sam Rivers for the summer. A discreet forty-one-year-old musician (three years older than Davis), like Davis he had grown up with bebop but showed a pronounced interest in free jazz, which he would foster. During the concert in Tokyo on July 14, 1964 (*Miles in Tokyo*, released in 1969), this tendency is detectable in his phrasing and sound, the content of his phrases, quite classic in "My Funny Valentine," elsewhere basically conforming to the original harmonic structure. Although more angular, discontinuous or saturated, sometimes irrupting in "So What," he seems relatively immune to the suggestions of the rhythm section, which he even occasionally neutralizes. In later interviews, this led him to categorize the quintet's music as "bebop." Wayne Shorter would not take the same approach as Rivers, which is why Davis and his sidemen begged him to join them as soon as they got back from Japan and learned that he was no longer with the Jazz Messengers.

IN THE BACKGROUND. The misunderstanding between Sam Rivers and Miles Davis' rhythm section exemplifies the rift developing in modern jazz. Emerging in the last years of the 1950s around leading figures like Cecil Taylor and Ornette Coleman, a new genre became predominant in the following decade, first called the "new thing," then "free jazz," after the title of an experimental work by Ornette Coleman recorded in 1960. The musicians who adopted it had, in the vast majority, sidestepped the technical requirements of bop, which they

Miles Davis on guard, Salle Pleyel,
Paris, October 1, 1964.
Photo Philippe Gras.

only skimmed as they learned on the job, generally in the world of rhythm and blues. They truly wiped the slate clean, radically denouncing the ways in which black music had managed to take hold in American society (regular rhythm meant for dancing, melodies and superficial expression for entertainment purposes). They likewise rejected the means modern jazz borrowed from "serious" European music to achieve a semblance of respectability (harmonic and formal complexity, instrumental virtuosity). Although the "free" musicians were not indifferent to the explorations of contemporary European music, they distanced themselves from it in their desire to renew ties with the spontaneous outpouring and raw expression of the African-American tradition at its most African, following a path that eventually led them to a candid interest in all non-European traditions. Melodic variation was carried to the extreme; improvisation dropped harmonic syntax in favour of free counterpoint; the melodic shaping, rhythmic profile and plasticity of sound exploded and crumbled; musical forms and their required progression dissolved into free collective roaming. All these characteristics must be considered case by case, for free jazz is far from uniform.

Spectacular in its challenge to the status quo, free jazz monopolized attention as it accompanied—more or less on purpose—blacks' political struggle. The campaign of non-violence headed by Martin Luther King ran up against brutal criminal resistance from the white community in the Southern States, then spread to the North in a climate of extreme tension that, starting in 1965, sparked riot after riot and brought about the radicalization of the movement through student factions. With the emergence of the Black Panther party and its anti-imperialist revolutionary stance, open to Marxist theory and in solidarity with the liberation movements appearing all around the world, new slogans like "Black Power" and "Black is beautiful" echoed the aesthetic position of free jazz.

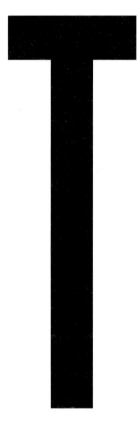

THE OTHER FREEDOM. Just as Miles Davis stayed on the sidelines of the social and political events underway (in fact, the majority of free-jazz musicians were not involved either), he considered free jazz with deep contempt. His allegiance lay elsewhere, founded on a less spectacular concept of freedom and risk-taking obscured by free jazz. The term "modal jazz" is sometimes used to designate anything unrelated to classic jazz, bop or free jazz at the time, but the label is too restrictive. The musicians of the second Miles Davis Quintet were the most significant exponents of this movement, which defies definition because it was so heterogeneous. What they had in common was a desire to assimilate everything that came within their reach. At the time, the tools Bill Evans borrowed from classical composers to advance the use of modes, Coltrane's vocabulary and the high-precision arithmetic developed by Elvin Jones and Tony Williams were at the core of this assimilation effort that would gradually open to other realms (popular black music, rock, world music). If the clean sweep was rarely total on the free side—musicians like Charles Mingus, Eric Dolphy, Andrew Hill and Sam Rivers found themselves on the cusp between two worlds—the free-jazz musicians' approach was more intuitive, less preoccupied with technique and theory, less concerned with finish and mastery than with the urgency of expression.

In the mid-1960s, once Miles Davis had become an internationally renowned star, he began playing the great halls of Europe's capitals. Opposite page: upon arriving at Paris' Orly airport, November 6, 1967. Photo Christian Rose.

Miles Davis' musicians broached the opposing concept of "controlled freedom" inherited from training that combined the discipline pervading the history of improvised jazz from Louis Armstrong to John Coltrane with academic knowledge. Herbie Hancock was first a young classical piano prodigy. Ron Carter graduated from the Manhattan School of Music. Tony Williams, the only one who showed a marked interest in free jazz, had studied with Alan Dawson at Boston's well-known Berklee School of Music. The music they turned to once Wayne Shorter joined them corresponded perfectly to this concept of controlled freedom, even if, in many cases, their daring brought them to the verge of losing control. In addition, they had the ability to react to what the others were playing, recalling the type of mutual listening evident in the Bill Evans Trio, referred to as "interplay."

AT THE BREAKING POINT. Wayne Shorter held a somewhat ambiguous place on this scene. A university graduate, he was a disciple of John Coltrane—perhaps the first and closest, since they practised together around 1958, when Coltrane was perfecting the "Giant Steps" changes, a harmonic system he explored on the record *Giant Steps*. However, he seems to have taken only what he needed from Coltrane. Though possessing a vocabulary incomparably more solid than that of Sam Rivers in 1964, in the swing machine of Art Blakey's Jazz Messengers, for which he was music director, Shorter did not necessarily display the technical verve of those around him, and doubts have been expressed about his sense of time, intonation and articulation. He was furthermore a stranger to the type of musical athletics into which hard bop could sometimes evolve. Throughout his career, he often appeared to wait patiently for the music to come to him, as his titles evoking Zen mystique suggest. Freed from the yoke of the Jazz Messengers and in contact with Miles Davis, he was reborn: "With Miles, I felt like a cello, I felt viola, I felt liquid, dot-dash, and colours started really coming."

In fall 1965, the new edition of the second quintet toured the great cities of Europe. If *Miles in Berlin* caused a sensation when it was released in 1969, fans' excitement was far greater in 1976 when Sony released some tracks in Japan that had been recorded during a two-week engagement at the Plugged Nickel in Chicago starting on December 21, 1965. However, it was Columbia's release of the entirety of these live recordings (*The Complete Live at the Plugged Nickel 1965*) that let listeners evaluate the incredible risks taken by the group, risks that had gone almost unnoticed at the time. This eight-CD box set reconstitutes three sets from the evening of the 22nd and four from the following evening, making it possible to compare different versions of the same number at an interval of a few hours. With tempos at the breaking point ("Walkin'," "Milestones," "So What," "Agitation," "All Blues"), in a sonic haze in which at times they seem to lose themselves then get their bearings from signals they send each other—for example, in the form of thematic reminders—the musicians engage in a parody of harmonic and rhythmic forms that periodically takes a dramatic turn. In "Stella by Starlight" especially, Tony Williams amuses himself by doubling the beat and then doubling it again, eventually nudging the group into the medium tempo that, in the 1964 version, was only simulated. This practice was still relatively new to jazz. Davis had tried it out in *Kind of Blue* by contracting the ten-measure structure of "Blue in Green" into five for the first piano solo and the saxophone solo, then into two and a half for the second piano solo. In 1965, he had the musicians he need-

10

In late December 1965, Miles Davis appeared at the Plugged Nickel. The recordings made in this Chicago nightclub attest to the boldness of the musicians of his second quintet.

ed to renew the experiment. Did this happen by chance or with intent? While the earlier "Blue in Green" shows cautious experimentation, at this point, the five players were taking up the challenge in the heat of the action, letting themselves go.

MILES SMILES. Miles Davis reluctantly agreed to the recording at the Plugged Nickel. He was not at his best. For the seven previous months, his health had kept him offstage. He needed a bone graft on his left hip joint in April 1965. Scarcely had he recovered from the operation when he broke his left leg, and in August, the failure of the graft required further surgery. The continuous use of painkillers combined with cocaine plunged him into deep paranoia. Worn down by jealousy, infidelities, conjugal violence and immature, even irrational behaviour, Frances Taylor left him in late 1965. In January 1966, Davis was immobilized for three months by a liver infection. During his convalescent walks in Riverside Park, he made the acquaintance of actress Cicely Tyson, who contributed to his gradual recovery.

NICKEL
TONITE
MILES DAVIS
DAVIS
CAFE
THE
PLUGGED NICKEL
Miles Davis

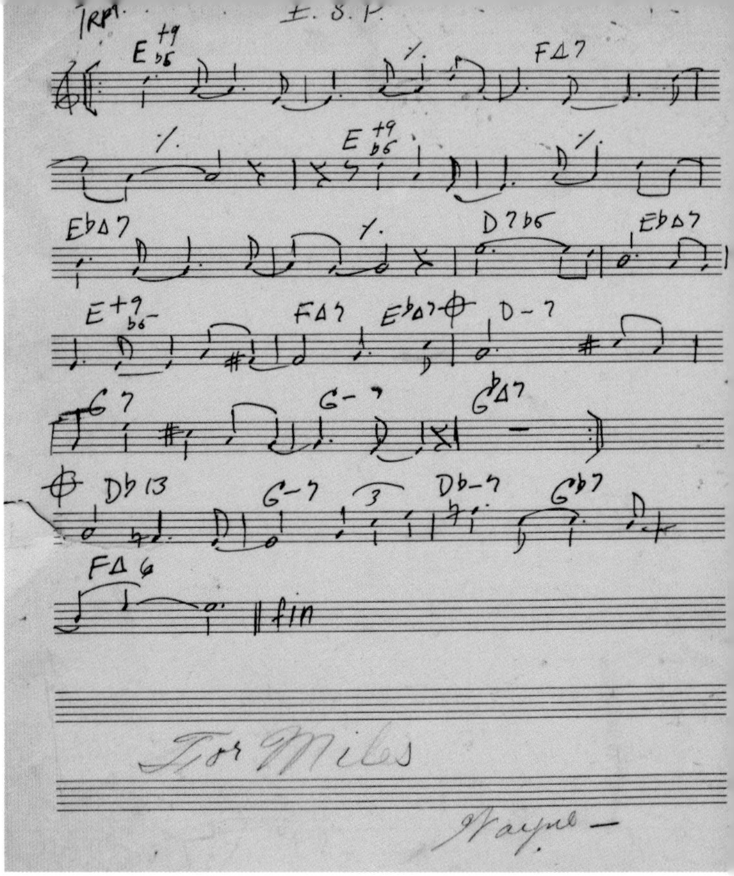

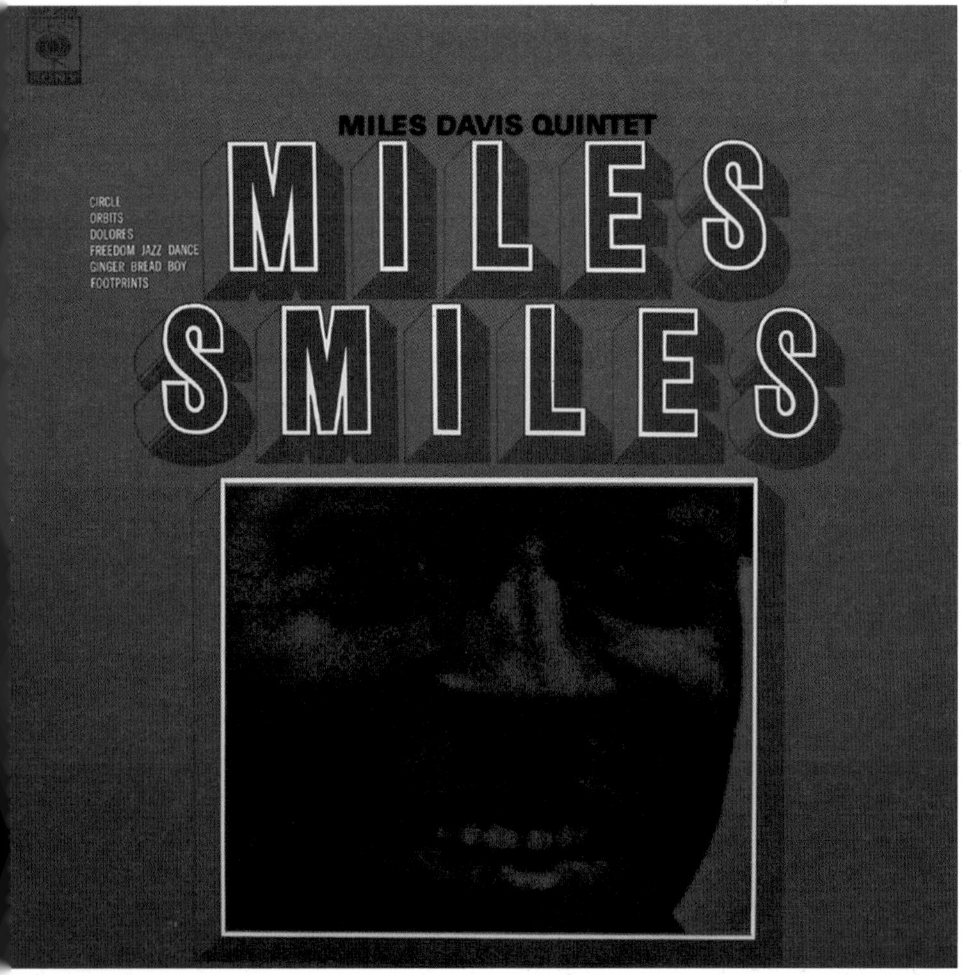

Between 1965 and 1968, Miles Davis made recordings that have become modern jazz classics. He had his girlfriends' faces appear on some of the record covers: Frances Taylor on *E.S.P.*, actress Cicely Tyson on *Sorcerer* and singer Betty Mabry on *Filles de Kilimanjaro*.

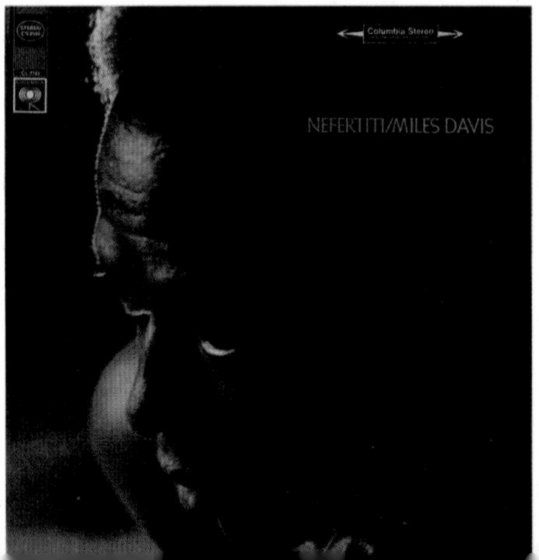

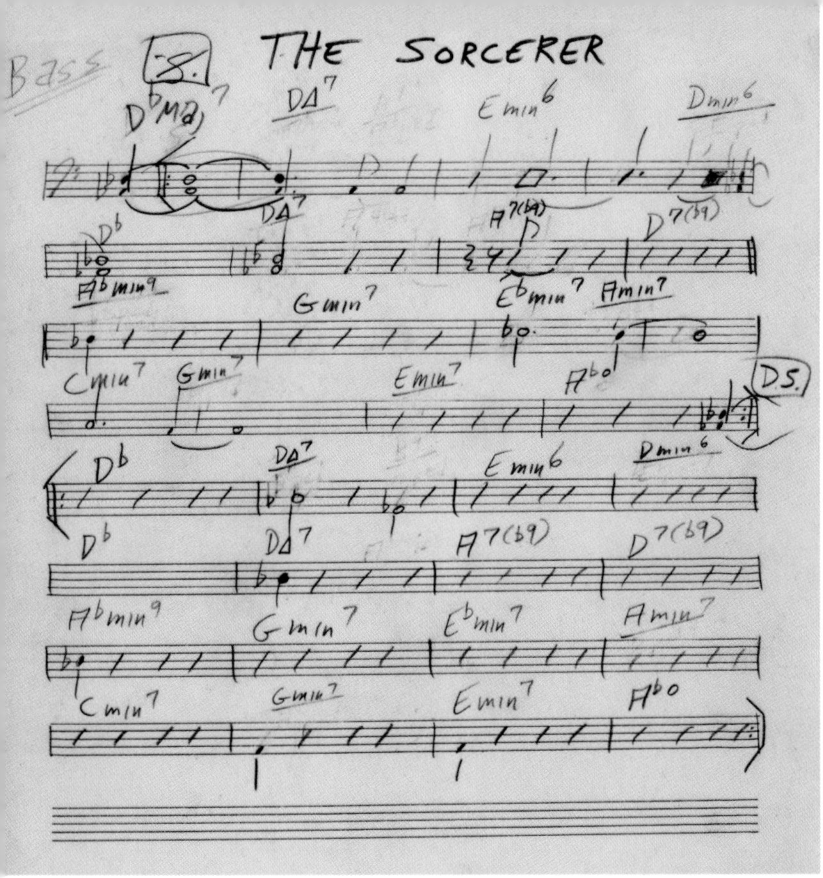

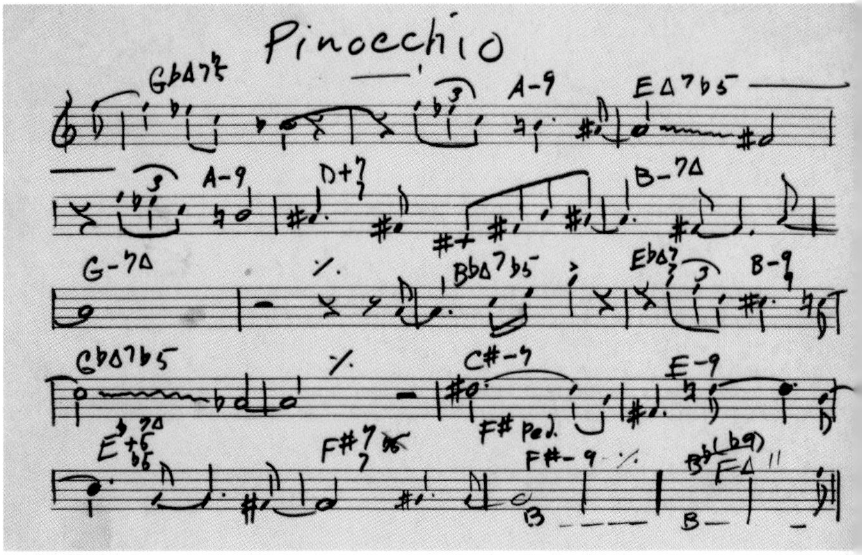

Wayne Shorter and Herbie Hancock contributed considerably to the renewal of Miles Davis' repertoire. Their compositions demonstrate harmonic and rhythmic practices and requirements incompatible with the standards' traditional form.

Reproduced here: the trumpet parts for "E.S.P.," "The Sorcerer" "Capricorn," "Pinocchio" and "Dolores," all by Wayne Shorter, and "Little One" by Herbie Hancock, as well as the bass part for "The Sorcerer," also by Hancock.

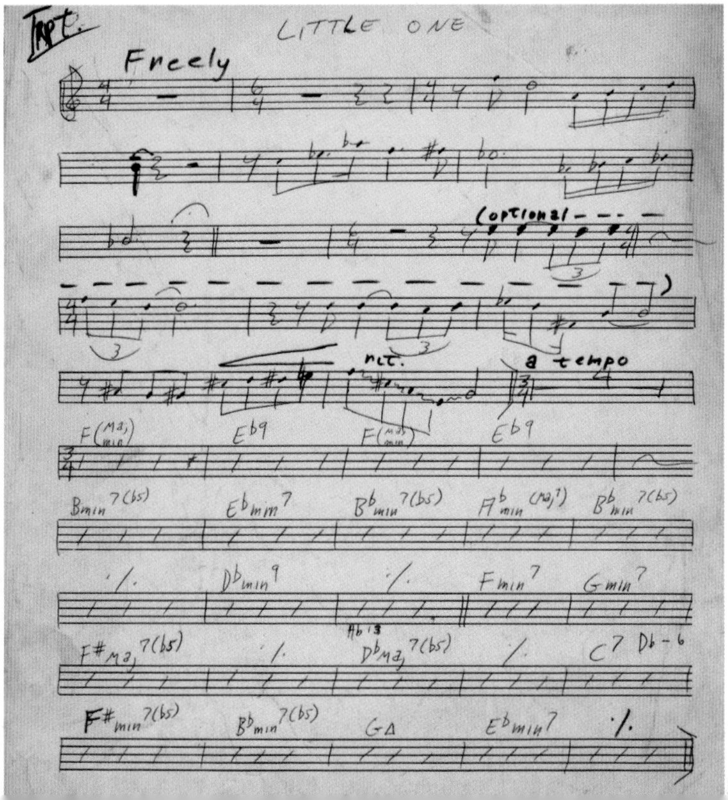

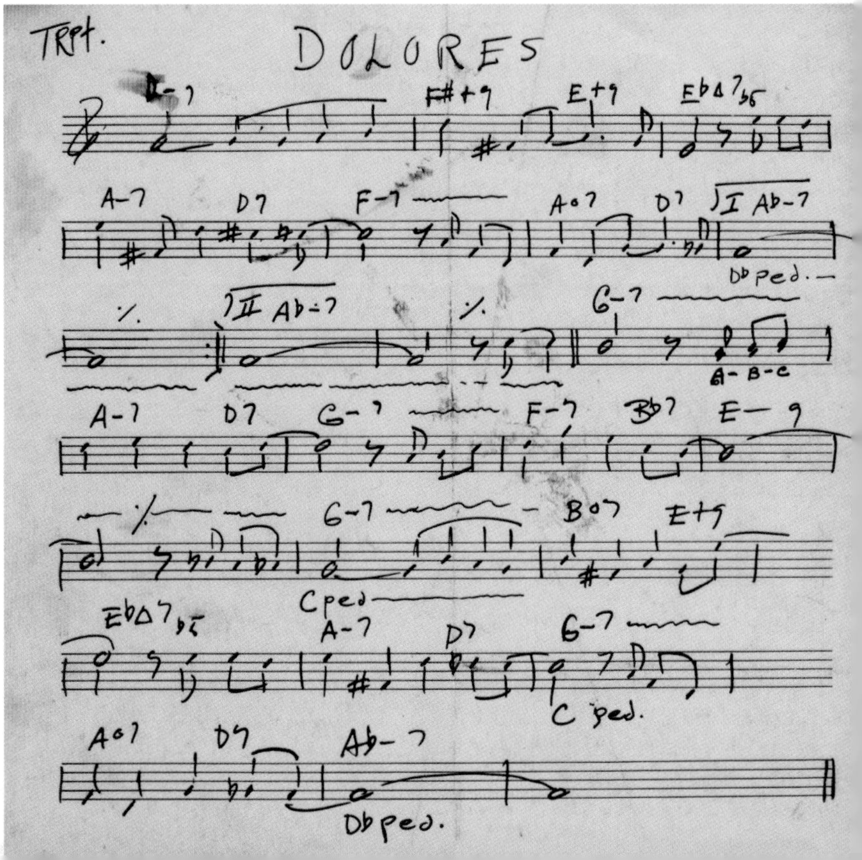

Four decades after their collaboration with the trumpeter, Herbie Hancock and Wayne Shorter have never failed to acknowledge how much they owe to Miles Davis. Pictured here in a Columbia recording studio, probably in 1968. Photo Corky McCoy.

Until the early 1970s, Davis kept in shape by boxing and swimming. This had an unquestionable effect on his trumpet playing, which in terms of phrasing and sound regained the summits of the late 1950s.

In spring 1966, Davis went back on the road with his quintet, in which Ron Carter, still much in demand, sometimes had himself replaced by Richard Davis, Gary Peacock or Reggie Workman. Tired of working the clubs, where alcohol and drugs were constant temptations, Davis spaced out his engagements and favoured concerts on university campuses. After the summer, he was back in form when he got his band together in the studio, reuniting with Teo Macero, with whom he had not worked for three years. The resulting record is called *Miles Smiles*. It followed the quintet's first series of sessions with Wayne Shorter, in Los Angeles in January 1965, during which they seemed to return to the vein of *Kind of Blue* while exploiting it much more openly. The material from this first series of sessions was released with the enigmatic title *E.S.P.*, the name of a composition signed jointly by Davis and Shorter, with a record cover on which, under the anxious eyes of Davis, Frances Taylor was to appear for the last time. Does the title refer to the state of telepathy (i.e. extrasensory perception) required for collective improvisation? That was indeed the quintet's frame of mind, as attested to by the pace at which *Miles Smiles* was recorded on October 24 and 25, 1966. The musicians saw the scores for the first time when they arrived at the studio. After skimming through them just once, they recorded them in a single take, with a freshness that recalls the Prestige sessions in 1956, except that these were original scores of a fairly unusual nature. The spontaneity of the sessions and the musicians' joyful playing are accentuated by the loose placement of notes in some tunes, not to mention the flubs audible on the recording, but also by Davis' interpellations and exclamations at the end of numbers.

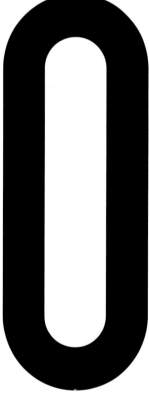

ORIGINAL REPERTOIRE. After *E.S.P.*, Miles Davis set aside the standards to focus on original repertoire, as he had done for *Kind of Blue*. This time, however, he featured his musicians' compositional talents. Tony Williams had begun to record his own repertoire with Blue Note (*Life Time*). Herbie Hancock had made his reputation with the hit "Watermelon Man" on his first record for Blue Note (*Takin' Off*) and since then had recorded four more. Ron Carter also composed. After *Introducing Wayne Shorter* (1959), almost exclusively penned by him, Wayne Shorter had become one of the Jazz Messengers' main sources of material. In the space of two years, Shorter had made seven records for Blue Note, including a great many masterpieces. He would compose others, notably during the sessions with Miles Davis in May 1967 that resulted in the record *Nefertiti* and, in June, *Sorcerer*, as well as previously unissued material released on *Water Babies* in 1976.

The new repertoire was radically different from the standards. A colour emanates from the recurrent use of the interval of a fourth. It comes up in the melodies (the first three notes of "E.S.P." are consecutive descending fourths; the first four notes of "Hand Jive" are an ascending fourth followed by a descending fourth). It is also present in the chords ("Eighty One"), where it readily replaces the more usual third, producing a strangeness that is neither major nor minor. The chords are often disguised, altered, hybrid, non-functional, creating an atmosphere of agnosticism in regard to the harmonic monotheism of bebop and the atheism—often more professed than actual—of free jazz. The modal progression inaugurated with "Flamenco Sketches" is back, thanks to musicians able to negotiate them with a freedom that, in "Agitation" and "Riot," is radically different from the careful and predictable development of the earlier forays in this genre. The structures, when not shifting ("Circle"), are unusual ("R.J.," "Dolores," "Limbo") and may be contracted ("Iris"). Swing-feel phrasing is no longer the rule: "Eighty One" alternates the even eighth notes of rock with the uneven ones of swing, but most often the drummer plays around with superimposition and ambiguity, while the time signature undergoes structural ("Black Comedy," "Limbo") or improvisational twists (constant ambiguities throughout "Footprints").

NEW RULES OF THE GAME. In this respect, the activism of the Ron Carter–Tony Williams tandem was of prime importance. Nevertheless, Miles Davis maintained a decisive influence in the way he adapted and "directed" his colleagues' compositions. He could alter their nature by encouraging the most unrestrained playing (as illustrated by a comparison of the version of "Footprints" on Wayne Shorter's record *Adam's Apple* with that of the Miles Davis Quintet on *Miles Smiles*), or by inverting their roles (as in "Nefertiti," where the saxophone and trumpet repeat the theme ad infinitum as an accompaniment to the rhythm section's collective improvisation). He often intervened in the content by changing the time signature (Herbie Hancock's "Madness," composed as a ballad in three-four time, became formally more abstract in the studio, cut to its final section and opening into a floating statement of the theme in a tempo three times as fast). In general, he divested the score of its complexities and excess weight, reducing it to static sequences into which the solo comfortably settles. "I don't want to play chords anymore," he often stated, while he forbade Herbie Hancock his "butter notes"—harmonic language's bad fat. Hancock often withdrew from the accompaniment and his improvisations were frequently pure melody, i.e. single notes unaccompanied by the left hand. "Time, no changes"—tempo, not chord progressions: this is how the musicians referred to their music. Ornette Coleman, whom Miles Davis had so decried, was no longer that far off, and Davis would end up recognizing that his own music was getting close to that of Coleman's trumpet player, Don Cherry.

On the 1967 European tour, where original compositions essentially replaced the standards, the quintet seemed to disregard the laws of gravity with no other safety net than a capacity for invention and interaction. This music still defies understanding today. When Miles Davis died in 1991, the newspaper obituaries evaded the matter of this as yet little understood second quintet, barely mentioning it between the first, with Coltrane, and the electric orchestras of the 1970s. However, in many ways, the 1960s quintet represents for the jazz of the past forty years what Louis Armstrong's Hot Five was to jazz in the preceding forty years.

In the 1960s, Miles Davis' success brought a rise in standard of living, the most explicit symbol of which was the acquisition of a Ferrari 275 GTB. Having been admitted to a certain show-business elite, the musician attracted media attention (he was interviewed by *Playboy* in 1962). Photos Hank Parker (above); Baron Wolman (opposite page, above); Corky McCoy (opposite page, below).

PER CUE.
UIPMENT CO.
5677·WJ

Photo Lee Friedlander.

ELECTRIC MILES ROCK DISTORTION

1968–1971

The year 1968 was a turning point. An unprecedented crisis of values arose from the tremendous tensions experienced by much of the youth in the Western world. The driving force of consumer society, this generation erupted under the double weight of an outdated, repressive capitalist society and the influence of the entertainment industries, which were igniting the collective imagination. At the same time, new thinkers began to speak about the alienation of consumption, the idea that the imperialist structure was transplanting the colonial framework, and the ecological limitations of growth. In the United States, this revolt, unleashed by the opposition to the military engagement in Vietnam and by the systemic violation of civil rights at home, manifested itself on a number of fronts: the sexual revolution and drugs, social equality, the revival of spirituality, women's rights, draft dodging and the rejection of urbanized ways of life. Riots followed Martin Luther King's assassination, and the black movement isolated itself even further, falling deeper into extreme radicalization and factionalism.

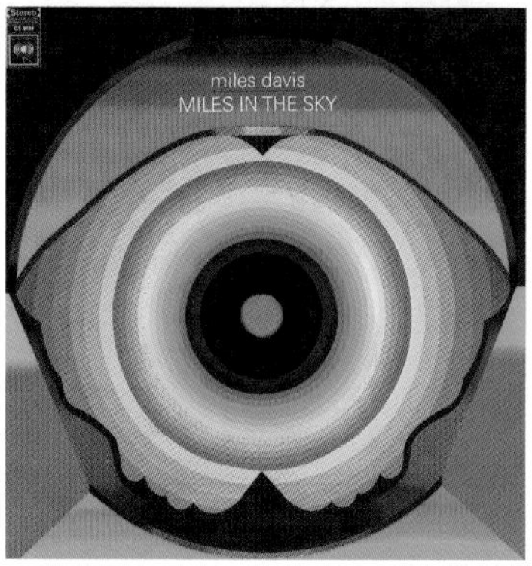

Influenced by Betty Mabry, whom he married in 1968 and who, under the name Betty Davis, made a name for herself as a sultry singer and sex symbol, Miles Davis changed his look and turned to rock. Columbia accompanied him in this new direction, using a psychedelic illustration for the record design of *Miles in the Sky*, a title clearly inspired by the Beatles. Photo Baron Wolman.

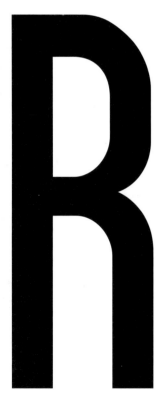

ROMANCE AND BUSINESS. For Davis, 1968 was pivotal for another reason: a new woman. Betty Mabry, whom he met in the spring of that year, was a twenty-three-year-old African-American woman embedded in the New York scene in the late 1960s. Writer of "Uptown," a song performed by the Chambers Brothers, model for the magazines *Ebony*, *Glamour*, *Jet* and *Seventeen*, and co-owner of the Cellar, a club popular among teenagers, she had been on the television show *The Dating Game* and was just starting a singing career. Mabry encouraged Davis to trade in his ties and classic grey suits for the exotically coloured, hippie-inspired clothes he found in shops in the Village. Soon, he grew an Afro just like Mabry's. She also introduced him to the rising black stars of the music scene, notably Sly Stone and Jimi Hendrix.

Mabry married Miles on September 30, 1968, and left him soon after, passing through his life like a tornado. This personal upheaval mirrored the shifts occurring on a larger scale. Western unrest was accompanied by the rise of new currents in music from various places (London, San Francisco, Los Angeles, Chicago, New York, Memphis) and of various styles (psychedelic rock and blues, folk-rock, soul, and rhythm and blues), which took to the stage at the Monterey Pop Festival in 1967. Clive Davis, the new president of Columbia, attuned to these changes, undertook the reorientation of his company's catalogue. As the label signed rock acts, it dropped its jazz artists (Thelonious Monk, Duke Ellington, Dave Brubeck). Miles Davis, who enjoyed handsome advance royalties as a star in the jazz catalogue, was retained, but under mounting pressure to adapt to the new reality. Clive Davis steered an aggressive promotional campaign to combine jazz and pop, which benefited rock bands with horn sections like Chicago and Blood, Sweat and Tears, and encouraged Miles Davis to move in this direction to appeal to a younger audience. Miles Davis was kept abreast of developments in new music through keyboardist Herbie Hancock and, to a greater extent, drummer Tony Williams, both of whom followed the scene closely. When journalist Leonard Feather visited the trumpeter in his hotel room, he was surprised to see Davis surrounded by records of white rock bands, soul and funk.

TOWARDS A GUITAR SOUND. In late 1967, Miles Davis started on a new series of recordings, during which he regained control of a repertoire that had mainly consisted of his musicians' scores. These he replaced with simple sketches, which would appear throughout *Miles in the Sky* (a title inspired by the psychedelic Beatles hymn "Lucy in the Sky with Diamonds") and on the collections of previously unreleased recordings, *Directions* and *Circle in the Round*. "Circle in the Round," the title of the first of these pieces, was recorded on December 4, 1967. It is an almost thirty-minute montage of sequences drawn from minimal material consisting of alternating pedal notes, continuously repeated figures and scattered solos. Rather than the expected melodic line, these provide ornamentation on a rhythmic continuum in which the drums emerge sporadically like the principal soloist. An instrument not heard before in Davis' work was introduced: the guitar. Several guitarists tried out for the band in the subsequent

Photo Guy Le Querrec.

Miles Davis at home, June 1969. His sumptuously decorated apartment on West Seventy-seventh Street, New York, which had a round layout, was full of decorative elements evoking Africa and black beauty. Photo Don Hunstein.

The scores for *Filles de Kilimanjaro* show the meticulous preparatory work that Miles Davis undertook with Gil Evans, although the latter was not explicitly credited on the record. This seminal album, on which the electric piano supplanted the standard piano, was greatly influenced by Jimi Hendrix and James Brown. Shortly afterward, however, written material was abandoned for an oral and informal way of working in the studio.

months (Joe Beck, Bucky Pizzarelli and George Benson), but none succeeded in meeting with Davis' approval. Herbie Hancock was invited to play the celesta, then the various brand names of electric keyboard (Wurlitzer, Hohner, Fender Rhodes). In May 1968, on a track found on *Miles in the Sky*, Ron Carter traded in his double bass for an electric bass guitar. A month later, acoustic piano and electric bass played together on the first sessions of *Filles de Kilimanjaro*, whose title refers to the shares Davis had in the Kilimanjaro African Coffee Company.

In summer 1968, Ron Carter and Herbie Hancock were replaced by two white musicians: the British bassist Dave Holland, discovered during a stay in London, and Chick Corea, who had just signed off on a masterwork for jazz trio, *Now He Sings, Now He Sobs*. On the two last tracks recorded for *Filles de Kilimanjaro* in September 1968, the acoustic double bass reappears, while Chick Corea is on electric piano. "Frelon Brun" was directly inspired by James Brown. "Mademoiselle Mabry," recorded in the presence of the woman Miles Davis would marry days later, begins with the first notes of Jimi Hendrix's "The Wind Cries Mary." However, Davis' rendition is far from being a straightforward copy; the vision that inspired him to draw from these two models was just as original as when he was inspired by the music of Ahmad Jamal, gospel and flamenco. The mention "Directions in music by Miles Davis" on the record cover indicates that, from that point on, he was sole composer. The failure to credit Gil Evans, who since December 1967 had been an important presence in the studio, puts into perspective the growing importance of producer Teo Macero. Evans freely shared ideas and gave advice, and even provided the score for "Eleven," which became "Petits Machins," credited to Davis. This was not unusual. Davis had earlier appropriated "Four" and "Tune Up" (by Eddie "Cleanhead" Vinson), "Solar" (which is none other than "Sonny" by Chuck Wayne) and "Blue in Green" (by Bill Evans), to name but a few examples. John Scofield encountered similar unfortunate experiences in the 1980s.

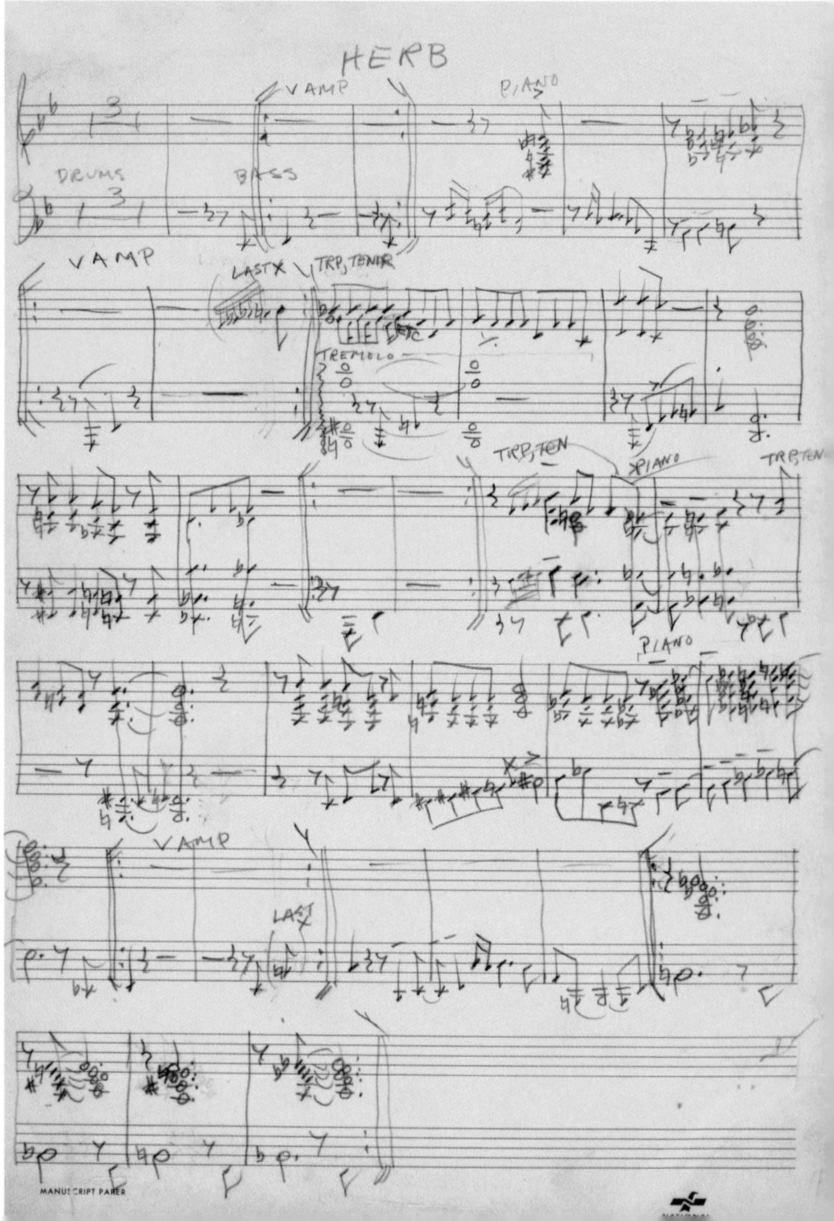

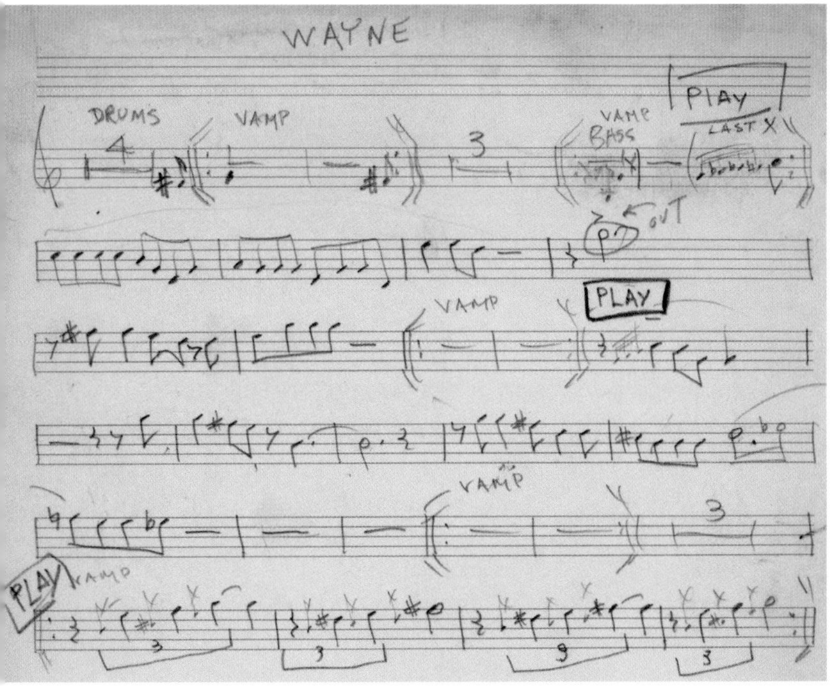

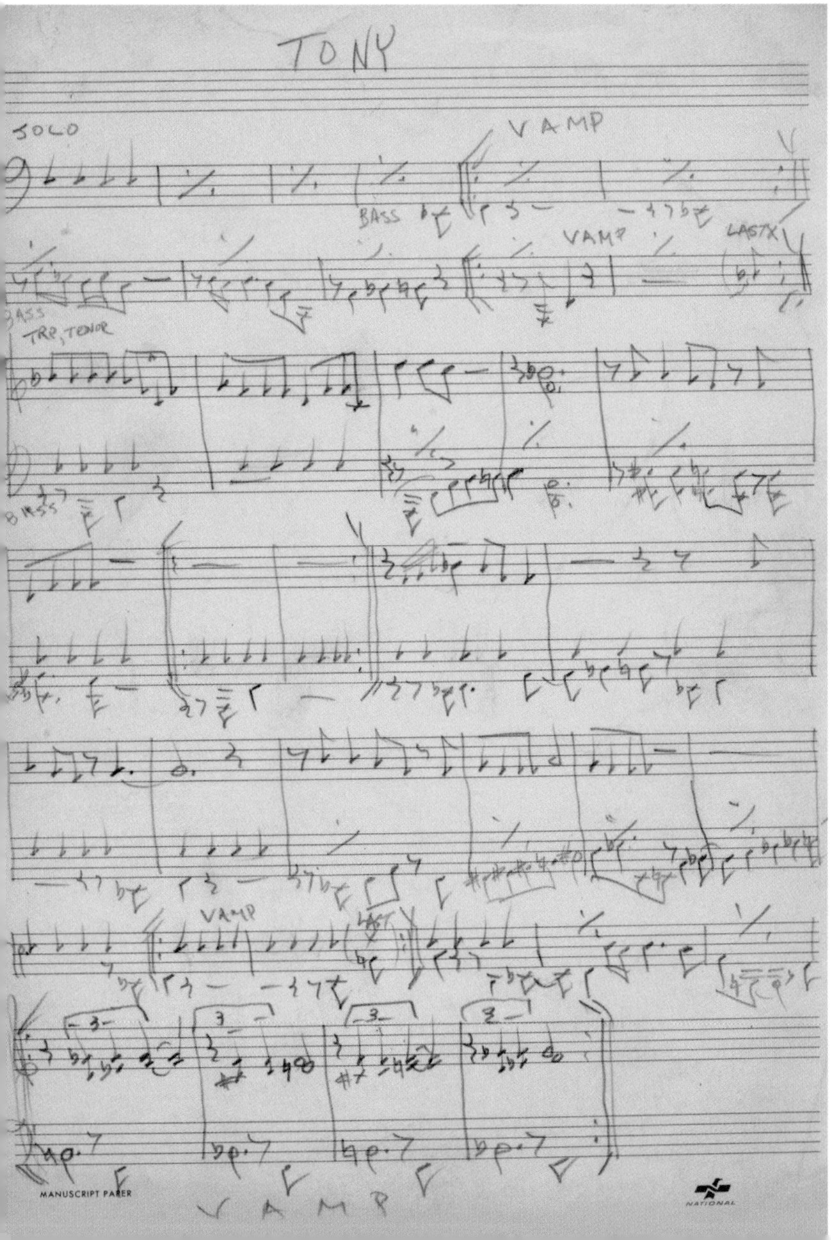

A new round of recordings began in November with an expanded quintet. Miles Davis added two, even three keyboards (electric piano and Hammond organ) played by Hancock and Joe Zawinul, while Jack DeJohnette and Tony Williams took turns on drums. In February 1969, a new guitarist entered the picture: John McLaughlin. A committed jazzman, he was a seasoned session musician and part of the British music scene, in which the lines between jazz, rock and blues were blurred. He had participated in various free-jazz events and just completed, along with saxophonist John Surman, a record for jazz quartet, *Extrapolation*. McLaughlin was a guitarist with a saturated sound inherited from Chicago blues; the density of his strongly articulated phrasing resembled the Coltrane-esque sheets of sound until then only captured by saxophonists. On Dave Holland's advice, Tony Williams convinced McLaughlin to leave London and join his new band, Lifetime. Miles Davis thought he had found the guitarist he had been looking for when he saw McLaughlin perform in New York the night he arrived in the city: "I was already moving towards a guitar sound in my music because I was beginning to listen to a lot of James Brown, and I liked the way he used the guitar in his music. I always liked the blues and always loved to play it. . . . [Now] I could feel myself starting to want to change. . . . I knew it had something to do with the guitar voice . . . and I was beginning to get interested in what electrical instrumental voicing could do in my music. See, when I used to listen to Muddy Waters in Chicago down on Thirty-third Street and Michigan every Monday when he played there and I would be in town, I knew I had to get some of what he was doing up in my music. You know, the sound of the $1.50 drums and the harmonicas and the two-chord blues. I had to get back to that now because what we had been doing was just getting really abstracted. That was cool while I did it, but I just wanted to get back to that sound from where I had come."

In a Silent Way marks the significant addition of the guitar to Miles Davis' music and his growing use of electric instruments, which saw the piano replaced by the keyboards of Joe Zawinul, Herbie Hancock and Chick Corea. On stage, the trumpeter's outfits made him look like more of a rock star than a jazzman. Photo Jean-Pierre Leloir.

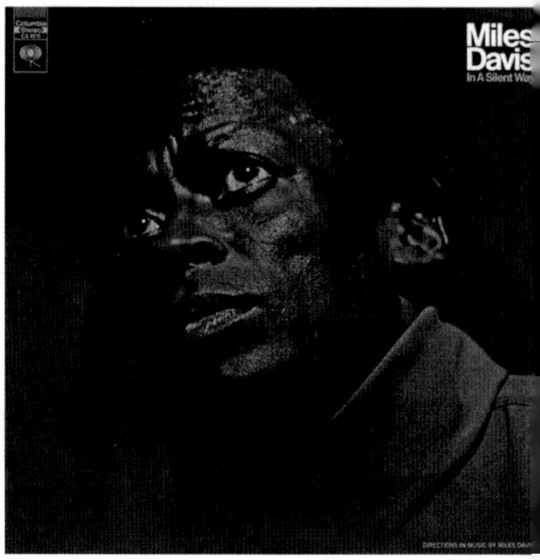

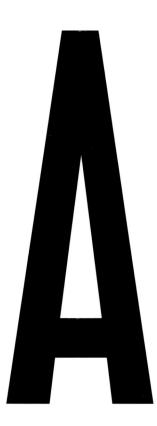

A PASTORAL VEIN. The recourse to a growing number of keyboards corresponded in part to a desire to return to the sound of the popular black music of the time, in which the accompaniment, often competing with the main melody, was played simultaneously on the bass, keyboards and guitar. This doubling had already made its appearance in the unison of the piano and bass on "Frelon Brun" and "Dual Mr. Anthony Tillmon," and would become a staple of Miles Davis' music. The reference to "two-chord" blues is proof of his desire to be rid of harmony's fetters, which would become an obsession over the next six years. John McLaughlin brought to Davis' music the saturated sustain of blues guitarists and the gritty rhythms of the guitars in James Brown's music.

Even so, at the February 1969 sessions, Joe Zawinul presented a score ostensibly at odds with Davis' stated intentions. In his work with the Adderley Brothers' funk band since 1962, Zawinul had become the electric-piano pioneer of jazz. He loved descriptive music. On a visit to his country of origin, Austria, he tapped into his childhood memories, and the resulting score fed into a fresh direction Davis was exploring. Culminating in 1969, this direction has sometimes been described as "pastoral," a new development in the art of the ballad, in which ambience and colour progressively override narrative and rhythm. Falling into this category, which was not exclusive to Davis, are "Flamenco Sketches" (inspired by Bill Evans); "Mood" (by Ron Carter); "Circle" and "Tout de Suite" (by Miles Davis); "Vonetta," "Sweet Pea," "Nefertiti," "Fall," "Sanctuary" and "Feio" (by Wayne Shorter); "Guinnevere" (which Davis borrowed from folk-rock singer David Crosby in late 1969); as well as numerous pieces by Joe Zawinul, namely "Ascent," "In a Silent Way," "Orange Lady" and "Gemini"; succeeded in 1971 by some scores by Brazilian composer Hermeto Pascoal, which became "Nem Um Talvez," "Selim" and "Little Church."

Taking one of Zawinul's scores, "In a Silent Way," Miles Davis decided to simplify the harmony. As was often the case, the trumpeter relayed his instructions cryptically, asking McLaughlin to play as though he did not know how. McLaughlin played the arpeggio of the first chord a guitarist learns, ornamented by the notes of Zawinul's theme. It was this hesitant statement of the theme, recorded without the guitarist knowing, that was used on the record. Then, Shorter (on soprano saxophone, which he had been playing more since November 1968) and Davis took turns restating the theme. These theme statements were edited in at the beginning and at the end with a recording made in the same session: "It's about that Time" was the result of a kind of jam session based on a series of vamps and directed by Davis, who moved around the studio to whisper instructions into the musicians' ears. Various fragments from the session were pieced together by Teo Macero to make up the B-side of the *In a Silent Way* microgroove LP. Using the same method, the first side, entitled "Shhh/Peaceful," consists of parts of a long improvisation on a pedal D, the minimalist ostinato of a Charleston cymbal and the harmonic daubing produced by the three keyboards. Davis' solo opens this suite, and is edited in to end the track, like a theme. Put together in this way, the record creates a sort of monochromic blue out of which emerges the red glow of the B-side, when everyone comes together briefly on the rhythm.

Despite their tempestuous relationship, the long-lasting collaboration between Miles Davis and Teo Macero (top row, 1970) was one of the most fruitful ever seen between an artist and his producer. An expert in studio techniques, Macero sound edited and sometimes reprocessed uncut material recorded live in studio to arrive at music that, when let loose on stage, occasionally bewildered listeners (below, at Ronnie Scott's, London, November 1969). Photos Don Hunstein (above); David Redfern (below).

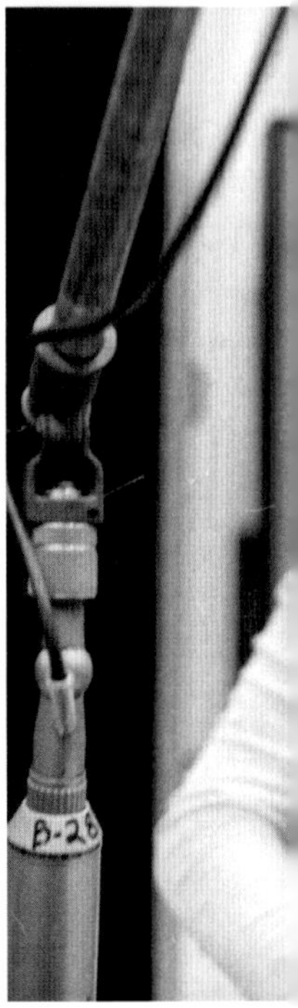

S**ESSIONS WITH DAGGERS DRAWN.** When the quintet was on the road, mostly during the summer festivals, they played their new, very different repertoire, the standards appearing only fleetingly. The group moved fast and furiously towards free jazz from the moment the trumpeter, after his first solo, left the stage to Wayne Shorter and to the Corea–Holland–DeJohnette trio in particular, who dove into a whirlwind of improvised sound, breaking the rules of harmony and even rhythm. When Davis went back to the studio in August, he took hold of the reins once again, still giving his musicians minimal instructions so they at least had something to go by. He surrounded the band with more musicians, depending on the track, including John McLaughlin, Joe Zawinul and Larry Young on electric piano; Bennie Maupin on bass clarinet; Harvey Brooks on electric bass; Jack DeJohnette, Don Alias and Lenny White on drums; and Jumma Santos on percussion. Davis took this opportunity to push the experience of *In a Silent Way* a little further by augmenting the palette, hastily handing out musical sketches with bits of melody and rhythm to provide some structure, and listening to takes to determine which parts to keep or edit, and where to add overdubs.

Although the mention "Directions in music by Miles Davis" still appeared on the record *Bitches Brew*, Teo Macero's post-production work on it was as essential as that of a film editor who, using rushes shot by the director, cuts, splices, formats and arranges. Starting from tapes that recorded continuously during directed but relatively informal jam sessions, Macero thought of a structure, sometimes isolating a short sequence and playing it back in a loop or inserting it in different places, like a thematic element. Although the relationship between Macero and Davis was stormy, the tension formed part of the latter's conscious or unconscious strategy, as was often the case. "I think *Bitches Brew* came out of a bitter battle that Miles and I had in the studio," Teo Macero later said, referring to the insults traded with Davis in the control booth during the sessions. At one point, when Davis entered the studio to cancel the session, Macero shouted at him, "Take you and your fucking trumpet, and your fucking musicians, and get outa here!" Surprised to see the musician pick up his trumpet as though he was about to play, the producer started rolling tape. Then the band started up as insults and obscene gestures were exchanged through the glass, and Davis challenged the producer to join him in the studio: "So I said, 'I'll go out.' I went out, stood right next to him, and didn't move. And he made all those fantastic tracks. . . . I said: 'You sonofabitch, you should be this way all the time—mean and miserable!'" The resulting tapes produced a double album, a very popular format since the release of Bob Dylan's *Blonde on Blonde* and Frank Zappa's *Freak Out* in 1966. In 1968, the Beatles came out with their famous *White Album*, Jimi Hendrix with *Electric Ladyland* and Cream with *Wheels of Fire*. In the 1970s, Miles Davis put out ten double albums.

Bitches Brew elicited a strong reaction: people either loved it or hated it, but the opinions of those from both camps were based on certain misapprehensions. Some critics saw the turn Miles Davis took as selling out, overlooking the fact that his highly abstract recordings were long, which prevented them from getting airtime through the usual hit-making

The dreamlike visions in the diptych (above) by surrealist painter Mati Klarwein (1932–2002), which was used to illustrate the record *Bitches Brew*, contrasted with the look of jazz at the time. Miles Davis called on the artist once more for *Live-Evil* (below). In 1969, the trumpeter appeared on the cover of *Rolling Stone* magazine, proving that his reputation extended far beyond the world of jazz.

ROLLING STONE
ACME No. 48 DECEMBER 13, 1969 UK: 2/6 35 CENTS
The ENVIRON MENTAL ISTS
ROBBIE ROBERTSON
MILES DAVIS

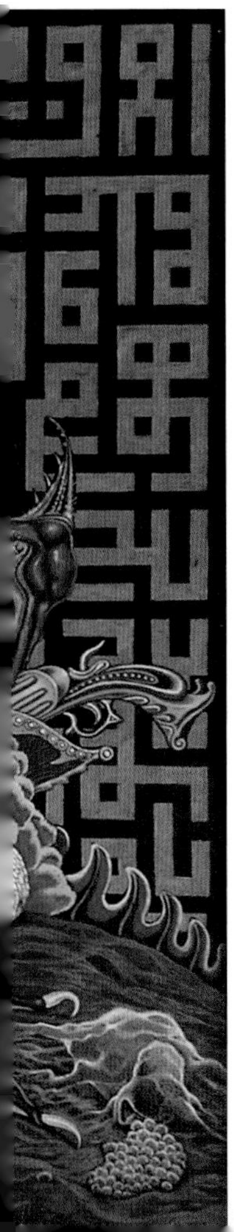

A boxing enthusiast and admirer of its champions, namely Sugar Ray Robinson (right, in a sweatsuit), in 1970 Miles Davis recorded the original soundtrack for a documentary on Jack Johnson, the first African-American world heavyweight champion. "Johnson portrayed Freedom," Davis wrote in the liner notes. Photos Corky McCoy (left); Thierry Trombert (opposite page).

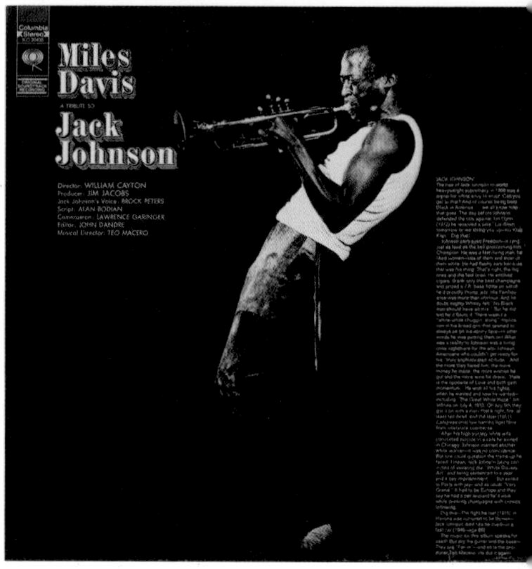

channels. The rock press, which, since the release of *Miles in the Sky*, had been following Davis, hailed *Bitches Brew* as revolutionary, unaware that the music on the last albums, from "Flamenco Sketches" to "Spanish Key," was the culmination of a steady evolution.
While his stage group was becoming more radical, Davis pursued a pastoral vein with his studio musicians in the winter 1969–70 sessions, bringing in new people, including the Brazilian percussionist Airto Moreira and members of what he called his "living room," sitarist Khalil Balakrishna and tablaist Bihari Sharma.

FORAY INTO FUNK. Nevertheless, in mid-February, a new series of sessions saw Davis reinforcing the funk direction he had first explored on "Stuff" (*Miles in the Sky*) and "Frelon Brun" (*Filles de Kilimanjaro*), in addition to the November 1968 sessions ("Splash," "Splashdown"). He constantly made Jack DeJohnette listen to recordings featuring rhythm-and-blues drummer Buddy Miles; DeJohnette grudgingly gave up the radically free style he had been playing on stage with Dave Holland and Chick Corea. Davis was navigating towards the funk rhythms of popular black artists—among whom James Brown was the fountainhead and Sly Stone the new messiah—inherited from African music's repetitive polyrhythms. The swing was replaced by the groove. The rhythm no longer provided an abundantly fertile ground for the soloist's voice, but rather intertwined with it to create a constantly rolling rhythmic machine that is driven by each interlocking component (guitar, keyboard, bass, drums).
When he went into the studio to record the music for a documentary on the African-American boxer Jack Johnson, Miles Davis temporarily let his usual collaborators go and called on Michael Henderson (an electric bassist who had experience working with soul bands, namely Stevie Wonder's group) and the unavailable Buddy Miles, who was replaced by Billy Cobham. When Herbie Hancock dropped by the studio unannounced, Davis invited him to jump in on electric organ, which technicians had to scramble to hook up as the band had already started recording. Davis had not initially planned for a keyboard, entrusting the harmony to John McLaughlin because of his ability to contribute syncopated touches to the groove created by the bass and drums. The session began to heat up with McLaughlin's boogie beat. By chance, the tapes were rolling. Miles Davis dove out of the control booth, where he had been chatting with Teo Macero, to join in what was to be a long jam session. The rest of *A Tribute to Jack Johnson* consists of edited sessions notably containing a riff borrowed from Sly Stone's "Sing a Simple Song." The record was to become a major work, but success was delayed: Columbia, failing to anticipate its impact, gave it inadequate promotion.

INSIDE THE TEMPLES OF ROCK. At this time, Clive Davis, the head of Columbia, was pushing Miles Davis to open for rock acts. At first, Davis refused to play for "those fucking long-haired white kids." However, he was willing to make concessions, on the condition that he play for black audiences. Accusing Columbia of favouring white rock music, Davis threatened to move to Motown, the number one label for black artists. But, after requesting not to be sold under the jazz label, he ended up

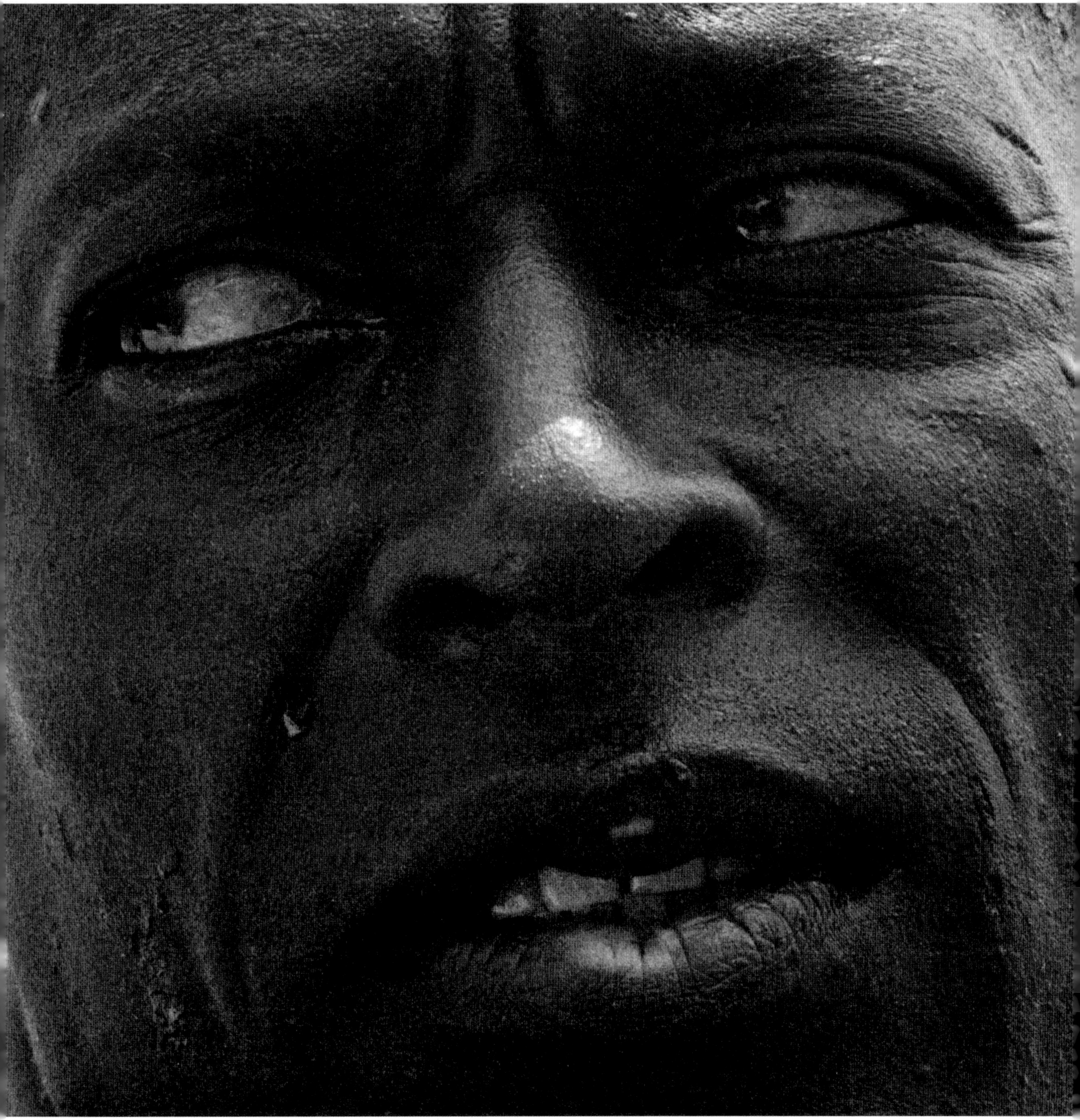

WOULD JACK JOHNSON DANCE TO THAT?

The last twenty seconds of "Yesternow." A voice rises over the strange, wild chords and a trumpet in a cloud of reverb: "I'm Jack Johnson. Heavyweight champion of the world. I'm black. They never let me forget it. I'm black all right. I'll never let *them* forget it!"

The deep, thundering voice enunciating these words is that of actor Brock Peters, who, in William Cayton's documentary, incarnates Jack Johnson, the first African-American world heavyweight boxing champion (1908).

Miles Davis recorded the soundtrack for this film in 1970; producer Teo Macero slipped in these few biting words right at the end of the record.

It is easy to substitute the name of the boxer with Miles Davis' in that passage. Same pride, same fight.

The importance of boxing to Miles Davis' very existence is obvious. He practised the sport, which fascinated him. Davis recounted to drummer Art Taylor, who was then interviewing the jazzmen he knew, that boxing was his only hobby aside from "making fun of white folks on television." Davis received journalists and photographers in boxing gyms, and insisted that his manager find him a gym where he could train at every stop on tour. Some musicians close to him shared his enthusiasm for the sport: drummer Stan Levey, his roommate when he first arrived in New York, and Red Garland, the pianist in his first quintet, were both former pros. Joe Zawinul often said that he and Davis spent more time comparing the relative merits of boxing champions than they did discussing their music.

In 1983, a Japanese journalist got in the star's limo, only to find Davis glued to images of Sugar Ray Robinson's triumphant knockout fight on the limo's television screen for the duration of the trip through New York City.

American race relations at that time produced a widely held view in the African-American community that the only two areas in which blacks were allowed to excel were sports and music. Boxing was, according to Miles Davis, the sport that most resembled jazz. He appreciated the individual styles, the mastery of mind over talent, the physical and mental control demanded by the performance. Above all, he recognized that boxing was a demanding discipline whose foundations—precision and quick reflexes—required long-term training that was useless without the freedom to be inspired, the stroke of genius, the knockout punch.

Davis boxed regularly. In 1952, when his drug addiction was dragging him under, he suffered the ultimate humiliation: Bobby McQuillen, not bothering to hide his disgust, pulled no punches as he refused to be Davis' trainer. Some months later, voluntarily confined under lock and key to a room at his father's, Davis went cold turkey. He succeeded, he said, thanks to the example set by Sugar Ray Robinson, model of discipline, excellence and integrity: "Sugar Ray was one of the few idols that I have ever had." Davis offered the boxer one of his trumpets in tribute. He admired this man, who, symbol of accomplishment and dignity, owed his success to his mind, his will and the power of his fists. Like Robinson, Davis had his own "Soldier" (a reference to Soldier Jones, Robinson's trainer), a man he could rely on, an alter ego in the shadows, a coach, the only person whose opinion counted: Gil Evans.

Boxing contributed to the musician's resurrection. His training loosened his body, relaxed his posture, helped him with breath control; on stage, one could witness Davis move his shoulders differently, become more cat-like, and match his legs, chest and neck movements to the development of a solo, making manifest the correlation between musical thought and its expression.

Davis moved like a boxer, but, in order to safeguard his career, he never actually fought in the ring. In the gym, everyone was well aware that his face could not be touched. He was confined to the punching bag, to shadow boxing, to dancing around an invisible adversary in the ring.

In the early 1970s, his music seemed to receive a jolt, as though the punches he could not deliver and his intensive training were being channelled on stage or in the studio. On very long tracks, or in pieces with the same sequences endlessly repeated, the music seems to loop over and over until the trumpet comes in, rending the saturated space with phrases that are less long discursive passages than a series of brief sequences unleashed with the expert precision of a well-placed jab.

David Liebman, saxophonist with the group at this time, compared the polished quality of Davis' cutting rhythms to a series of hooks, a careful combination of impulse, timing, rhythm and controlled power. In his autobiography, Davis recalled that, in the studio, his obsession could be summarized by a single image: "Would Jack Johnson dance to that?" For Davis, the champion's fancy footwork set the pulse.

VINCENT BESSIÈRES

VINCENT BESSIÈRES IS A JOURNALIST AND FORMER ASSISTANT EDITOR OF THE MAGAZINE *JAZZMAN*. HE IS CURATOR OF THE EXHIBITION *WE WANT MILES*, ORGANIZED BY THE CITÉ DE LA MUSIQUE, PARIS (OCTOBER 2009– JANUARY 2010).

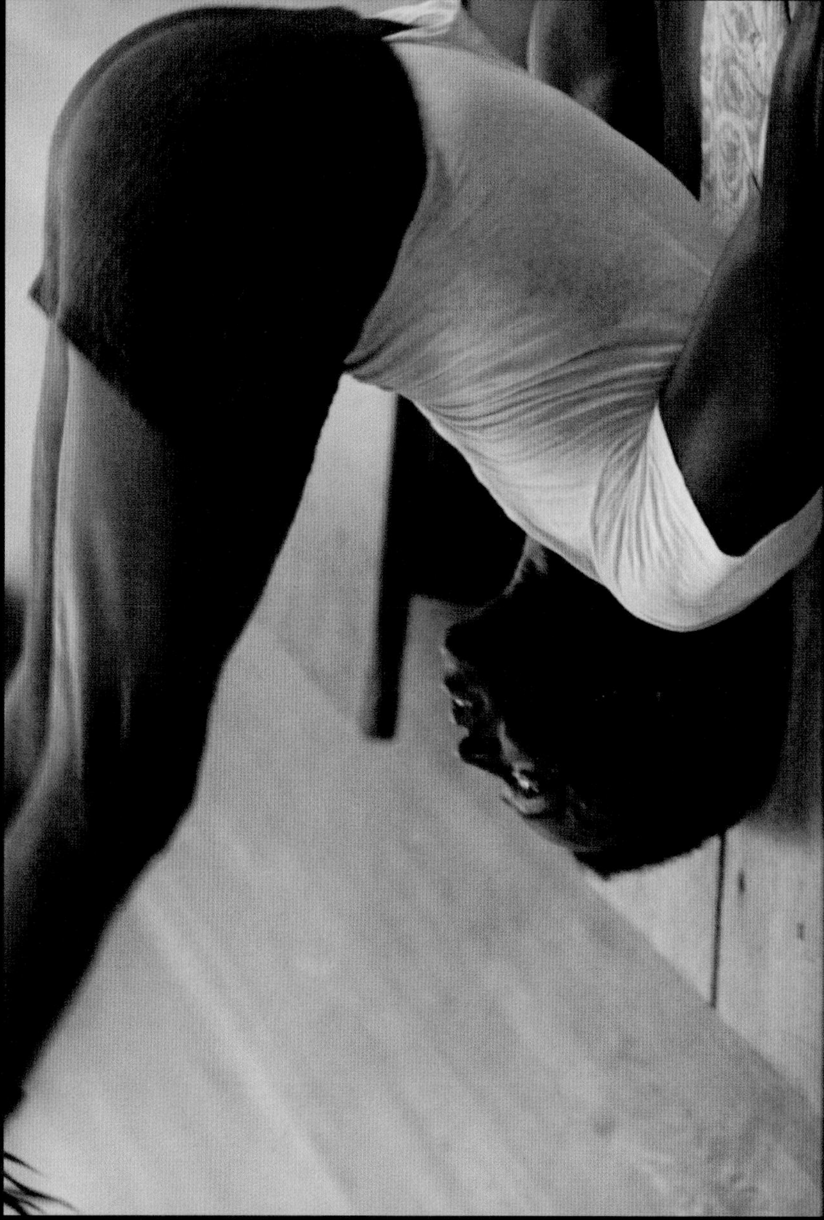

Photos Corky McCoy.

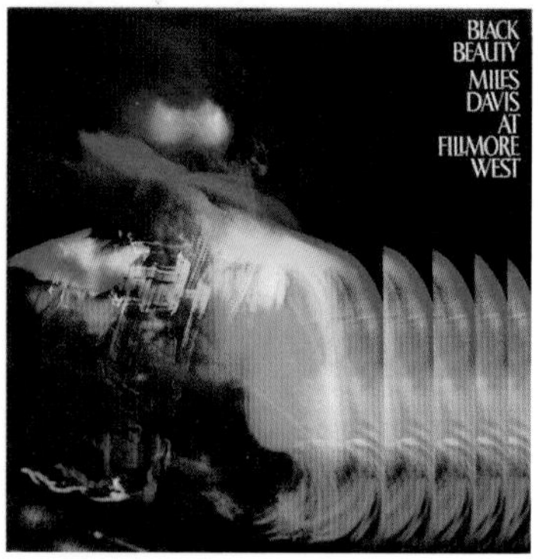

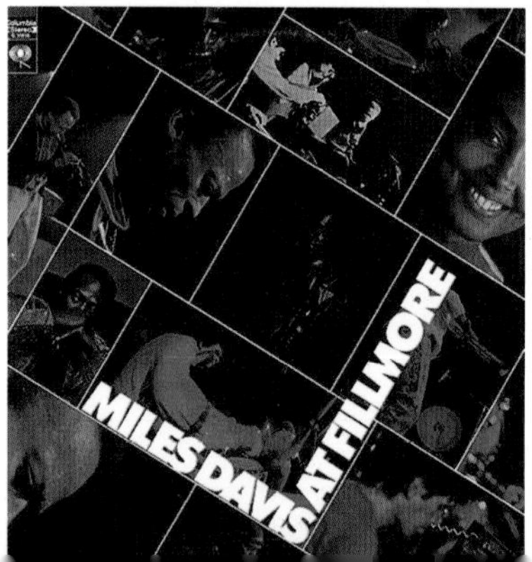

Backed by Columbia, Miles Davis was invited to perform in two of the big rock venues of the time—Fillmore East, New York, and Fillmore West, San Francisco—in 1970 and 1971, and to be billed on the same psychedelic posters as popular groups, including the Grateful Dead. The record label issued some recordings of these concerts. Photo Fred Lombardi (opposite page).

accepting to open at the temples of rock, Fillmore East and Fillmore West (these concerts were recorded and sound edited by Teo Macero as double albums), and at the Isle of Wight Festival. Airto Moreira's varied percussion now coloured the music of the stage group. Wayne Shorter was replaced by Steve Grossman (on soprano saxophone rather than on tenor, the better to break through the wall of sound produced by the rhythm section), then by Gary Bartz (on alto and soprano saxophone). In late spring, Keith Jarrett was invited to play a no-name organ to contrast with the electric effects Chick Corea usually added on the Rhodes. The positioning of the two keyboards at opposite ends of the stage, in addition to the subpar sound system Davis had acquired, kept the two keyboardists from hearing each other. Chaotic sound ensued, amplifying the free-form solos of Dave Holland (now always on electric bass) and Jack DeJohnette.

Corea and Holland soon left to form the Circle quartet with one of free music's leading figures, saxophonist Anthony Braxton. Alone on keyboards, Keith Jarrett worked towards cleaning up the band's sound, at times focusing more on rhythm, espousing the chucking rhythms of funk guitar and the ecstatic inflections of gospel and soul, at other times playing with greater lyricism, all the while maintaining a great deal of spontaneity. Although possessing a beautiful melodic agility, Michael Henderson's bass guitar lines, powerfully anchored in the tempo, did not blend well with the free impulses of drummer Jack DeJohnette. Davis took advantage of the recording session at the Cellar Door in Washington in December 1970 to call in John McLaughlin for some extra spice on the last day; the resulting tracks, along with various studio pieces from that year, were put on the compilation double album *Live-Evil*.

GB
MOLE-RICHARDSON LTD.,
CHASE ROAD, LONDON, N.W.10.
965 6834.

In August 1970, Miles Davis performed at two major rock events that marked the period, the Isle of Wight Festival in the United Kingdom (p. 153: "backstage" with Betty Davis) and Tanglewood in Lenox, Massachusetts (below, with Gary Bartz). Photo Amalie R. Rothschild.

Photo K. Abe.

ON THE CORNER FUNK BEAT

1971–1979

The musicians who had participated in Miles Davis' first electric experimentations went on to form groups at the forefront of jazz rock that were modelled on the rock band: Tony Williams' Lifetime; John McLaughlin's Mahavishnu Orchestra; Wayne Shorter and Joe Zawinul's Weather Report; Chick Corea's Return to Forever. They played greatly amplified music propelled by the powerful beat of the electric bass and drums, characterized by showy instrumental technique and coloured by the diversification of electric sounds, mostly due to the synthesizer. World music, funk and progressive rock were important influences. While free jazz seemed to be on its last legs, these bands spread their positive message at the major festivals and captured the attention of a disenchanted, mainly white audience for whom spiritual exoticism and ecological concerns were transplanting the revolutionary ideals of the 1960s. Despite having contributed to its development, Miles Davis disregarded this well-intentioned jazz rock, which, with Columbia's backing, achieved a certain commercial success that exceeded what Davis' more radical music could aspire to. The dark, righteous Afrofunk direction he was taking echoed the brutal repression

In 1970, tired of playing to an audience largely made up of young white hippies, Miles Davis decided to anchor his music even further in the black culture of rhythm and blues and funk, evidenced mainly by his decision to include bassist Michael Henderson (opposite page), who had worked with the Motown label. He also changed his look by growing an Afro. Photos Corky McCoy (left); Jean-Pierre Leloir (right).

that fell upon the black movement, deeply dividing its more extremist ranks. The feelings of bitter resentment among African Americans fed into his music. Numerous black performers freed themselves from the record labels' control to produce their own music that expressed their convictions in no uncertain terms: "When the Revolution Comes" by the Last Poets and "On the Other Side of Town" by Curtis Mayfield came out in 1970; the next year, "What's Goin' On" by Marvin Gaye, "Respect Yourself" by the Staple Singers, "There's a Riot Goin' On" by Sly Stone and "The Revolution Will Not Be Televised" by Gil Scott-Heron were released.

For Davis, the causes of bitterness were legion. After his divorce from Betty Mabry in 1969, he had begun to see two pleasant young women at the same time: Marguerite Eskridge (pictured on the cover of *Miles Davis at Fillmore*) and Jackie Battle. Both tried to convert him to their spiritual views and health regimes. They encouraged him to follow various diets and engage in relative abstinence. However, the eventful life of their mate turned out to be incompatible with their temperaments. On October 9, 1969, while Davis was dropping Eskridge off at her place, a car stopped by his Ferrari. Five shots fired at the couple went through Davis' car door. Once on the scene, police began by searching the Ferrari, where they conveniently found marijuana, which Davis never used. He and his girlfriend were taken to the police station and later released without being charged. Then, a few months later, Davis was pulled over because his Ferrari was not up to code. The brass knuckles he had been carrying since the October encounter with police fell out of his bag, which meant he had to spend a night in jail for a weapons violation. Eskridge left him in 1971, when she was pregnant with Erin, Davis' youngest son, born April 29. Davis' drinking and cocaine use increased, even though his health was beginning to give him trouble: he was suffering from a stomach ulcer, gallstones and joint pain.

A BAND UNDER PRESSURE.

In 1971, Airto Moreira left the band, followed by Jack DeJohnette. Miles Davis was on his way to Europe in October, so Leon "Ndugu" Chancler took over on drums and Don Alias and James Foreman (a.k.a. Mtume) filled the two percussion spots. Whereas Moreira's playing had added more colour, Mtume contributed to the groove. Tensions had begun to build within the band with the arrival of saxophonist Gary Bartz, and it came to a head when Mtume joined. Bartz founded NTU Troop, a band that sought to reconnect with music's African roots. Mtume was a radical Africanist. Bassist Michael Henderson came from the world of rhythm and blues as well as funk, and had no special affinity with jazz. Keyboardist Keith Jarrett, despite his Afro, was the band's only white member. Although his music was not without elements of soul and funk, his background in classical music and the harmony-based language of Broadway musicals strongly connected him to white culture. He hated electric instruments and, as a classical concert per-

Miles Davis at home, New York, 1971.
Photos Anthony Barboza.

Miles Davis went to Jimi Hendrix's funeral in September 1970, with Betty Davis (right) and Jackie Battle (left), whom he was seeing at the time. The guitarist's untimely death brutally closed the subject of collaboration, which the two musicians had been toying with for some time. Photo Bob Peterson.

former, demanded that the band's stage manager tune his Fender Rhodes every night. Jarrett chose to be there for Davis, but did not disguise his dislike for Davis' current tastes in music or his contempt for the other band members, who reciprocated the feeling. Davis went out of his way to turn everyone against each other, forbidding them from taking Jarrett's lead by saying, for instance, "When Keith starts playing that Catholic school shit, lay out, don't play, don't follow him." Davis was fascinated by the pianist and his ability to improvise out of nothing. This bandleader knew exactly what he wanted from his band members and deliberately encouraged opposition and tension between them.

The standards and original compositions of the second quintet had been completely eliminated from the repertoire, which now consisted of pieces distinguished by the succession of bass riffs played throughout the different sequences. Miles Davis would employ this minimalist vocabulary as the framework for long improvised suites until 1975. Musicologist Enrico Merlin later meticulously catalogued these sequences as "coded phrases." The canonical form of the twelve-bar blues had been abandoned. Now that rock was raiding the blues, Davis told his musicians: "Let the white folks have the blues." Yet the blues colour and its blue notes were pervasive. Davis now only ever played the electric trumpet, whose sound was usually altered by the wah-wah pedal, recreating the phrasing and sound of Jimi Hendrix's guitar. With his back to the audience, facing his musicians, Davis used looks and gestures to direct changes in tempo and instrumental entrances and exits, while the trumpet called the transitions.

Meanwhile, Davis had not managed to renew his music. In early 1971, suffering from depression, he spoke again about retiring. He had not set foot inside a studio since June 1970. Overlooked by the Grammy Awards in early 1971, he accused the record industry of being 99% controlled by white people and told *Jet* magazine he was associated with the Mammies for Black Recording Artists, which involved cam-

Miles Davis had a music room at home, where he would listen to tapes recorded in the studio and plan out his records (opposite page). It was in this room in 1972 that Davis, along with the young British arranger-composer Paul Buckmaster, laid the groundwork for the record *On the Corner*, on which are found the mixed influences of Sly Stone, Stockhausen and East Indian music. Davis' interest in the latter led to the addition of sitarist and percussionist Badal Roy (below) to the band. Photos Mark Patiky (above); Urve Kuusik (below).

paigning black disc jockeys to support music by black artists. Nevertheless, Davis did not manage to appeal to young African-American audiences. On November 26, 1971, for a performance at the New York Philharmonic, he spent half his fee giving away free tickets in black neighbourhoods. In March 1972, he hired Ramon "Tiki" Fulwood, a drummer with the most inventive funk bands of the time, Funkadelic and Parliament. The following month, a gallstone operation forced Davis to break up his band.

A LUSH GROOVE. A new, unexpected figure helped reignite Miles Davis' creativity. In 1969, Davis met Paul Buckmaster, a classically trained arranger-composer and cellist who played music somewhere between experimental rock and pop. He gave Davis a recording containing abstract melodies over a basic rhythm; in return, the trumpeter invited Buckmaster to stay with him in May 1972. A keen admirer of Karlheinz Stockhausen's music, Buckmaster introduced his host to a whole new world. When at home, Davis usually played his James Brown, Jimi Hendrix and Sly Stone records all day long; these he now alternated with recordings of the German composer's "Gruppen" and "Mixtur." In the same way that Stockhausen blended traditional instruments and electronic music, the two men set out to combine funk rhythms and abstract forms. Davis also listened with keen interest to his guest play the Prelude to Bach's Cello Suite No. 1. The development and interweaving of rhythmic and harmonic ideas drew Davis' attention to the music of Ornette Coleman, whom he had initially dismissed outright. Davis even said he felt a bond with Don Cherry, the trumpeter of the historic Coleman quartet, who had become a pioneer of the fusion of jazz and Eastern traditions.

Davis went into the studio on June 1, 1972, with musical sketches devised by Buckmaster not unlike the minimalist instructions the trumpeter had been giving since *Kind of Blue*. The lineup recalled the studio bands Miles Davis had surrounded himself with in 1969. The group included three keyboards (Chick Corea on synthesizer, Herbie Hancock on electric piano and Harold "Ivory" Williams on organ); guitar (John McLaughlin); electric bass (Michael Henderson); drums (Jack DeJohnette); two percussionists (Don Alias on congas, Billy Hart on hand percussion); and members of Davis' "living room": Collin Walcott on electric sitar and Badal Roy on tablas. The musicians were chosen at the last minute; the young saxophonist David Liebman was contacted on the very day of the studio session, as he was waiting to see his doctor. When Liebman got to the studio, where the session was already in progress, all he heard was the percussion and the buzzing of the other instruments, which were plugged directly into the mixing board. Liebman found himself without headphones in front of a microphone, pushed there by Davis, who whispered "E flat" in his ear. Liebman began to play amid the confusion of the first session. Paul Buckmaster's instructions were soon disregarded.

The music recorded that day, and five days later with a slightly different band, make up the record *On the Corner*. Drawn by Corky McCoy, the characters on the record cover depict Harlem types. These figures were clearly intended to illustrate Davis' desire to

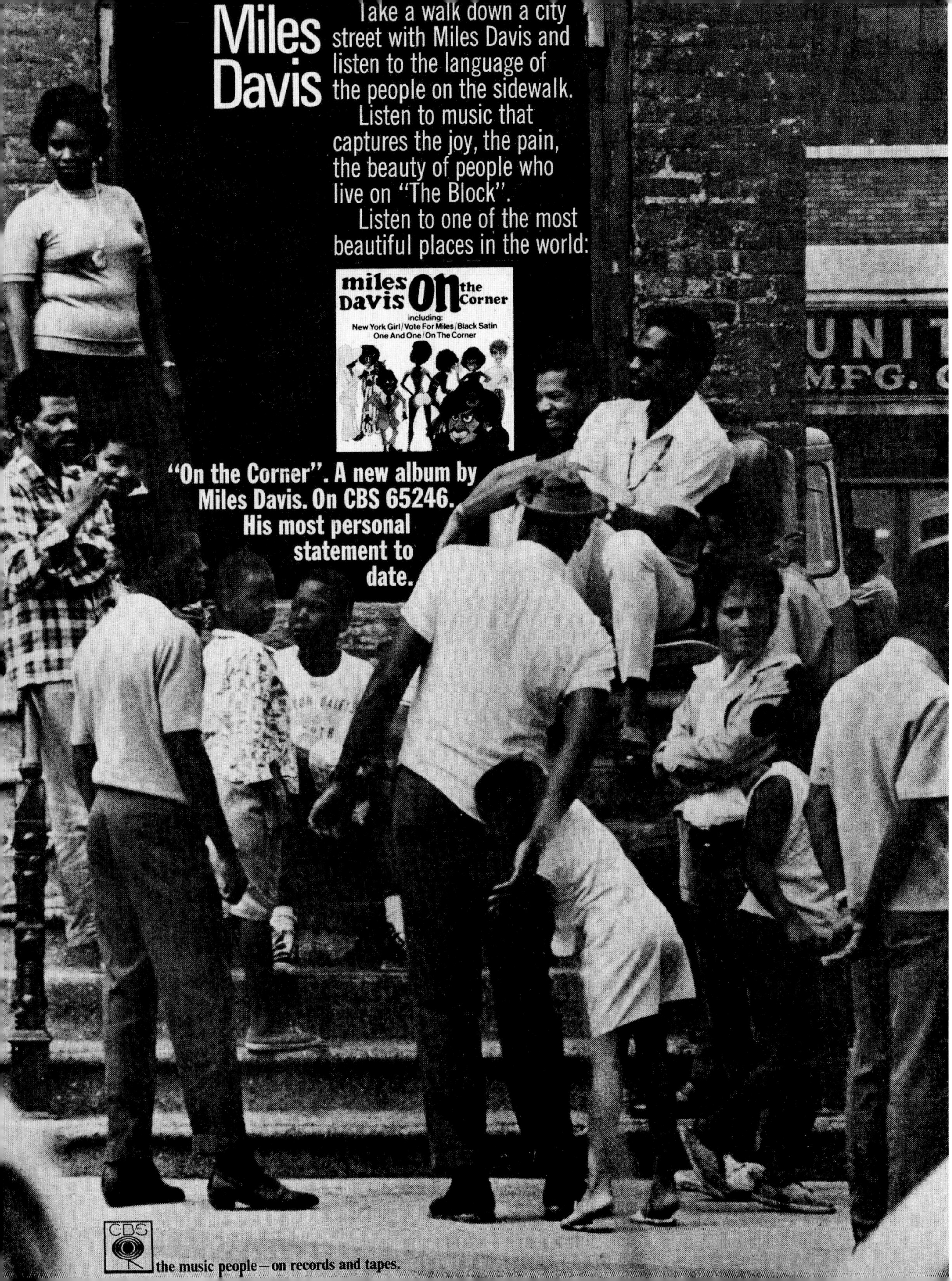
Miles Davis
Take a walk down a city street with Miles Davis and listen to the language of the people on the sidewalk.
Listen to music that captures the joy, the pain, the beauty of people who live on "The Block".
Listen to one of the most beautiful places in the world:
miles Davis On the Corner
including:
New York Girl/Vote For Miles/Black Satin
One And One/On The Corner
"On the Corner". A new album by Miles Davis. On CBS 65246. His most personal statement to date.
UNIT
MFG. C
CBS
the music people—on records and tapes.

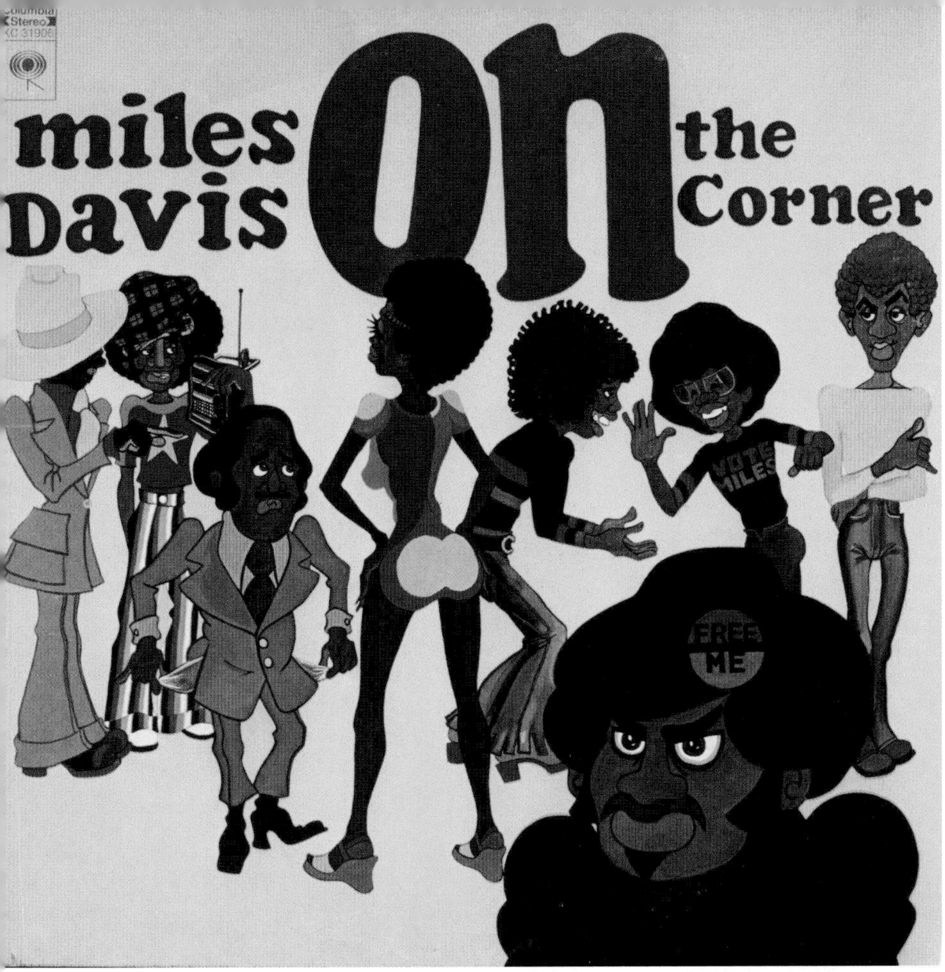

In an attempt to draw attention to his desire to have an impact within the African-American community, Miles Davis asked cartoonist friend Corky McCoy to illustrate his record covers.

McCoy's characters are supposedly based on types found on the streets of Harlem, who kill time "on the corner." Columbia echoed this approach in its ads (opposite page).

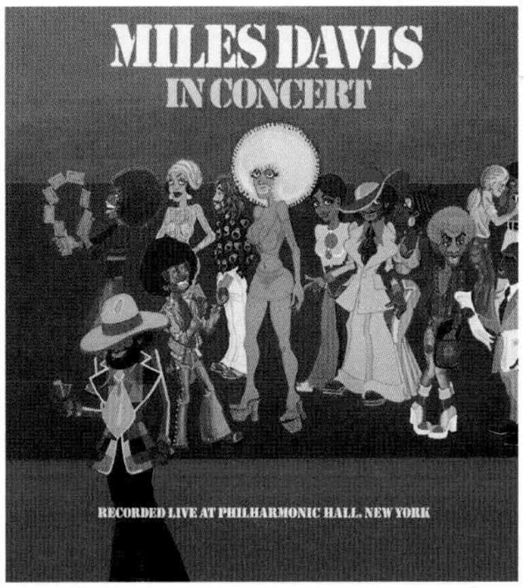

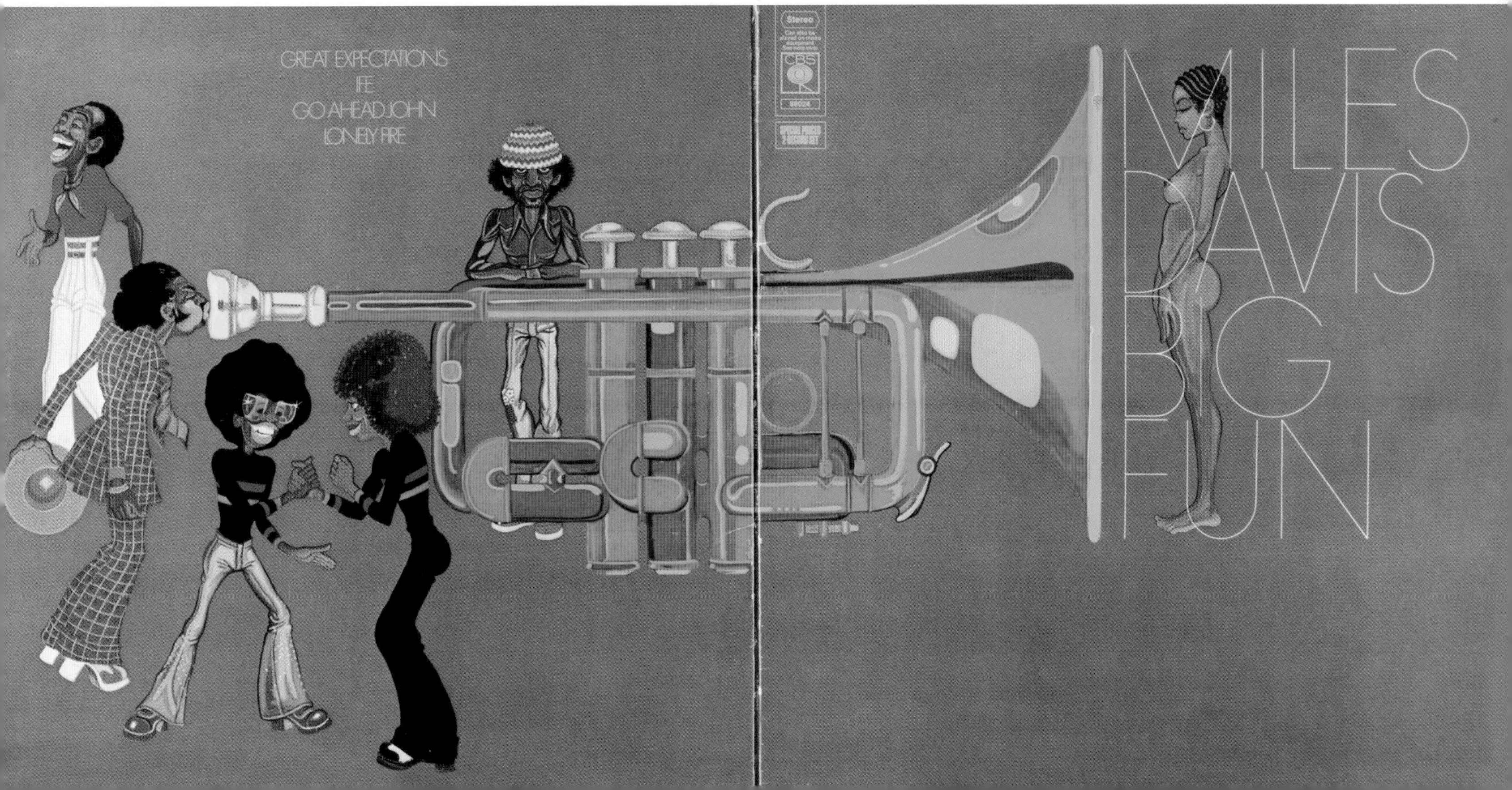

Miles Davis equipped his trumpet with an electric device that allowed him to modulate his sound with a wah-wah pedal identical to the type used by guitarists. The sounds he produced led him to reconnect with some of blues' expressiveness. Miles Davis in Paris, November 1973.
Photos Christian Rose.

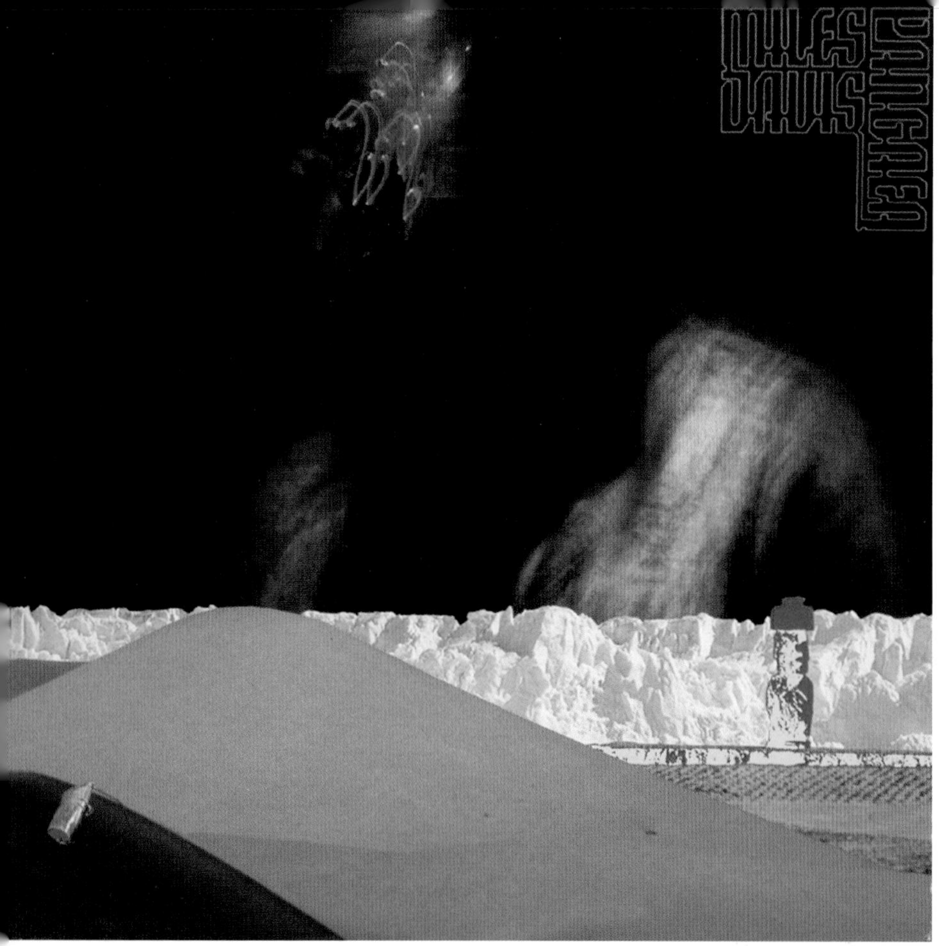
MILES
DAVIS
PANGAEA

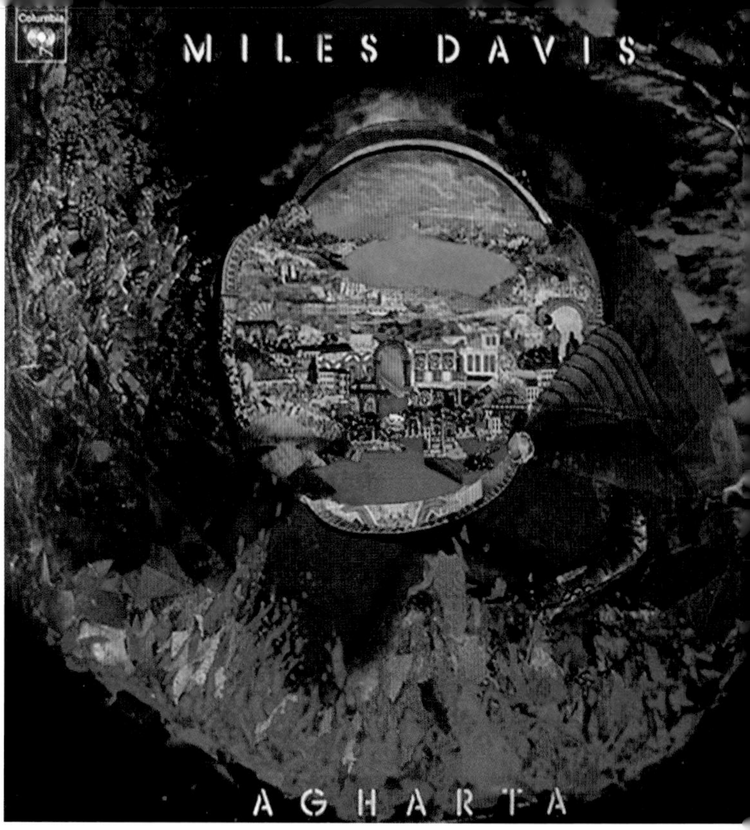
Columbia
MILES DAVIS
AGHARTA

MILES DAVIS
DARK MAGUS

AGHARTA
MILES
DAVIS

Apart from *Get Up with It*, the last albums Miles Davis recorded before retiring—*Dark Magus*, *Pangaea* and *Agharta*—are concert recordings consisting of long jungle-of-sound sequences in which form is difficult to perceive. The music's mystery was underscored by the esoteric nature of the titles, bestowed only after the event, which the cryptic cover illustrations only serve to heighten.

appeal to African-American audiences. Though the record was misunderstood upon release, it became a cult classic twenty years later among electro-jazz and drum-and-bass circles, where it was appreciated as a seminal work. Even more so than *Bitches Brew*, which had influenced the pioneers of ambient music, including Brian Eno and Jon Hassell, *On the Corner* deals with intricately textured sound. The repeated motifs are only intelligible when tied together. Carried by a relentless beat, these motifs form a lush groove within which improvised lines get lost in the anonymity of the rhythmic collective. Moreover—as he had done in the past to confound biased critics—Davis did not credit the musicians who contributed to the record. At the time, the trumpeter told his supporting musicians, "Don't finish your idea; let [the band] finish it."

This is how Davis took Charlie Parker's approach to polyrhythm to the extreme and reduced James Brown's groove to an abstraction. Pushing instrumental negation to the limit in sessions held sporadically over 1972, there is no trumpet on "Rated X." Instead, Davis pounded out sustained long chords on a synthesizer while the sound engineer periodically cut the rhythm channels, a technique known as on-off. The two words, "on" and "off," appear on either side of the *On the Corner* cover.

Hints of this process, also called stop and go, are found in his earlier work, beginning in 1968, but Miles Davis only became fully aware of it during his conversations about Stockhausen with Paul Buckmaster, and he began to apply it in his live shows.

BLACK MAGIC. Initially, Davis was not very successful at reproducing his music on stage. *Miles Davis in Concert*, a double album recorded in September 1972 at the New York Philharmonic, resulted from the attempt. In January 1973, he managed to convince David Liebman to join his regular group. This disciple of John Coltrane was hardly taken with what he heard, but he had a vague sense that something interesting was going on, so he decided to take the plunge. The same can be said of Al Foster, who continued to play drums for Davis until 1984. Trained in the school of swing, bop and hard bop, Foster infused pounding funk drums with his signature blend of strength and fluidity.

A new guitarist signed on in the spring. Like others before (and after) him, Pete Cosey came on stage without any rehearsal. However, Cosey was no neophyte—he had made a career for himself as a guitarist with Chess Records, the main blues label in Chicago, where he had played with Etta James, Howlin' Wolf and Muddy Waters; he had added his personal touch to Waters' record *Electric Mud*, a mix of Chicago blues and psychedelic music. Cosey had been a member of Chicago's Association for the Advancement of Creative Musicians (AACM), which promoted African-American artists. Deviating from the stereotype of the warring or erotic guitar hero, he appeared with Davis' band seated at a table bearing hand-percussion instruments, electronic devices and a small synthesizer. Using alternative guitar tuning, Cosey recreated the harshest aspects of Jimi Hendrix's instrumental music, while Reggie Lucas' guitar powered the rhythm section's syncopation.

March 30, 1974, after Columbia dispatched a team to record Davis at Carnegie Hall (*Dark Magus*), Miles Davis brought two musicians on stage without any rehearsal: saxophonist Azar Lawrence, who was not kept on, and guitarist Dominique Gaumont, who stayed on for a few

Miles Davis and David Liebman (above), Mtume (below, left) and Reggie Lucas (below, right). Photos Corky McCoy.

ON STAGE WITH MILES DAVIS

On Friday night, January 12, 1973, I got on the bandstand for the first time with Miles Davis, at the famous rock venue, Fillmore East, all plugged in (my horns—tenor, soprano—and flute were all drilled to accommodate microphone pickups that day for amplification). As for the band members, I only knew tablaist Badal Roy, who was with me was on the *My Goals Beyond* recording with John McLaughlin in 1972, and drummer Al Foster from jam sessions in my loft over the past several years. That I had no idea what I played or what happened on the bandstand that night would be an understatement. The energy, volume and sheer textural density was overwhelming. After the gig, I returned to the Village Vanguard across town in time for the remainder of the first set to finish the engagement I had with drummer Elvin Jones' group, with which I had been working for two years. The night before, Elvin had graciously granted me leave, saying, "If Miles Davis wants you, you have to go!" On the most significant night of my professional life, it felt like I had gone from the future back in time, from the twenty-first to the twentieth century, from some sort of space-like rock music to the familiar sounds of bebop.

For the first few months before he cut the personnel down, the instrumentation consisted of tablas, electric sitar, guitar, organ, drums, congas, bass, Miles and me. Playing mostly concerts and relatively short sets, it took me months to truly "hear" what was happening and what my place was in the music. You had to figure out what to do on your own. There were no written charts, and Miles said almost nothing to me or anyone else from what I could observe about the music. With this edition of Miles Davis' group, live performance was the main event. Miles was the quintessence of a true jazz musician in that he trusted, invested in and savoured the moment: spontaneity was everything.

The period when I was with him (January 1973—May 1974), before he took a "sabbatical," can be seen as further development towards more and more abstraction of the earlier innovations from the late 1960s, highlighting the incredible speed of change during this period from what was in a sense jazz-rock to rock-jazz, all a matter of which musical element was being emphasized: increased use of electronics resulting in a thicker and varied textural density (wah-wah pedal on the trumpet; use of the Yamaha organ; chorus and delay effects on my saxophone; Mtume's drum machine, Pete Cosey's percussion instruments); more "accidental" harmonic dissonance (two, and for a period three, guitarists playing together; atonal organ chords played by Miles); even less use of formal compositional devices, with forms and melodic statements replaced by an almost total reliance on simple and extended vamps as well as a continuation of Miles' penchant for ongoing segues between tunes; increased rock/funk underpinning in which rhythms overlapped and were spread out between various rhythm-section instruments (similar to some of Sly Stone's music); solos that were not so much developed as they were episodic, short vignettes.

Miles' playing, though fundamentally retaining the main ingredients of his basic style, changed in some dramatic ways. The use of the wah-wah pedal and microphone pickup on the trumpet meant that the very unique and incredibly individual trademark sound that Miles Davis had on his horn was transformed. Whether it was the effect of how he heard himself through the pedal or other contributing factors, his playing became even more rhythmically pronounced than previously (above all, Miles was ALWAYS a rhythmic improviser) as well as very focused towards the middle of the beat. The best jazz musicians treat pulse with a loose and flexible attitude, pushing and pulling the beat at will. I have always thought that Miles' sense of pulse was among the most accurate of any jazz musician in history. This "jabbing" rhythmic style became interspersed with flurries of notes consisting of indistinguishable pitch runs and the occasional long tone thrown in. All of these stylistic mannerisms were played in a dry sonic context without reverb or delay, heightening the stark nature of Miles' rhythmic approach even more.

His note choices ranged from very diatonic/in-the-key lyrical phrases combined with blues-scale motifs to completely out-of-tonality asides. Of course, whatever came out of his horn still retained a melodic contour, with nursery-rhyme-type melodies thrown into the mix on occasion. All of this, as always in Miles' case, was executed with élan, bravura and a unique sense of space and timing which remain historically the most distinct aspects of his overall style. There is no doubt in my mind that during this period Miles was thinking within a specific set of parameters concerning his trumpet playing.

Previous years had seen Miles play a solo, leave the stage, returning often in the middle of someone else's statement to start up again, usually after the piano solo. During my time, he was an ever-present force on stage, which had its effect on the sidemen. Not only did he not leave the stage, but he would also stand with his back to the audience, staring at all of us through gigantic, impenetrably dark sunglasses! Marking the beat physically with his body, nodding in the direction of someone to solo, he might unexpectedly cue the band to execute uneven "stop" time episodes in the midst of a phrase, a traditional device from older jazz styles. And there was the Yamaha organ, which was a kind of precursor to the whole keyboard technology. Miles would splash down clusters and triads at will, thereby orchestrating the live performance even further. Though the format of our live performances was loose, it wasn't predictable, meaning the music could change drastically from night to night. To sum it up, Miles was a real and looming force on the bandstand, whether he was actually playing or not.

As mentioned earlier, when Miles went on stage, past and future didn't exist. It was all about the present tense, the essence of true improvisation and what most jazz musicians strive for daily when playing. I have recounted to students and interviewers how concentrated Miles became in the moments before we hit the bandstand. Quiet, subdued and seemingly deep in thought, the whole band could sense his vibe before we walked out. It wasn't so much dramatic as it was penetrating, and you could feel that serious business was about to commence. For me, it was a lesson in owning and trusting the moment, two intangible aspects of playing that I have tried to absorb into my own musical personality. Miles had complete confidence in whatever gesture he made, whether in his own playing or in directing the band. One never felt a second of doubt. This meant that anyone within playing range could, by osmosis, transfer Miles' strong sense of conviction and self in his own playing. I certainly doubted myself to some degree at that stage of my life, but with his energy in such close proximity, I had no time to think about it. This is particularly true in the recording situation. You realize that when the light is green, anything you play may be heard anywhere, anytime and forever—the ultimate judgment day! Thinking about the posterity of a recording can easily become a nerve-wracking experience, depending upon one's personality. But with Miles Davis, you just had to concentrate and be on his case—watching, listening and ready to jump into the fray when called upon.

The lessons I learned from being around Miles Davis took a decade or more to firmly take root. They pertained to everything from instrumental grafts gathered from observing Miles' trumpet style, which I have incorporated into my playing on the soprano saxophone, especially in the rhythmic realm; being in the moment; focusing the other musicians' energy as a function of leading a band; but, most of all, gaining the confidence necessary to allow musical events to occur with spontaneity and regularity. In the 1980s especially, I would find myself thinking of Miles in the middle of a solo, which would alter or inspire a fresh direction.

As Miles once reminded me in dramatic fashion, being with him made me in some ways part of the jazz bloodline back to Louis Armstrong. Consequently, I have tried to maintain the integrity and honesty that I observed and experienced with Miles and Elvin Jones. I had the best possible training a person could ask for—a real-time apprenticeship with masters of the art—Emperor Jones and the Prince of Darkness, Miles Davis—a privilege and honour that I have gladly accepted with a concomitant sense of responsibility during my allotted time on this planet. For that opportunity, I am eternally grateful.

DAVID LIEBMAN

DAVID LIEBMAN'S CAREER HAS SPANNED NEARLY FOUR DECADES, BEGINNING IN THE 1970S AS THE SAXOPHONIST IN BOTH ELVIN JONES' AND MILES DAVIS' GROUPS. HE HAS PLAYED ON NEARLY THREE HUNDRED RECORDINGS WITH OVER ONE HUNDRED UNDER HIS LEADERSHIP OR CO-LEADERSHIP. IN JAZZ EDUCATION, LIEBMAN IS A RENOWNED LECTURER AND AUTHOR OF SEVERAL MILESTONE BOOKS: *SELF PORTRAIT OF A JAZZ ARTIST*, *A CHROMATIC APPROACH TO JAZZ HARMONY AND MELODY* AND *DEVELOPING A PERSONAL SAXOPHONE SOUND*.

Photos Corky McCoy.

Several attempts were made to get Miles Davis back into the studio after his retirement. Below: The session band of March 2, 1978, produced only one track, unreleased to this day. Photo Don Hunstein.

months, adding an additional solo voice directly inherited from Jimi Hendrix. The electric guitar had definitively done away with the European grand piano, and the keyboards only persisted in the form of the Yamaha YC45 organ used but rarely by Davis himself. Saxophonist David Liebman continued to represent the European instrumental and harmonic legacy, drawing on his background in both Coltrane and classical music. Even though he had quickly absorbed Davis' lessons on dynamics, phrasing and dramatic energy and effects, his virtuosity and attachment to the elaborative virtues of jazz set him apart from the polyrhythmic collective of percussion, guitars and bass. When, in June 1974, Miles Davis paid tribute to Duke Ellington, who had died a few weeks before, with a static piece on the electric organ drawn out over thirty-two minutes, David Liebman felt a bafflement that compounded his feelings of isolation within the group.

The saxophonist left to form his own band, which would combine the influences of Miles Davis and John Coltrane. He was replaced by Sonny Fortune, a black alto and soprano saxophonist and flutist, who had a more linear post-Coltrane approach than his predecessor. However, the individual voice lost almost all of its importance in this jungle of sound, somewhere between lush growth and decomposition, documented on two double albums, *Agharta* and *Pangaea*, recorded in Osaka over two concerts held on the same day in February 1975. The music now functioned as inextricably dense organic matter carried by a big groove periodically interrupted by the bandleader's gesture to stop, his way of recreating the on-off effect in live performance. In early April, during the second half of a concert in Boston, Miles Davis invited Sam Morrison, a young tenor saxophonist who he felt bore the Coltrane torch, to join him on stage. Sonny Fortune packed his bags. Despite this new direction, the trumpeter's stage appearances became sporadic. He cancelled all of his concerts in October 1975. There would be no more shows until spring 1981.

RETIREMENT. Nothing was going right for Davis anymore. As far as the music went, he had perhaps reached the end of the line. He was exasperated by the success of white jazz-rock bands, and had failed to attract African-American audiences, despite the radical turn his music had taken towards funk. His stormy relationships with his sons Miles IV and Gregory reminded him of his personal failures, and he fell deeper into depression. His health problems multiplied, aggravated by his use of drugs and painkillers on top of the drinking. On October 9, 1972, he crashed his Lamborghini into a guardrail and broke his ankles. He had to use crutches for months, and the casts he had to wear made his bad hip worse. He broke his heel again in 1973, after trying to climb his garden wall in a fit of paranoia. In 1975, his hip worsened to the point that it repeatedly dislocated, and he had to undergo another hip replacement in December. He also suffered from sickle-cell anemia, bursitis, a stomach ulcer, recurrent pneumonia and nodules on his vocal cords. In addition, Davis led an erratic life riddled with various incidents: in 1972, a neighbour accused him of holding her hostage; in February 1973, he was arrested for carrying an automatic weapon.

Also in 1973, Jackie Battle broke off her relationship with Davis. He stopped going out, holing himself up in a giant mess in near total darkness, the sole source of light the flickering television set he kept on at all times. His growing solitude and boredom were broken only by the visits of a dwindling number of friends, fleeting acquaintances, freeloaders, dealers and rats. His contract with Columbia expired at a time

A recluse in his West Seventy-seventh Street apartment, Miles Davis lived behind drawn curtains, cut off from the world and emerging from his home only rarely. Photographed at home right before making his public reappearance. Photo Teppei Inokuchi.

when his cocaine habit was costing him $500 a day. The record company put him on retainer—a benefit up until then only extended to pianist Vladimir Horowitz—in the hope of seeing him return to the studio, but Davis had stopped playing and listening to music, and lost touch with new developments in music. When he was encouraged to play again, he replied, "Play what? I played it all before." Some writers have claimed that the accounts of this period, for instance in the autobiography Davis wrote with Quincy Troupe, are exaggerated. As with tales of the 1950s, Davis took pleasure in dramatizing his descent into hell. His manager, Mark Rothbaum, later said, "The house didn't get that dirty, and when it did, it got cleaned eventually. And the stories of all the women, they're bravado stuff. Miles did not fuck scores of women. . . . He was with Trixy, and he was with Loretta. And he was ill."

While waiting for his return, Columbia continued to put out compilation records of previously unreleased material—double albums for the most part. In 1974, *Big Fun* and *Get Up with It* covered the electric period with recordings made since 1970; in 1976, *Water Babies* delivered some unknown gems from 1967 and 1968; Columbia's Miles Davis catalogue from 1955 to 1970 was combed through to make *Circle in the Round*, released in 1979, and *Directions*, in 1981. Gil Evans took a turn trying to rekindle Davis' interest in music by bringing up an old project involving Puccini's *Tosca*, but nothing ever came of it. Several recording sessions were organized between 1975 and 1978, but when Davis was feeling co-operative, it was to play the keyboard, and Columbia never released any of the material. Beginning in 1978, the jazz department's new vice-president, George Butler, began to pay Davis daily visits. One time, Davis told Butler that he had an idea. Davis went to the piano, played a chord, but no sound came out. None of the keys worked. On Davis' birthday in 1979, Butler had a piano delivered to Davis' home. Diplomatic negotiations were undertaken to get him to open the door. That evening, Davis phoned Butler, said "thanks," and hung up just as brusquely.

Photo Anton Corbijn.

STAR PEOPLE GLOBAL ICON

1980–1991

The electricity had been cut off in Miles Davis' apartment. Lit only by candlelight and without air conditioning to relieve the heat of the summer of 1979, the atmosphere was suffocating. British arranger-composer and cellist Paul Buckmaster was witness to this scene of decline. Davis had brought Buckmaster to New York in the hope of rekindling the experiments that had resulted in *On the Corner*, in 1972. While in New York, Buckmaster spent some time with Gil Evans, who, having twice failed to reignite Davis' career, quickly lost interest in the whole affair. Twice, Buckmaster put together a band, but both times Davis did not show up for rehearsal. Fully registering Davis' deterioration, he sounded the alarm. Davis' sister Dorothy arrived from Chicago to put her brother's life back in order. To help with the intervention, she called Cicely Tyson, who had remained close friends with Davis ever since their romance in 1966–67. Possessive and protective, Tyson isolated Davis from everyone else. They would marry in 1981. Brushed aside, Paul Buckmaster headed back to London. Then, another figure entered the picture: Dorothy Davis' son, Vince Wilburn, Jr., would bring his uncle out of "retirement."

T

HE MAN WITH THE TRUMPET. Dorothy Davis made it clear to her brother that it was time to help out the young man he had encouraged to take up the drums at the age of six. Young Wilburn had been performing in Chicago, playing funk, soul and fusion, most notably with AL7, a group that Miles Davis first overheard during a phone conversation with his sister. The group was made up of keyboardist Robert Irving III, guitarist and singer Randy Hall, bassist Felton Crews and Wilburn on drums. AL7's music was closer to the hits of the time rather than the sonic abstractions pioneered by Davis over his last active ten years. Rejecting the group that guitarist Pete Cosey had pieced together for him yet again, Davis brought AL7 to New York in April 1980, at Columbia's expense, and started following their rehearsals over the telephone. As a replacement for saxophonist Glenn Burris—too bop for his liking—Davis brought in a student of David Liebman's called Bill Evans, just like the pianist on *Kind of Blue*. Davis joined the group in the studio, only to discover, when he finally brought in his trumpet, that he had lost much of his technical ability. In June, the band headed back to Chicago before Davis had recorded his parts, which he ended up doing in January 1981, at which point he realized that he needed to go in an altogether different direction.

It would be the first about-face to mark the last ten years of his life. On the eve of his return to music, was Davis hesitant to adopt the "bubblegum" music, as he called it in his autobiography, of his nephew's friends? He would give these musicians time to mature, and sooner or later, he would bring them back to play integral roles in his new band. At the time, critics of his latest entourage—David Liebman, Al Foster, Cicely Tyson and the young Bill Evans, who had become his confidant—saw this as an indulgence. Davis built a group around Al Foster with his new saxophonist, guitarist Barry Finnerty and percussionist Sammy Figueroa. With the motto "no drummer, no band," Davis knew he could count on his old partner in crime from 1972–75. For this project, Bill Evans recommended Marcus Miller. Bassist and multi-instrumentalist with impressive musical training, Miller would play an important role in Davis' life for years to come. The spirit of these new sessions was much more open, featuring simple jam sessions based on melodic hooks, different from prior collaborations. Seeming to recognize the creative impasse he had arrived at before retiring in 1975, in these sessions Davis moved away from the sonic confusion of the 1970s. With the exception of the nod to classic jazz on "Ursula," with its walking bass and barely disguised swing, the music still relied on powerful, hammering drums and highly syncopated bass. However, this music was sharper, clearer, with solos clearly distributed throughout. The pieces—lighter, more melodic and controlled—were shorter than in the past. As the sessions continued and his playing grew more assured, his young collaborators convinced Davis to abandon the wah-wah pedal, which he had been using to hide his technical weaknesses. To record the piece that would become the title track of the album *The Man with the Horn*, Davis brought in a new guitarist that David Liebman had introduced to Bill Evans: Mike Stern, former student of the prestigious Berklee College of Music in Boston.

A

CHANGED AMERICA. In fall 1981, the release of *The Man with the Horn* was a major media event during a time of great change. Discouraged by the failures of Communism, dissension was dead. The intellectual and artistic elite in the West let themselves be seduced by money and the media, which fostered the acceptance of a certain type of unbridled capitalism ushered in by Ronald Reagan, elected president of the United States in 1980. Reagan championed military spending at the expense of social programs,

Davis at home preparing for his return to the stage in 1981, surrounded by the young musicians who would accompany him (bassist Marcus Miller, guitarist Mike Stern, percussionist Mino Cinelu, saxophonist Bill Evans, as well as his old friend, drummer Al Foster, who was older). As in the past, Gil Evans (centre) helped out with these work sessions. Photos Teppei Inokuchi.

creating an even wider gap between the rich and the poor. Disadvantaged African Americans were the first to be affected, while, at the same time, affirmative action was helping to introduce a new, African-American bourgeoisie to the seats of power: Andrew Young was elected mayor of Atlanta in 1982 and Colin Powell appointed Chairman of the Joint Chiefs of Staff in 1989.

By now taught academically the world over, jazz relinquished its avant-garde ambitions, which renewed its commercial appeal, prestige and image, notably through advertisers and a media that often sought out Miles Davis. The jazz featured in the media could be divided into two main camps. On one side, fusion, with its jazz-rock lineage, was accessible, with simple melodies and catchy rhythms. Destined for FM radio under the moniker "smooth jazz" and inspired by Caribbean, Brazilian and African exoticism, fusion was also distinguished by the more obvious elements of funk (notably, virtuoso bass lines featuring percussive, slap-bass techniques) and by recording techniques that had been developed for soul, pop and disco music. Employing the technical developments and new array of sounds available to electronic music (synthesizers, programmed beats, sequencers), fusion was often carefully constructed, instrument by instrument, in the studio, resulting in a relatively cold sound.

On the other side of the not so clearly defined aesthetic divide, and much less accessible, jazz students continued to play traditional, acoustic instruments to explore, more or less audaciously, the potential of interactive improvisation, applying their solid technical ability and unprecedented theoretical knowledge. This new science of improvisation embraced the potential of classical European harmony with its modal and polytonal traditions, while borrowing heavily from the rich heritage of the 1960s: the legacies of John Coltrane, Bill Evans (the pianist), Davis' second quintet and Ornette Coleman. At the heart of this movement, young African-American jazzmen closed ranks around hard bop—a communal reflex. They presented this music, now called "neo-bop," as the classical music of their culture. Some of them saw this music as a form of resistance to white pop music and to hip hop, the expression of ghetto violence and misery.

TEMPORARY REPRIEVE. After cutting himself off from the music scene for five years, Miles Davis had to reposition himself on the musical chessboard. He explored the soft ghetto music of smooth funk as played by his young protégés from Chicago, as well as the music of the young virtuoso improvisers introduced to him by David Liebman and his disciple, Bill Evans. These two poles defined Davis' music in the first half of the 1980s. At the same time, he immediately distanced himself from the neo-boppers, calling their music retrograde, singling out the person spearheading this group, Wynton Marsalis, as his favourite target—and Marsalis responded in kind.

The record *The Man with the Horn* may appear to lack coherence. The two pieces from the Chicago group that made it onto the record opened up Davis' music to a new audience, ensuring his success throughout the 1980s, but they also attracted harsh criticism from unforgiving jazz aficionados. Those who enjoyed his music from the 1970s preferred the improvised nature of the other tracks, even though they seemed toned down compared to the electric and rhythmic storms found on *Agharta*. In particular, Mike Stern's unbridled solo on "Fat Time," the opening track, garnered a great deal of attention. However, the guitarist's flat-

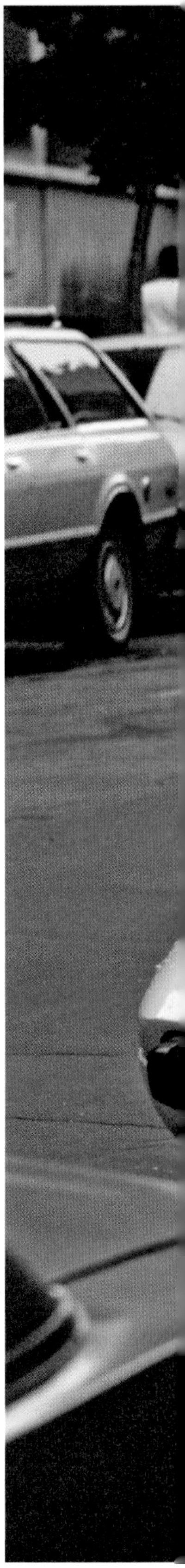

Influenced by Cicely Tyson (above right, before Davis' departure for the Kix concert in Boston, June 1981), Miles Davis assumed a healthy lifestyle based on a vegetarian diet, Chinese medicine and regular swimming (opposite page), which helped him recover his health after years of deterioration. Photos Anthony Barboza (left); Teppei Inokuchi (right).

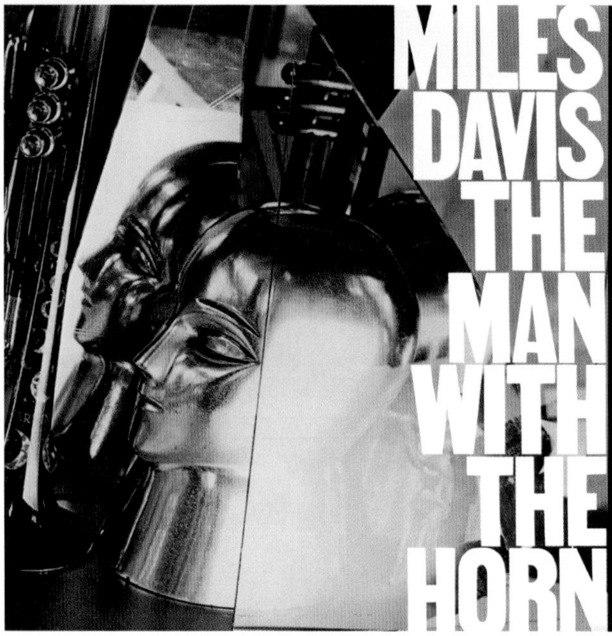

Miles Davis' comeback albums, recorded between 1980 and 1983, are distinguished by the prominence of the guitar, played by either Mike Stern or John Scofield (opposite page), as well as by Davis' growing fascination with synthesizers, which he would play on stage. Photo Didier Ferry.

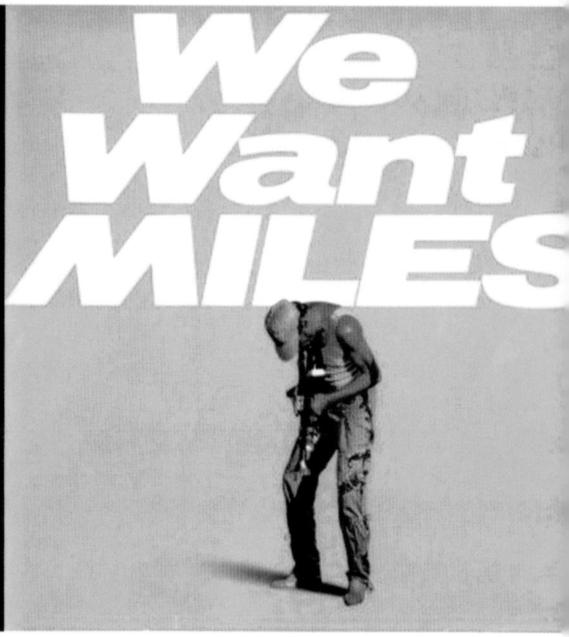

out rock style did not please everyone, especially those who were delighted to see Davis playing with renewed lyricism and, at times, swing (as on "Ursula"), which he had abandoned during his electric period. These ambiguities set the tone for the band's first public appearances, recorded by Columbia at the Kix club in Boston between June 26 and 29, 1981, and at Lincoln Center in New York on July 5, 1981. Percussionist Mino Cinelu from Martinique joined the band. Although the relaxed atmosphere at rehearsals had left the players somewhat unprepared, on stage the music rapidly took shape. The set consisted of two tracks from *The Man with the Horn* (the stately yet saturated wash of guitars that introduced "Back Seat Betty" would be used to open Davis' subsequent shows) as well as "Kix" and "My Man's Gone Now" by George Gershwin. The first song surprised audiences with the hybrid nature of its rhythms, which borrowed from jazz-swing, reggae and funk, while the second piece, dominated by a rhythmic swing, indicated a return to melody, though the original melodic line was cleverly disguised. Another difference was in Davis' stage performance. From this point on, Davis would use a wireless microphone, allowing him to move around as he played.

During the summer tour, a light-hearted new song became a crowd-pleaser. "Jean-Pierre" was a syncopated and bluesy readaptation of the lullaby "Dodo l'enfant do" that Davis had heard Jean-Pierre, son of his first wife, Frances Taylor, sing as a child in the 1950s. Precursors of this song can be found in the formulas Davis had occasionally used in his improvisations since 1958. Recorded in Japan, this track would become the hit from the compilation album *We Want Miles*, which also included live tracks from the Kix and Lincoln Center concerts, released in 1982. The tour revealed Davis' fragile health, as he succumbed to recurrent pneumonia in addition to suffering from diabetes. In January 1982, when Cicely Tyson went to Africa to work on a film, Davis fell back into his bad habits of smoking, drinking and cocaine use. Subsequently hospitalized, he suffered a stroke that left his hand paralyzed. According to his doctors, he would never play the trumpet again. As soon as she returned, Tyson brought Davis to a doctor of Chinese medicine who treated him with acupuncture, Chinese herbs and a strict diet. Tyson took Davis swimming every day as therapy and encouraged him to do keyboard exercises for his hand. Slowly, Davis got back to the trumpet. In April of that year, he toured Europe, but he was noticeably exhausted.

CHROMATIC FUNK AND SYNTHESIZERS.

Davis' next record, *Star People*, was recorded between summer 1982 and February 1983. Tom Barney replaced Marcus Miller on bass and John Scofield was brought in to help out Mike Stern, who was struggling with his drug problem. Scofield was another graduate of Berklee College and had played in David Liebman's quintet two years earlier. His improvisational techniques were more cultivated than Stern's, and when it came to rock, his touch was more subtle. Also, he was a remarkable interpreter of the blues, a genre Davis revisited with the songs "Star People" and "It Gets Better." "Star People" was a return to the type of playing featured on the 1954 album *Blue Haze*, while "It Gets Better" was inspired by bluesman Lightnin' Hopkins. "Come Get It," whose introduction covers the opening chords of "Back Seat Betty," consists of a feverish jam session over a basso ostinato inspired by Otis Redding. Paul Tingen, the biographer who wrote about Davis' electric period, uses the term "chromatic funk" to describe an

MILES
STAR PEOPLE

OB-Xa

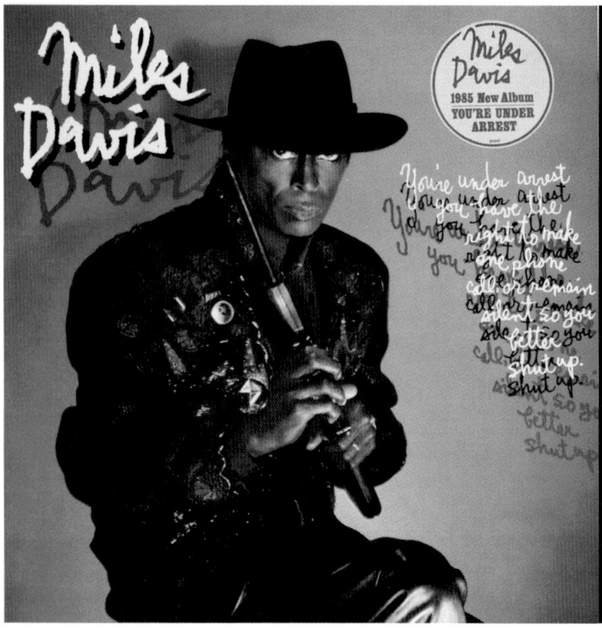

Machine gun or pistol in hand, Miles Davis poses like a thug for the cover of *You're under Arrest* (1985), clad in flashy clothes and holding a trumpet engraved with his name, presaging imagery that would become standard for gangsta rap. Photos Anthony Barboza.

aspect of the repertoire's sound that consisted of angular, chromatic, virtuoso melodic lines, in contrast to Davis' interest in the latest forms of popular black music. Often, Davis would take fragments of solos transcribed by Gil Evans and rework them in the studio. On "Star on Cicely" (based on a solo by Mike Stern), "Speak" and "It Gets Better" (both inspired by John Scofield solos), the guitar and saxophone play these fragments in unison.

The musicians began to complain about producer Teo Macero's outdated sound-editing techniques. This would be Macero's last record with Miles Davis. The greatly altered drum sound and Davis' synthesizer parts seem equally out of place. However, it is regrettable that, aside from the two songs recorded live during this period ("Come Get It" and "Speak"), Columbia never released concerts from the period, which showcased John Scofield's natural feel for the blues, the clever angularity of his playing and his brilliant rhythmic placement, which proved influential.

On *Decoy* (recorded in summer 1983 and released in May 1984), Scofield took over all duties on guitar, transcribing three new solo pieces again played as a single theme on "That's What Happened" taken from "Speak" on *Star People*. Davis renewed ties with members of his group from *The Man with the Horn*, bassist Darryl Jones and keyboardist Robert Irving III, who would also act as music director and co-producer, along with Davis' nephew, Vince Wilburn. Daryl Jones' heavily percussive and metallic sound intensified and modernized the funk colours of the bass. With his abilities as a multi-instrumentalist and his knowledge of programming, Irving would make the synthesizers credible, but he would also push the songs into pop territory. As Davis regained his health, *Decoy* bridged the gap between this new approach and the chromatic funk heard in Scofield's playing. On "Decoy," "Robot 415" and "Code M.D.," Irving assimilated Davis' ideas about harmonics and angularity, but his use of synthesizers and programmed beats threatened the cohesion of the record, which was less than forty minutes long—producer George Butler had decided that a large portion of the recorded material was not sufficiently commercial to be released. To fill out the LP, it was necessary to add two live tracks, "What Is It" and "That's What Happened," recorded during the Montreal Jazz Festival on July 7, 1983, at Théâtre Saint-Denis.

A TENTATIVE TURN. Bill Evans began to complain that the music was becoming too heavy and that it did not leave enough room for improvisation. On stage, the saxophonist had apparently been relegated to the sidelines. In September, Branford Marsalis came into the studio and laid down exceptional improvised tracks for *Decoy* ("Decoy" and "That's Right"). Davis tried in vain to get him to join the group. In November 1983, Evans drew his own conclusions: he left the band at the same time as percussionist Mino Cinelu, who was replaced by Steve Thornton.

The band's repertoire was increasingly turning towards pop when they recorded *You're under Arrest*, on which synthesizers and drum machines were even more in evidence. The initial plan was to rework popular songs arranged by Gil Evans. Begun in the fall of 1983, recording was interrupted while Davis underwent hip surgery, followed by a bout with pneumonia. The sessions recommenced in January 1984, but Gil Evans seemed to lose interest. In May, Davis took advantage of the arrival of saxophonist Bob Berg to

record a series of informal chromatic-funk jam sessions, setting aside the ballads. The only ballads that remain are "Something on Your Mind" by the disco tandem D-Train, "Human Nature," written by Steve Porcaro for Toto but recorded by Michael Jackson, and "Time after Time" by Cindy Lauper. Marking a return to ballads, "Time after Time" brought Davis the same success in the 1980s that he had enjoyed with "Autumn Leaves" in the 1960s. With the exception of "Time after Time," the other ballads had to be re-recorded because, in late 1984, Davis decided to redo all the songs in just a few days.
Davis reworked another extract from a John Scofield solo for the title song "You're under Arrest," replaced Al Foster with his nephew on certain pieces and called in John McLaughlin for the songs "Ms. Morrisine" and "Katia." The opening track on the record, "One Phone Call/Street Scenes," is a curious narrative montage that explores the numerous times Davis had been arrested by police. With overdubs of sirens, screeching tires, whistles, cocaine sniffing and the click of handcuffs, the song features the voices of Sting, Marek Olko (the Polish promoter who arranged for Davis to play in Russia) and Davis himself. The record ends with another *mise en scène* in the form of a medley: the lullaby "Jean Pierre" is followed by a nursery rhyme played on celesta, meant to sound like a music box, and accompanied by the voices of children and the synthesized sound of nuclear explosions. As bells toll the death knell, Davis says, "Ron, I meant for you to push the *other* button." Was Davis talking to sound engineer Ron Lorman, or to Ronald Reagan, who had just been re-elected after launching his Star Wars weapons program? On the record cover released in fall 1985, Davis stands at the ready, clutching a toy machine gun. The record's drift towards demagogy, its lack of coherence, the overuse of a click track and drum machine led Al Foster to take his leave in January 1985, after twelve years of faithful service. John Scofield would also leave the band the following summer.

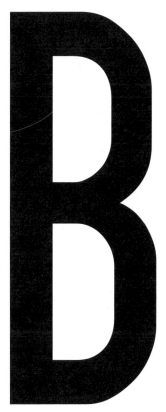

BREAK, BREAK-UP AND BETRAYAL. Although *You're under Arrest* was an immediate success, the jazz world was still concerned about Davis' future. Then something happened to dispel these worries. On December 14, 1984, he received the Sonning Music Award in Copenhagen, created by the widow of Danish writer Carl Johann Sonning. For the occasion, Danish trumpeter Palle Mikkelborg was commissioned to write an orchestral suite for the Danish Radio Big Band. Written in seven movements, one for each colour of the rainbow, the score was titled *Aura*, in reference to Davis' aura. Mikkelborg—who drew inspiration from Davis and Gil Evans, as well as Charles Ives and Olivier Messiaen—attributed a value on the chromatic scale to each letter of the alphabet in order to compose a score based on the names of Davis and previous recipients of the award, including Igor Stravinsky, Leonard Bernstein, Olivier Messiaen and Isaac Stern. Flattered, Davis agreed to play on the last movement, "Violet," at the award ceremony; he then initiated a long jam session at the end of the concert. In mid-January 1985, he told Mikkelborg that he would like to record the piece. Davis returned to Copenhagen with Vince Wilburn on January 31, and took advantage of John McLaughlin's being in town to recruit him for the project. This time,

In Copenhagen in 1985, Miles Davis recorded *Aura*, a long suite written by Danish trumpet player Palle Mikkelborg as a tribute to Davis' aura. For the first time in over twenty years, Davis was featured as a soloist backed by a large orchestra. Photo Kirsten Malone.

Davis played all seven movements of the suite, except for "Indigo," a tribute to his second quintet featuring the piano, a piece that reminded him how much he disliked looking back. In spite of the inadequacies of the electronic drums, Mikkelborg's sumptuous score covered, without nostalgia, the ambitious creativity of the important records by Miles Davis and Gil Evans. Even so, Columbia waited four years before releasing the album, and it came and went virtually unnoticed. Davis never forgave the label for this. In the meantime, he signed with Warner.

Davis condemned Columbia for ignoring him in order to focus on the new star of jazz trumpet, Wynton Marsalis, and for undermining his success with younger audiences by continuing to market his music as contemporary jazz. These were not Davis' only concerns. Too controlling, Cicely Tyson was behind the departure of Chris Murphy, Davis' road manager since 1973, as well as Mark Rothbaum, his manager since 1978. She turned Davis' affairs over to two lawyers whom Davis would soon accuse of incompetence. Their break-up was costly, and Davis had to sell his famous home on West Seventy-seventh Street—the place he had just renovated according to Tyson's wishes. The couple had become used to living the high life, with two New York apartments and a luxurious beach-side mansion in Malibu. Davis needed money. His new manager, David Franklin, arranged a million-dollar contract with Warner, but soon after signing, Davis took issue with the terms concerning publishing rights. As a result, Davis announced that he would no longer write music, leaving others to compose his repertoire. There may have been another reason for his discontent: he was quick to understand that if the new label was going to promote his music as pop, he would lose his creative freedom as a musician. Warner's risk-averse managers insisted that Davis make radio-friendly music along the lines of smooth jazz.

FORGOTTEN PROJECTS. Tommy LiPuma, Miles Davis' new producer at Warner, immediately rejected the sessions of September 1985, as well as the stage group that had contributed to them. These musicians would never again appear on any of Davis' records. Several of his works were left unfinished: with Paul Buckmaster, the originator of *On the Corner*; with bassist Bill Laswell, who had produced Herbie Hancock's *Future Shock* two years earlier; and with Steve Porcaro of Toto, with whom Davis had already covered the song "Human Nature." Davis resumed work with one of his nephew's associates, Randy Hall, who had written the two radio hits on *The Man with the Horn*. Having become a successful singer and producer himself, Hall also collaborated with multi-instrumentalist Zane Giles. The two would begin composing for Davis in the spirit of British producer Trevor Horn—whose work with Frankie Goes to Hollywood and Art of Noise was characterized by an extremely heavy use of the new music technology. An impressive group of collaborators was expected, including Al Jarreau, Prince and Chaka Khan. This new project, called *Rubberband* (taken from a song by Hall and Giles), gave rise to a period of intense studio work in Los Angeles involving Giles (guitar, bass, drums, drum programming, keyboards); Randy Hall (guitar and programming); Adam Holzman, Neil Larsen and Wayne Linsey (keyboards); Cornelius Mims (bass); Glenn Burris and Mike Paolo (saxophone); Steve Reid (percussion);

Designed to showcase Miles Davis' sound and meet the expectations of Warner Bros. producer Tommy Lipuma (bottom, seen from the back), the album *Tutu* was recorded in 1986 (opposite page) and completed thanks to the multi-tracking techniques of Marcus Miller (bottom left).

Vince Wilburn (electronic drums); and Mike Stern (guitar). Enthusiastic about the project, Davis prepared to go on tour with the band. However, the project was suddenly put on hold for no apparent reason—and no explanation is offered in Davis' autobiography. Of the twelve pieces recorded between October 1985 and early 1986, only "Rubberband," "Wrinkle," "Carnival Time" and "I Love What We Make Together" (rebaptized "Al Jarreau," after the singer for which it was written) would be performed by Davis' regular group.

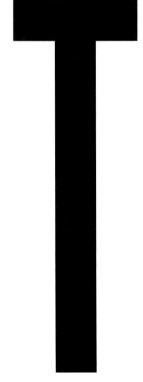

THE RETURN OF MARCUS MILLER. Although the *Rubberband Sessions* ran counter to the tastes of jazz aficionados, it also turned out to be too audacious for Warner's target market. Almost by chance, another project came along, between January and March 1986. Miles Davis commissioned music from keyboardist George Duke and sent him a recording of the group Irakere, who played a mix of traditional Cuban music, jazz and rock. Duke came back with demos of three pieces all recorded with machines, including "Backyard Ritual." Davis decided to use the song as recorded—including the faux saxophone solo, which Duke called "a stupid little saxophone"— rather than using real musicians, except for the percussion tracks and some bass lines from Marcus Miller. Miller had come a long way since *The Man with the Horn* and *We Want Miles*. Along with his skills as a bassist and multi-instrumentalist, Miller had also gained significant experience as a producer, composer and arranger, having worked with David Sanborn, Aretha Franklin and George Benson. He now offered to work on new pieces for Davis at Capitol Studios in Los Angeles.

With the help of synthesizer programmer Jason Miles and the new overdubbing technology, Miller developed a series of machine-based orchestrations upon which he added his own parts (bass, guitar, soprano saxophone, bass clarinet and drums) and then layered the songs here and there with percussion tracks by Paulinho DaCosta and Steve Reid, drum tracks by Omar Hakim (on "Tomaas") and electric violin by Michal Urbaniak (on "Don't Lose Your Mind"). Once all the pieces were in place, Davis joined Miller in the studio to play the trumpet parts. Although hearing the songs for the first time, he did all of his tracks in one take.

The resulting *Tutu*, with its lush arrangements of minimalist melodies ("Tomaas" and "Splatch"), peaks with the eponymous opening track and "Portia," a splendid homage to Gil Evans' *Sketches of Spain*. In a completely different vein, a cover of the song "Perfect Way" by Scritti Politti emphasized the problems Davis had encountered with "Human Nature." In fact, Miles Davis was satisfied to reuse the arrangements that had given the hits of the period their appeal, sticking closely to the original, often banal melodies by simply substituting his horn for the vocals with little variation. Nor does it appear that he was able to make these songs his own, in contrast to his visionary arrangements that so well parodied the standards in the 1950s. It was perhaps Davis' inability to take ownership of the music that led Prince to back out of a collaboration that was already well underway, as Davis, Jason Miles and Paulinho DaCosta had already laid down their tracks for the song "Can I Play with U?" that Prince had sent in during the *Rubberband Sessions*.

Featuring portraits by photographer Irving Penn, *Tutu* was a huge commercial success. Photos Guy Le Querrec (left); Irving Penn (right).

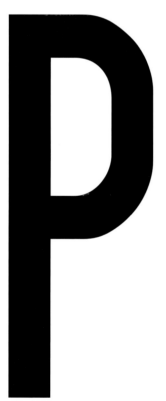

P**RINCE AND THE OTHERS.** Davis was fascinated with Prince, whom he compared to Duke Ellington for his musical colour and to Thelonious Monk for his rhythm. In addition, Prince claims to have recordings of his jam sessions with Davis. There are pictures (bootleg copies) of a New Year's Eve benefit concert at Paisley Park Studios in Minneapolis, when Davis played with Prince's band for a few minutes. "Full Nelson," the closing track on *Tutu*, comes very close to Prince's sound. In the past, however, Davis knew how to keep his distance from influences such as Charlie Parker, Ahmad Jamal or James Brown. Never had he attempted to get Jamal or Brown into the studio. One scheduled session with Jimi Hendrix was scuttled due to ill will on the part of Davis and drummer Tony Williams.

Another change was becoming apparent in Davis' approach. The trumpeter, who, since leaving the Charlie Parker Quintet, had rarely put himself at the service of other musicians, began to play as a sideman—and moreover, for singers. Vocalists, of course, held a special place in Davis' world, but when it came to his own band, he was the singer. In 1985, he collaborated with the cream of the show-business crop on the record *Sun City* by Artists against Apartheid. Davis was supporting a cause he believed in, much the same way he called his record *Tutu* after South African archbishop Desmond Tutu. At the end of 1985, he recorded Steve Porcaro's instrumental "Don't Stop Me Now" with the pop group Toto. In 1987, Davis accepted an invitation from Scritti Politti to record the song "Oh Patti." In 1988, he recorded with one of his favourite funk groups, Cameo; Italian singer Zucchero; and his friend, soul singer Chaka Khan (notably on "Sticky Wicked," by Prince). In 1989, Davis recorded two tracks for his saxophonist Kenny Garrett on the album *Prisoner of Love* and participated in the cover of "Birdland" (by friend Joe Zawinul), the hit appearing on Quincy Jones' record *Back on the Block*. Davis also played eight tracks on *Mystic Jazz*, a record by little-known Italian keyboard player Paolo Rustichelli. In 1990, he paid tribute to singer Shirley Horn, a former protégé whose career in New York he helped launch, by accompanying her vocals on the title track of *You Won't Forget Me*.

Working with Marcus Miller in 1987, Davis found himself involved with film scores again (thirty years after he recorded *Ascenseur pour l'échafaud*) on a film by Mary Lambert called *Siesta*. Set in Spain, the film led Miller to write some pretty sequences, in the vein of Gil Evans for *Sketches of Spain*, using the same technical toolbox heard on *Tutu*. Working with Robert Irving, Davis had already recorded music for "Prisoners," an episode of *The New Alfred Hitchcock Presents*, in 1985, and for the film *Street Smart* by Jerry Schatzberg in 1987. After appearing on the small screen in an episode of *Miami Vice*, playing a pimp, as well as in the series *Crime Story*, he played a trumpet player in the film *Dingo* by Rolf de Heer. For the same film, he shared trumpet duties with Chuck Findley in a series of compositions by Michel Legrand, who, for the first time, brought Davis back to his music of the 1950s. If Davis was retracing his steps on the soundtrack for Dennis Hopper's 1990 film *The Hot Spot*, it was less for nostalgic reasons than as a heartfelt tribute to the fathers of the blues with John Lee Hooker and Taj Mahal.

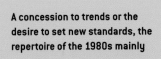

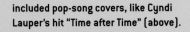

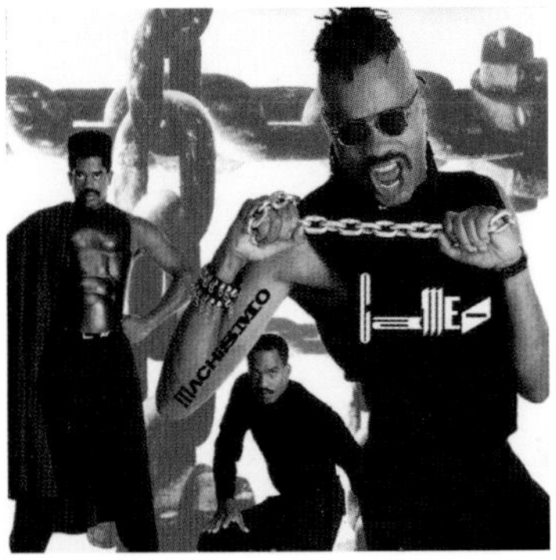

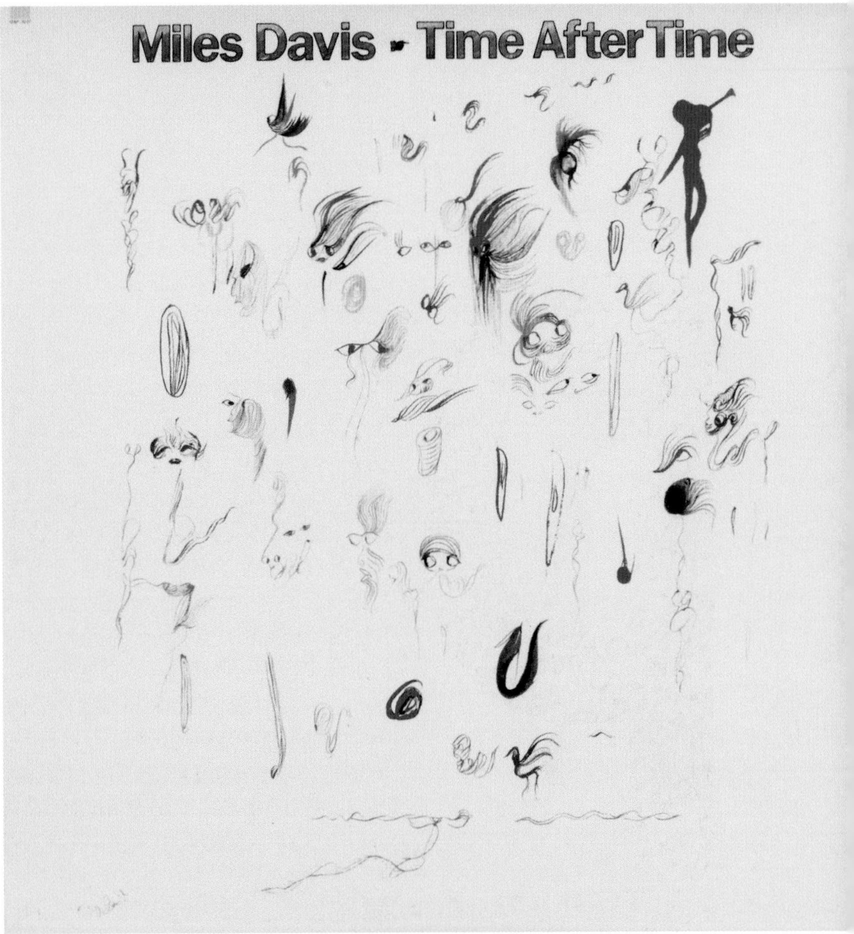

Having become a media icon and flashy show-biz figure in the 1980s, Miles Davis was in demand to appear in ads (for Honda scooters, bottom right), to support major causes (anti-apartheid with *Sun City*, top left and centre), to be featured on records (Cameo, Chaka Khan, Scritti Politti, and Kenny Garrett's first record) and even to appear on television in *Miami* Vice (bottom centre) and in the films *Scrooged* (right) and *Dingo* (top right).

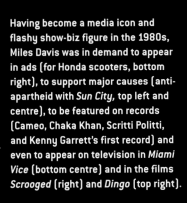

A concession to trends or the desire to set new standards, the repertoire of the 1980s mainly included pop-song covers, like Cyndi Lauper's hit "Time after Time" (above).

ROUTINE AND MUSICAL CHAIRS. During this time, Miles Davis' group continued to tour. In spite of his fragile health, Davis was constantly on the road between 1985 and 1988. Surprisingly, Warner allowed many concert recordings from this period to languish rather than releasing them. Warner seemed to have lost or forgotten the tapes until five years after Davis' death, when, in 1996, the corporation finally gave way to demands by Davis' management to release a compilation of these live recordings. Even then, Warner released a single record rather than a double album, as had been put forward. It was necessary to turn to the cassette and DAT tracks taken from the soundboard recordings Davis had insisted on making every night so that he could listen to each performance and give his musicians feedback. The heads of Warner seemed to dread releasing music beyond their control and too far outside the norm for them to earn the sort of returns they expected. Meanwhile, many jazz lovers found that the band had fallen into a routine repertoire pinned in by static grooves and constricted by arrangements overloaded by synthesizers. All of the soloists would leave one by one: guitarists Mike Stern and Bobby Broom, saxophonists Bob Berg and Gary Thomas, pianist Kei Akagi and percussionist Mino Cinelu. All complained of replaying, night after night, the arrangements for *Tutu* or the pop and funk records from which Davis borrowed to fill out his repertoire. Improvisation no longer had much place in the music, and when the reins did go slack, the solos suffered from a lack of interaction with the rhythm section.

The group seemed split in two. On one side were the freedom-loving jazzmen. On the other was the rhythm section. When out of Davis' shadow, these perfect technicians of funk and soul would blend into the background as accompanists or producers on tracks by popular singers. From 1985 until Davis' death, the rhythm section played per-

In the mid- to late-1980s, concerts became real spectacles, with designed set-pieces, such as large signs displaying the musicians' first names, which Miles Davis flashed during solos. Opposite page: at Le Zenith in Paris, November 1989. Photo Annie Delory.

petual musical chairs, without ever compromising the group with major changes. In addition to Benny Rietveld, a member of Prince's entourage, the bass was played by friends of Davis' nephew from Chicago: Angus Thomas, Felton Crews, Darryl Jones and Richard Patterson. Beginning in October, a parade of musicians filled the two keyboard spots aside from Davis', including Bobby Irving, Adam Holzman, Joey DeFrancesco, John Beasley and Kei Akagi, who remained the sole keyboard player from the end of 1989 until he was replaced by Deron Johnson in 1991. The percussion setup also doubled when Steve Thornton was joined by Marilyn Mazur between October 1985 and June 1986. Mino Cinelu returned in 1987, followed by Ruby Bird, Marilyn Mazur for a second time, Munyungo Jackson, John Bigham (on electronic percussion) and Erin Davis, Davis and Marguerite Eskridge's son, from June to November 1990. After this period and until Davis' death, the percussion seat remained vacant. For just a few months, the saxophone chair was doubled with a second tenor, Gary Thomas.

THE LAST ACCOMPLICES. Although he appreciated the solo brilliance of guitarist Robben Ford, who played a more straightforward blues than John Scofield, Miles Davis began to search for an African-American guitarist. In October 1987, he finally found the man he had been seeking. Player of the instrument dubbed lead bass, his concept of a hybrid between lead guitar and bass, Joseph "Foley" McCreary would occasionally assume the role of a post-Hendrix blues-rock soloist. Above all, Foley knew how to integrate his playing into the orchestral polyrhythms, much like the guitars in the music of Prince or James Brown. Previous to this development, Davis' group experienced a major shake-up in personnel, with Ricky Wellman replacing Vince Wilburn on drums in February 1987. Davis borrowed Wellman from Chuck Brown's Soul Searchers, the force behind the creation of go-go music in Washington, D.C., in the 1970s. Begun as a reaction to disco, go-go was a mixture of funk, Latin, jazz and African musical forms. Wellman's technical virtuosity, the breadth of his musical vocabulary, his sense of space and subtlety added fluidity to Davis' music, which was strengthened by Foley's arrival. There was a profound understanding between the two musicians and the trumpet player. Another musician gained Davis' confidence at this time. Alto saxophonist Kenny Garrett was a member of the band from February 1987 onwards, aside from a brief stint in summer 1989, when he was replaced by tenor saxophonist Rick Margitza.

Unlike most of his jazz colleagues, Garrett felt at home in Miles Davis' band, where he was given ample room to improvise. The saxophonist had worked at the highest echelons of jazz with the Duke Ellington Orchestra under the direction of Mercer Ellington, and Art Blakey's Jazz Messengers. While he was well versed in contemporary jazz, he was also immersed in funk and had a good sense of what the public wanted. Garrett would play long, heated choruses without any extreme, post-Coltrane bursts. Instead, he would combine the light, swirling incisiveness of alto bop with the hyper-rhythmic stabs of the James Brown horn section, where his ascending runs would rest on recurring, swirling formulas, intended to inspire and refresh the soloist and grab the public's attention. Often, Garrett would finish pieces in which he was invited to solo as though it were impossible to play after him. More than any other musician in the band, Garrett would play the game of call-and-response that Davis had adopted since the beginning of the 1980s. On stage, Davis would move from one player to the next, to slip an enigmatic suggestion or two, to show encouragement, to pay a compliment or to make a nasty remark. Increasingly, Davis directed his band with a look, addressing the other musicians with his trumpet to announce an impromptu change of direction, remodelling the overall sound from one concert to the next after listening to a recording of the day's concert, long into the night.

On stage in 1987, head to head with guitarist Foley and saxophonist Kenny Garrett, two of his favourite musicians during his last years. Left: bassist Darryl Jones. Photo Guy Le Querrec.

In February 1987, Miles Davis participated in a fashion show at the Tunnel club in New York for Japanese designer Kohshin Satoh, whose clothing he liked. Also invited was Andy Warhol, who acted as train-carrier for the "Dark Magus." Photo Susumu Shirai.

Painting and drawing became increasingly important to Miles Davis later in life. Davis used his own work as cover art on his records, notably for the cover of *Amandla*.

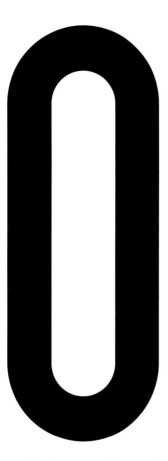

ON THE ROAD WITH MILES. Depending who you talked to, whether it was soloists like John Scofield and Bob Berg or the rhythm section, appreciation for Miles Davis' music differed during this period. The rhythm musicians observed another way of understanding the orchestral work, paying careful attention to the precise mechanics of the groove rather than taking risks with an improvised narrative. Live in concert, the band would sculpt scenarios and refine the nuances, achieving perfection in its domain and showcasing Davis' god-like abilities. Davis' musicians remember a man far different from the legend: warm, caring, attentive, joyful and filled with humour. As for Davis, he certainly managed to savour his return to life, success and good fortune. He obviously appreciated the company of the young musicians under his tutelage. One can see the blend of paternalism and mentorship in the careful attention he paid to his young protégés. Davis had developed an aura that made one forget the flipside of his personality, when he could be contemptuous, arrogant, rude, cruel, pitiless, capable of physical violence, prone to intimidation, and tempted to play the bad boy. Nevertheless, making music with Davis was still an unparalleled education.

The musicians, often discovered by Davis' colleagues, were invited to learn the group's repertoire by listening to the available recordings. The luckiest would be invited to attend rehearsals at the beginning of the tour organized by the group's artistic director (Robert Irving and then Adam Holzman) based on the new songs, sometimes in the presence of Davis. Most often, they would get on stage without rehearsing, only encountering Davis, who seemed more preoccupied by their attire than the music, just before going on. Miles Davis—who for years had refused to pay attention to the public, delivering his music without compromise—began to direct his band like a real entertainer, engaging in all sorts of on-stage antics, introducing his band using large signs, responding to shouts, smiling and grimacing at the audience (depending on his mood), and singling out pretty girls in the front row. Davis' costumes, with their ample sleeves and extravagant trouser legs, created by famous designers like Issey Miyake, Gianni Versace and his own protégé, the Japanese stylist Kohshin Satoh, helped to conceal the sickly silhouette of a man living on borrowed time.

Davis' passion for haute couture coincided with his interest in drawing, something he practised every chance he got, at home and on tour. Cicely Tyson had gotten him started during his convalescence in 1982, and his first drawings appear on the cover of *Star People*. When he broke up with Tyson—they divorced in 1989—another woman came into his life. In 1984, Jo Gelbard became his painting teacher and then his collaborator in 1988. When Davis found a new apartment overlooking Central Park, Gelbard decorated the place and moved in with furniture from the Memphis Group, founded in Milan by designer Ettore Sottsass. Under the influence of this school of design, the pair began painting together and planned to design sets for Davis' concerts. After Gelbard introduced Davis to the work of African-American painter Jean-Michel Basquiat, Davis began to integrate various media into

abstract paintings in which he deconstructed African-inspired masks and totems. The cover of *Amandla*, released in fall 1989, features the mention "Cover art by Miles Davis and Jo Gelbard."

AMANDLA'S PARADOX. As was the case with *Tutu*, Marcus Miller wrote almost all of the music for *Amandla*, aside from one song each by John Bigham and George Duke. On *Amandla*, recorded on and off between June 1987 and January 1989, live musicians take precedence over electronics. However, the album was not recorded live, but rather in parts, instrument by instrument. Miles Davis was more present than he had been for *Tutu*, although he was sometimes content to make suggestions by telephone—a method he had developed since the making of *Decoy*. This way he could avoid long days in the studio, which also suited Warner's rigid approach to production. He would only arrive at the requested time to record and re-record his part until it was perfect. Except for the omnipresent Kenny Garrett, the members of the group (Foley, Wellman, DeFrancesco) make only occasional guest appearances on *Amandla*. The move to use Omar Hakim, the last drummer for Weather Report, as well as many percussion instruments, highlighted the desire to move away from jazz and explore the rhythmic diversity of the music of Africa and the African diaspora. Meanwhile, Davis' great interest in zouk (music originating from the French Caribbean) revealed his narrow-minded view of newly popular world music, which he could only see through the prism of commercial success. With this mindset, Davis did not make much use of guitarist Jean-Paul Bourelly, who could have opened his eyes to prospective musical styles of the day—with which Davis had seemingly lost all contact. In fact, right from the first improvised notes in the studio, Tommy LiPuma's gaze let the guitarist know that he was an undesirable intruder on the album.

Joe Sample's return to acoustic piano on the ballad "Amandla" momentarily reconciled Davis with his jazz audience, though some fans considered the piece to be Davis' renunciation of jazz. On "Mr. Pastorius," Marcus Miller had Davis play without a mute at a time when the trumpet player was concealing his vulnerability behind a Harmon. In addition to this, something unexpected occurred during the recording of this ballad, with its refined harmonies. Miller had planned a simplified funky-blues sequence, upon which Davis would improvise without harmonic constraint, typical of his style at the time. At the beginning of his solo, Davis signalled to Miller that he wanted play on the original thematic harmonies in the old-fashioned way, with a regular walking bass, as he did in the time of Paul Chambers. As soon as Davis had finished at the studio, Miller brought in Al Foster, who laid down a traditional swing pattern as tears of joy sprang from his eyes. The result was captivating, but only served to make *Amandla* an enjoyable but less cohesive and powerful album than *Tutu*. Although only semi-successful by its author's own admission, and barely noticed by pundits, the song "Jilli" garnered attention for self-taught multi-instrumentalist John Bigham, whom Davis had taken under his wing for a while. Bigham would write other songs for Davis, but they would never satisfy producer Tommy LiPuma.

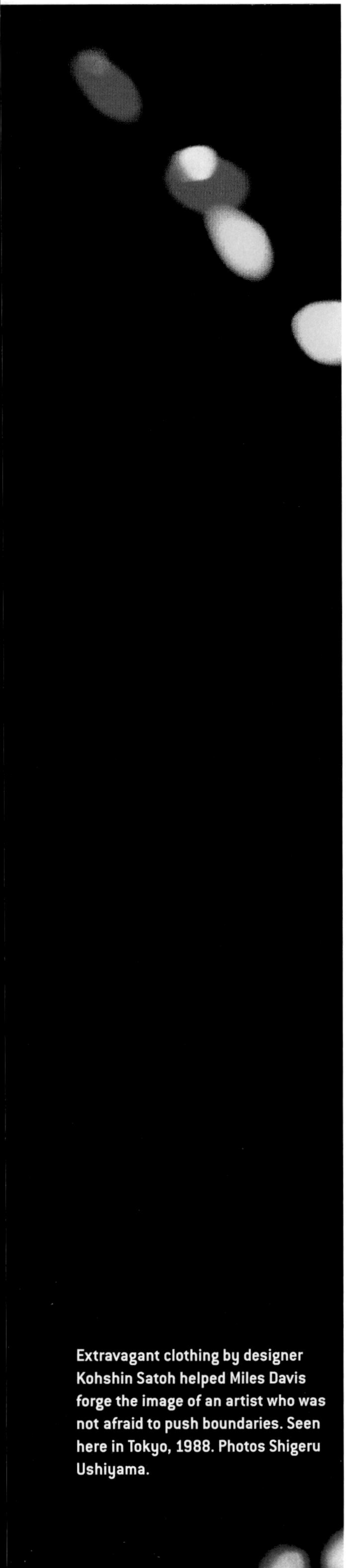

Extravagant clothing by designer Kohshin Satoh helped Miles Davis forge the image of an artist who was not afraid to push boundaries. Seen here in Tokyo, 1988. Photos Shigeru Ushiyama.

Compromise or sudden reversal? The man who once played with his back to the audience began acknowledging his audience at the end of his concerts. Opposite page: at the "Jazz sur son 31" festival in Toulouse, France, October 20, 1987. Photo Guy Le Querrec.

R**ETRO JAZZ AND HIP HOP.** After the convalescence from pneumonia in winter 1988–89, tours became less frequent. Even though he had changed his ways, Miles Davis was a man worn out by sickness, medication and paranoia, which was affecting his relationship with Jo Gelbard. He talked about retiring like a gentleman farmer as his father had and spending time with the horses that he owned on the West Coast. He also spoke about making a record with Prince, whose pieces he had included on the program in spring 1991. On July 8 of that same year, he got involved in a project that went against his natural instincts. Under friendly pressure from Quincy Jones, who was conducting an oversized orchestra, Davis agreed to play Gil Evans arrangements at Montreux. However, he did it ungraciously, sulking through rehearsals and leaving Wallace Roney to play in his place during most of a program that no longer fit his musical language or his technical abilities. On the other hand, he put on his own retrospective concert, "Miles and Friends," at the Grande Halle de La Villette for the JVC Festival in Paris two days later. Going back to *Dig* (1951), he showcased the musicians who had been associated with his career: veteran Jackie McLean, Wayne Shorter, Herbie Hancock, Chick Corea, Dave Holland, Joe Zawinul, John McLaughlin, Steve Grossman, Al Foster, Bill Evans (the saxophonist), John Scofield, as well as members of his regular group. Some saw this as his goodbye.

Over the same period, Davis was involved in the recording of a new album produced by Easy Mo Bee. Still unsuccessful at reaching young African-American audiences, Davis could not resist the world of hip hop—a street culture born in the ghettos of the 1970s that covered a wide range of artistic expression. In musical terms, hip hop is based on the pairing of an MC (master of ceremonies) and a deejay. The MC practises the verbal art of rap. The deejay delivers the musical accompaniment, using two turntables and a collection of vinyl records to create riffs by selecting brief passages from the album (breakbeats) and to produce rhythms by rapidly spinning the record back and forth under the needle (scratching). Slowly, turntable work was combined with beat boxes, electronic keyboards and samplers, which could reproduce any sound or series of sounds for appropriation. Sequencers would complete the deejays' arsenal by enabling them to create recurring melodic fragments known as loops.

In early 1989, Miles Davis took part in the recording of Quincy Jones' *Back on the Block*, an ambitious super-production bringing together major figures from the jazz world and the new stars of soul, funk and hip hop. Davis had been searching for a less cumbersome production method in which he could be more involved. Russell Simmons, co-founder of Def Jam Records, introduced Davis to rap production, with its small budgets and quick-and-dirty solutions, as opposed to albums with enormous budgets, like *Amandla*. Employing hip-hop producers recommended by the heads of Def Jam, Davis decided to work with Easy Mo Bee (Osten S. Harvey, Jr.), a twenty-six-year-old rapper and producer. Charmed by their lack of formal training, Davis partnered Easy Mo Bee as co-producer with his manager Gordon Melzer. More collaborators were lined up: Deron Johnson, keyboardist for Davis' regular group, was enlisted to ensure that Easy Mo Bee's pieces were cohesive; John Bigham was commissioned to write several tracks; and Prince had sent Davis some songs to use. Davis was also in contact with other rappers like Flavor Flav and Chuck D of Public Enemy, as well as Nikki D. Conceived as a double album, the recording of *Doo-Bop* began in July 1991. Easy Mo Bee laid the foundation for each track with a drum machine and sampler, and Davis laid trumpet over top. Deron Johnson then added the organ and bass lines on the synthesizer. When Miles Davis died in September 1991, only six tracks had been finished: "Mystery," "The Doo-Bop Song," "Chocolate Chip," "Blow,"

MILES IN THE ARTIST'S STUDIO

So here I am, at his place in Manhattan, on Wednesday, June 5, 1991, around 11 a.m., and all I can think of is that the place looks like an artist's studio.

The rest is history.

After four endless days waiting, Miles Davis agrees to see me three times. First round: fierce and hard (like a boxer, poised, taking hits, dodging and deflecting a shower of blows, on his toes).

Second round: he disappears, vanishing into thin air and leaving me alone. I figure, all is lost. Goodbye interview, questions and answers. Loafers, asses, pigs and hangers-on: I know the list by heart of those abler than me whom he dismissed without even a goodbye.

Third round: More than just his outfit has changed, which becomes apparent during one of the most intense days of my life. Why? I have no idea. He's gone now. At one point, he wanted to see me for the whole month of August, for me to move in.

The first impression is of an artist's studio: canvases on easels, half-used tubes of oil paint, stretchers leaning against the walls, some materials—charcoal, pencils, pastels, inks, nothing for the oils—green plants, a coffee table of precious wood, a bowl filled with fresh fruit, and two trumpets: the red one we know so well, and the second made of glass, a gift for a birthday or a jubilee year, I don't remember which. And no, I don't touch the trumpets. Not a drop of paint is on the floor, yet nothing is covered, not even the furniture. This artist's studio is spick and span, without any evidence of work taking place.

Musicians who paint, draw and take pictures, among other things, are hardly taken seriously. This is not very bright of us: Milt Hilton's photographs deserve more than a cursory glance. Who doesn't melt before Louis Armstrong's collages, with their detailed exuberance? And have you ever seen the fanciful birds drawn by Michel Portal? At the end of his life, Django Reinhardt painted between fishing excursions. Louis Sclavis exhibits his instant photos. Daniel Humair's abstract acrylics are renowned among painters. . . . Each of these various forms of expression pulses with a beat that we often—to protect ourselves, perhaps—consider with good-natured arrogance, affectionate disdain, benevolent condescension . . . in short, with contempt.

The first drawing Miles Davis ever gave me, dated Wednesday, July 3, 1985, depicts black figures on a white background, the silhouettes of African women. One of the record covers (Which one? I should check) is in the same vein: African women with generous posteriors and shorn heads. Davis executed this drawing on his feet, and with a direct flourish, he signed it. This took place in Lyon, a return trip for a brief interview. He talked about the blues—he was going back to it, he said with the subtle aggression we all use when afraid, afraid the other person isn't listening properly, afraid the other person just doesn't get it.

The following July 14, in Montreux, I saw his two concerts back to back (4 p.m. and 8 p.m.). Yes, these were the glory days, when people said he couldn't play anymore, when he turned his back to the audience, when he sat on his hands—and so on.

The second drawing, in grease pencil, depicts an African mask or a live model. Davis sketched it on the back cover of an invitation while standing in the doorway of his home, just before we parted in June 1991. The invitation announced the exhibition of his paintings at the Nerlino Gallery, 96 Greene Street. In it, a figure floats against a black background, while some words appear in the spaces in between: "FOR US / WAIT TO YOUR HEAR / WHAT PRINCE WROTE."

Flashback to June 5, 11 a.m.: at Miles Davis', you have to wait. He is looking for just the right moment, nothing more, nothing less. Before he comes down, the reigning WASP conducts herself as befitting her rank. As for me, I settle into a corner with my kit, consisting of tape recorder and other devices, index cards and notes. I'm ready. He descends, presents himself as cold, hostile, and speaks only of money. He is testing me. I hold my ground. In any case, a stroke of luck—he doesn't doubt for a second that I'm no slouch in terms of my English. And we're off. He takes a unique approach to the first move. There I am, flabbergasted, and he chooses the corner directly opposite me, by the window, the most uncomfortable spot possible for me. I have to give it to him. What artistry! The bell rings. The stare-down: a boxer's trick. I'm in awe. My insignificant hardware is just lying there, useless. I've let my guard down.

In his corner, he holds himself like a surly kid. Sometimes he looks like he's eleven, sometimes eleven million. He is exactly sixty-five.

Miles Davis at home resembles Miles Davis on stage. On stage, particularly over these past ten years, he has been assembling small groups, just like relaxed musicians entering the studio. Offering, invitation, exchange. He travels from one to the other, which is where he gets his reputation for playing "from the back." His back to whom, exactly? Not to his drummers, in any case. At home he does the same thing: he walks around, and makes everybody else walk around too. He wanders from canvas to canvas. He makes you do the same. He drags his leg, all those hip operations. . . . He has the air of a wounded adolescent, or death warmed over. His animal eyes are the most human in the world, encircled by a thin line of azure blue set off against luminous porcelain. When he has finished with his calculated dramatics, his observation round, he becomes himself again: timid, elegant, delicate, extremely polite, brash.

At the start, he talks only of painting, describing each work. His paintings are figurative, heavy, fuelled by a furious

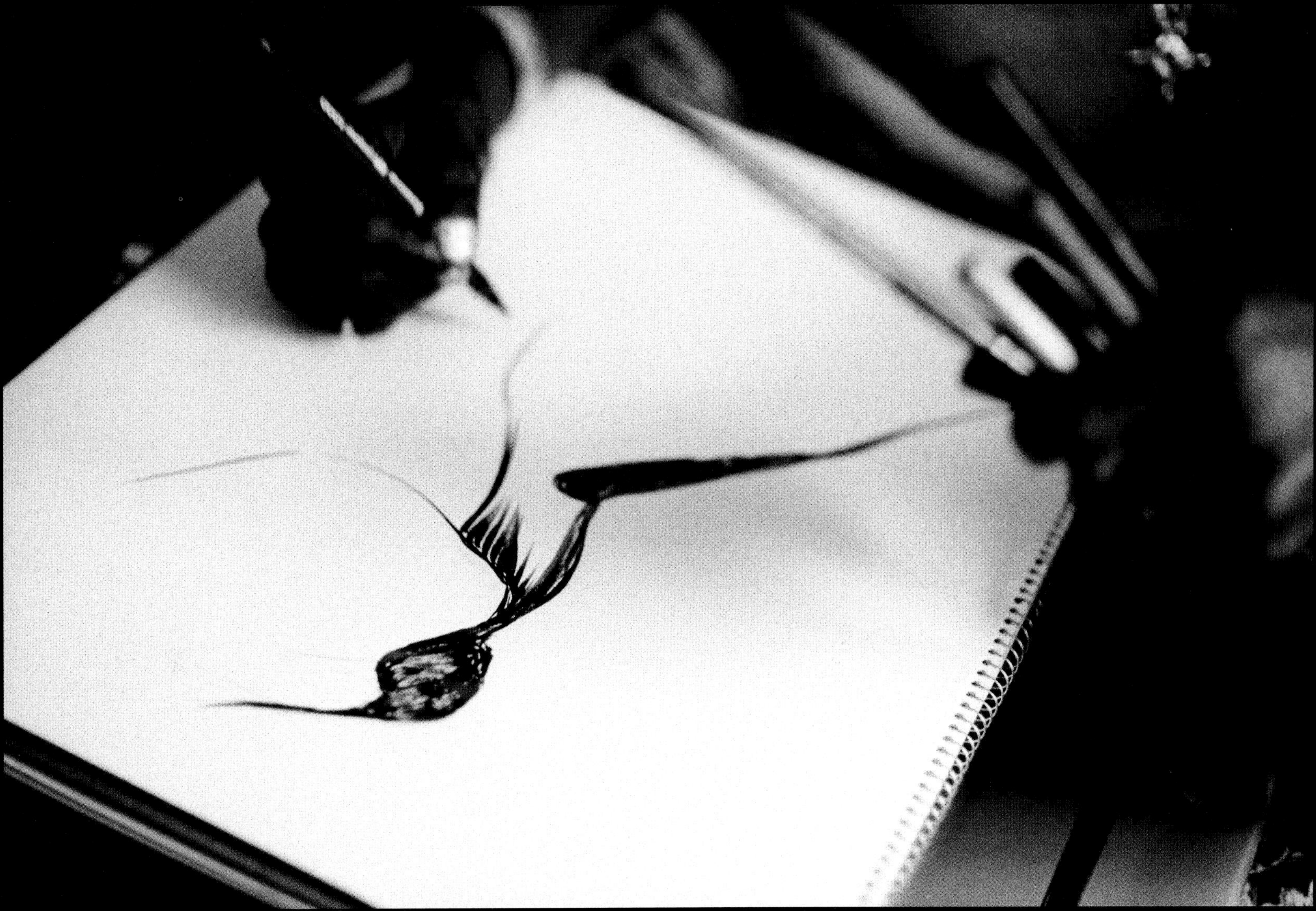

Photo Shigeru Ushiyama.

painting, the motivation of which is beside the point. My recorder is just lying there, across the room. I try to pay attention to what he's saying, really trying, but he doesn't make it easy. He is by turns rude, polite, pleasant, difficult, stylish, delicate. His hands dance like birds. He moves, draws, talks in his shaky voice. His voice sounds exactly like his music. Like the blues, some would say. It's true. But he also does it on purpose.

"You've never painted a self-portrait?"

"Mercy! I have seen my head enough."

"But I've seen one, I'm sure of it, no?"

"This is Jo, Jo Gelbard, my wife. I paint with her; she draws me all the time. You see this eye? That's my eye."

"Your face, you're saying that it has—"

"—has what?"

"—has changed over the course of your life."

"It won't stop changing. I have forty different faces. My body is changing. The body remembers everything. I change when I swim. It becomes this or that. I don't want it to be like that anymore. The air is much better in California, but here, in New York, is where the energy is. I want to get more into painting, more into the shapes and colours that occur to me."

"You draw women. What is your favourite part of the body?"

"The ass, the bum, you too, right?" He plays a few notes on the synthesizer. "I hate these damned chords. Gil always said that the chord is lost. The chord stands alone. Until we play the next one. Every first chord sounds strange. Then the next enters in harmony with first, and it sounds good; now we can start to play. It's a fine balance, see? Like painting."

I do see. Timid sorcerer. The observation ritual over, he transforms. He disappears (telephone, conversation, the WASP lady offers me orange drinks, time passes, I think about this interview, limited to three discussions about painting). He changes, his clothes too; he has a thousand outfits. He descends the Moulin Rouge staircase again, face fifty years younger, black silk shirt open to reveal a bare torso, and leather pants. A turban is wrapped around his now arranged hair. He is a hundred thousand years old. He looks like his long-deceased mother—he says so himself. He is reborn; he looks maybe sixteen. We can talk! The canvases gaze at us from the walls. The infinite interview.

FRANCIS MARMANDE

UNIVERSITY PROFESSOR FRANCIS MARMANDE IS ALSO A COLUMNIST FOR *MONDE* AND *JAZZMAN*. HE IS THE AUTHOR OF *LA CHAMBRE D'AMOUR* (DU SCORFF) AND OF *L'INDIFFÉRENCE DES RUINES* (PARENTHÈSES).

Miles Davis leaves Le Zenith in Paris by limousine, September 20, 1986. Photo Claude Gassian.

Eternal angry young man or genius mellowed by the years? Portrait of an ageless Miles Davis. Photo Annie Leibovitz.

"Sonya" and "Duke Booty." The record was completed with a cover of "Mystery," cut short and subtly remixed, as well as two Davis solos, taken from the *Rubberband Sessions* in winter 1985–86 and built up by Easy Mo Bee.

THE END. What would have happened with *Doo-Bop* if Miles Davis had lived longer? It is tempting to think that he had arrived at a decisive turning point. After the radical choices he made from 1964 to 1975, his music had become increasingly formulaic, as though he had succumbed to the over-cautiousness of the 1980s—an evolution in which Davis seemed to be a spectator, steadily surrendering his autonomy to those who had taken charge of his destiny, culminating in his reluctant covering of the Gil Evans repertoire at the Montreux Jazz Festival a few weeks before his death. *Doo-Bop* had the potential to help him break away from this situation. Hip hop is a raw art form, an expression of reappropriation, and the sound of his last record is populated by the memory of vintage keyboards already sought after by acid jazz and which would become popular in music at the turn of the twenty-first century. If Davis had lived through the 1990s, would he have heard the advances in freestyle rap and the emergence of drum and bass, and jungle? Would he have explored the more creative aspects of electronic music? Would he have witnessed the immediate impact of his music from the 1980s giving way to the profound and persistent influence of his second quintet and the growing importance of his groups from the 1970s on the music of this century? During the 1980s, Miles Davis was a man cut off from the world, allowing his helplessness to show. Journalist Claude Carrière recounts the following anecdote: on his way out of the venue at the Nice Festival surrounded by bodyguards, Davis saw his old friend Clark Terry trying to reach him, but he was powerless to help Terry break through the line of defence. Already, by the mid-1970s, Davis was kept abreast of the music scene solely by hearsay. Francesca Spero, in charge of relaying Def Jam's suggestions about hip hop, recalls that Davis was shielded from the more radical productions of the time and provided access only to music that was melodious and jazzy. These accounts correspond to Branford Marsalis', who chastised Davis for running after a musical reality that had passed him by. David Liebman has the feeling that when Davis returned to the stage in the late 1970s, he had no idea which way to go because he had lost contact with the creative musical scene and had missed the emergence of musicians who could have fed his music during that period: "He should have chosen guys like (guitarist James) Blood Ulmer or (drummer) Shannon Jackson or (guitarist) Vernon Reid." Ulmer and Jackson were part of the "harmolodic" funk movement pioneered by Ornette Coleman; Reid was the founder of the Black Rock Coalition in 1985.

THE LAST RAGE. At the beginning of September, Miles Davis was admitted to St. John's Hospital in Santa Monica with yet another case of pneumonia. He died on September 28, 1991, at the age of sixty-five. Rumours propagated by the media suggested that Davis had died from AIDS. While he certainly had many opportunities to contract it, he had developed recurrent pneumonia and infections well before the emergence of the virus. That he had survived the combined ravages of sickle-cell anemia and chemical addiction for so long was miracle enough. Does it really matter either way? The answer to this question will not reveal anything of importance about the artist, his work or his legend. After speculating about the cause of death, British biographer Ian Carr settles the matter by describing Davis' last moments: refusing to be intubated to help his breathing, he became so enraged that he had a massive stroke and fell into a coma. Miles Davis died of rage just as he had lived, marked since youth by the furious tornado that ravaged St. Louis in 1927.

MILES RUNS THE VOODOO DOWN

VINCENT BESSIÈRES

The Sorcerer, the Prince of Darkness, the Dark Magus . . . Miles Davis was the dark angel of jazz. Veiled in an aura of mystery, he was always fascinating and inaccessible, steeped in the extremes. He bore down like an occult force, an alchemist who transformed the nature of music, an augur of the jazz to come, the voodoo master who brought music to parallel worlds. In 1969, the year he went electric, inspired most likely by Jimi Hendrix's "Voodoo Child," Davis highlighted the inherent "blackness" of his music by calling one of his tunes "Miles Runs the Voodoo Down." However, Davis' music was not "black" because it was a form of black spiritual, but because it at once absorbed and rejected the inherent radiance that jazz had maintained since its origins. In opposition to the masterful luminosity of Louis Armstrong, the joyous beat of Count Basie's swing, the serene majesty of Duke Ellington and all else that came before him, Davis created an art form that dwelt in the shadows, turned the game into a serious drama and deliberately broke the rules. Contrary to what had been heard before, Davis imbued his music with the freshness of the cool, the drama of flamenco, the intentional subversion of traditional forms, a dizzying brew, jabbing beats. With an unshakeable commitment to his ideals, he drew his sidemen after him. These sidemen—with a few notable exceptions (John Coltrane, Bill Evans, Wayne Shorter)—once freed from his authority, left the darkness for brighter climes. Davis himself continued to seek out new ground, the unmentionable and unknowable, the illicit. Davis believed in jazz's ability to transform itself.

Though he would keep coming back to it, Miles Davis rejected the dialectic of the blues, the suffering transmuted to lament, the human condition subsumed by song. While a student at Juilliard, Davis challenged a teacher's slavery-based description of the blues by explaining that he—the child of a well-to-do family who never wanted for anything—could play the blues perfectly. Proud of his culture, Davis did not believe that jazz should be limited to the African-American community, and he refused to accept that it was a set language forced to adhere to strict codes requiring only athletic virtuosity. Davis' life and words expressed the apparent paradox between his desire to root himself in the music of his people and the fear that he would be trapped by his culture. To Davis, the genius of black musical expression was its endless capacity to find new directions. In this way, Davis upset jazz. He turned the music inside out, refracting it through an interplay of mirrors of which he was the master. Where jazz tended towards repetition, he took the opposite course. While immersed in the sound of the swing-era big bands as a child, Davis revelled in the frenzy of bebop as a teen. Given Charlie Parker's and Dizzy Gillespie's blessing, he assembled a group surprising in its use of soft tones and the novelty of its arrangements. Was this the birth of the cool? Immersed in the blue haze, inspired by the astringency of Thelonious Monk's music, he brought in the tenor madness of saxophonists Sonny Rollins and John Coltrane. The traditional chord progressions bored him, the road already travelled fatigued him, so he reduced them to a minimum, instead favouring modal scales to rise above the fray. He eschewed the stable Rolls-Royce of the rhythm section for the nervous, unforgiving nature of a Ferrari. Davis' "second quintet" was the speedster that would restore his appetite for risk and the thrills that came with it. Yet, the liberties and opportunities presented by this venture gave way to a sulphurous brew of atmospherics and sudden storms saturated with electricity and rent by guitar distortion. Then, once again, he made a major shift. The funk pulse became the heartbeat of his music. Interwoven with the rhythms of the African diaspora, he created a sonic tapestry pierced by the distorted voice of his trumpet, now plugged into a wah-wah pedal. Where could he go after all that noise? Davis resisted this deluge of sound with silence. When he did return, it was to play nursery rhymes and songs. After playing with the best musicians, Davis now believed in synthesizers and machines, and a young Marcus Miller proved he was onto something. Then, when pop was on the rise, he elected to re-engage with the sounds of the street, clearly anticipating jazz's association with hip hop.

Miles Davis gave jazz movement, which was both its good fortune and its tragedy. He invalidated all notions of a jazz "tradition," adopting instead one overriding conviction: if jazz stayed stuck in the past, it would die. This notion has not pleased everyone; it is the diametrical opposite of the comfortable and the routine, of instant gratification. Few could (or can) attain these lofty goals—that is the tragedy. Davis adapted jazz to the revolution, his achievement all the more awe-inspiring because it endures. His shadow looms over the landscape of twenty-first-century jazz, kept alive by those who knew and worked with him and who are now considered major figures of the period, as well as by all those who bear some part of his artistic legacy.

Due to its versatility, Miles Davis' music still illuminates the field of jazz by the sheer number of fruitful avenues it opened up. The concepts developed with his Birth of the Cool nonet shaped the possibilities of arrangements within a medium-sized band and introduced new instrumentation to the jazz band. A half-century later, the records issued by Prestige remain a bible for those still exploring the virtues of the standards and cultivating the expressivity of the canons of the form. *Kind of Blue* completely expanded jazz's horizons, giving currency to the use of modals still alive today. Davis embraced silence, understatement, the use of carefully selected notes, a mastery of space and time. His way of playing songs ushered in and gave legitimacy to an "alternative" way to play the instrument that resisted the ostentation and technical fireworks traditional to the trumpet. Gil Evans' orchestral colours turned big-band composition on its head—blurring lines, expanding the sonic palette, opening up harmonies. The "controlled freedom" of the second quintet has become a reference point for much of contemporary jazz, and band members are now lauded for their creativity individually and collectively, their full worth finally recognized. Aside from providing jazz with a new branch on the family tree, Davis' conversion to electricity introduced trumpet players to the ambiguity of their instrument to such a degree that from that point on, most would have to assume two personae, one acoustic and one electric. The overlapping polyrhythms of his Afrofunk period anticipated complex meters inseparable from the groove, nourishing the contemporary jazz world. His use of the wah-wah pedal with the horn would inspire a whole coterie of jazz and electronic musicians, for whom texture and the shape of the sound—totally transformed by electricity—would play a more important role than the phrase itself. The covers of the pop years led him to draw on the existing repertoire to create new standards, while showing that machines could be effective in developing a whole new sonic environment. Although Davis' experiment went unfinished, the encounter with hip hop highlighted its natural propensity to connect with jazz, which has since led to numerous attempts at hybridization.

Certainly, Miles Davis is not the only hero to loom large in the history of jazz. Nor is he the only influential figure in a musical form torn between celebrating its glorious past and looking forward to inventing its future. But he is the person to look to when conservatism and skepticism rear their ugly heads. Everyone, it can be said, likes Miles Davis—even if not everyone likes "all Miles Davis." More than the archetype of the cool musician—deliberate, distant, elegant, uncompromising—Davis is the incarnation of audacity and invention. Miles Davis is jazz. And he is a legend. The two have been staring each other down for more than three-quarters of a century. One cannot exist without the other; one is inconceivable without the other. At the heart of what is intrinsically jazz—a confrontation of individual voices in the warp and weft of the century—Davis' uniqueness is, above and beyond the emotions it provokes, exemplary. But Miles Davis, the one and the many, with a Gemini personality (as he himself emphasized) that successfully evaded all attempts to pin it down, remains something of an enigma. The exhibition *"We Want Miles"* is a tribute to an artist whose work has maintained its appeal and whose mystery and magnetism live on. We wish to take this moment to thank all those who have helped us get a little closer to both the work and the man.

ILLUSTRATIONS

The photographs and record covers reproduced in the catalogue and appearing in the exhibition are indicated by an asterisk in this list of illustrations.

Abbreviations:
BNF: Bibliothèque nationale de France, département de l'Audiovisuel, Fonds Charles Delaunay, Paris; IJS: Institute of Jazz Studies, John Cotton Dana Library, Rutgers, The State University of New Jersey, Newark; INA: Institut national de l'Audiovisuel; LAJI: Los Angeles Jazz Institute; MDP: Miles Davis Properties, LLC, Los Angeles; NYPL: The New York Public Library for the Performing Arts, Astor, Lenox and Tilden Foundations, Music Division, Teo Macero Collection; SME: Sony Music Entertainment, New York.

Cover
* Portrait of Miles Davis, about 1958.
p. 4
Miles Davis, Antibes-Juan-les-Pins Jazz Festival, July 1969. Photo Jean-Pierre Leloir. © Jean-Pierre Leloir.
p. 10
View of Fifty-second Street, New York, 1947. Photo William P. Gottlieb. © William P. Gottlieb/www.jazzphotos.com.
p. 12
Left to right, top to bottom:
* Miles Davis (right) and his brother Vernon (2nd from the left), Easter 1939. © Courtesy of Anthony Barboza Collection. * View of a street in St. Louis, Missouri, after a tornado, 1927. © Historical Manuscript Collection, University of Missouri, St. Louis. * Miles Davis, his sister Dorothy Mae, his brother Vernon and his mother, Cleota H. Henry Davis, Easter 1939. * Dorothy Mae (right), Miles Davis' sister. * Miles Davis' father, a recent graduate of the school of dentistry at Northwestern University, Evanston, Illinois. * Miles Davis at age eight or nine. © Courtesy of Anthony Barboza Collection.
p. 14
* Charlie Creath and his Jazz-O-Maniacs, St. Louis, about 1922 (left to right): Sammy Long (alto saxophone), Willie Rollins (C melody saxophone), Marge Creath (piano), Charlie Lawson (trombone), Charlie Creath (cornet), Alexander Lewis (drums). © Frank Driggs Collection.
p. 15
* The Dewey Jackson Orchestra, Castle Ballroom, St. Louis, 1937 (left to right): Willie Rollins (alto and baritone saxophone), Bradford Nichols (tenor saxophone), Clifford Batchman (alto and baritone saxophone), Eugene Phillips (guitar), Earl Martin (drums), Dewey Jackson (trumpet), Wendell Black (trumpet, actor), Robert Parker (piano), Singleton Palmer (double bass). © Frank Driggs Collection.
* Floyd Campbell's Singing Syncopators, St. Louis, 1929 (left to right): Clifton Byrdlong (alto saxophone), Sammy Long (alto saxophone), Harvey Lankford (trombone), James Barlow (double bass, tuba), Floyd Campbell (drums, vocals), Gus Perryman (piano), Walter "Crack" Stanley (trumpet), William Calloway (banjo), Cecil Thornton (tenor saxophone). © Frank Driggs Collection.
pp. 16–17
* Eddie Johnson's Crackerjacks, St. Louis, 1932 (left to right): Freddie Martin (alto saxophone), Singleton Palmer (tuba), Ernest "Chick" Franklin (tenor saxophone), Walter Martin (alto saxophone), Lester "Spareribs" Nichols (drums), Benny Jackson (banjo), Winfield Baker (trombone), James Talphy (trumpet), Harold "Shorty" Baker (trumpet) and, seated, Eddie Johnson (piano). * Original St. Louis Crackerjacks, 1936 (left to right, top to bottom): Elmer Ming (trumpet), William "Bede" Baskerville (guitar, arrangements), Levi Madison (trumpet), Freddy Martin (alto saxophone), Nick Haywood (drums), Austin Wright (singer), Kermit Haynes (tuba, double bass), Chick Finney (piano), George Smith (trumpet), Ernest "Chick" Franklin (tenor saxophone) and Walter Martin (alto saxophone). * The George Hudson Orchestra, St. Louis, mid-1940s. Back row, left to right: Singleton Palmer (double bass), John "Bones" Orange (trombone), Earl Martin (drums), Ed Batchman (trumpet), George Hudson (leader, trumpet), Fernando Hernandez (trombone), Robert Horne (trombone), Willie Rollins (baritone saxophone), Tommy Starks (alto saxophone); front row, seated, left to right: Jimmy Britton (vocalist), Robert Parker (piano), Clark Terry (trumpet), Paul Campbell (trumpet), Cyrus Stoner, Sr. (trumpet), Bill "Weasel" Parker (tenor saxophone), Cliff Batchman (alto saxophone), Edgar Hayes (tenor saxophone). © Frank Driggs Collection.
p. 18
*Eddie Randle's Rhumboogie Orchestra, Club Rhumboogie, Elks Club, St. Louis, December 31, 1943 (left to right): unidentified (drums), Tommy Dean (piano), Irvin "Broz" Woods (trumpet), Miles Davis (trumpet), unidentified (tenor saxophone), unidentified (alto saxophone), Walter Martin (alto saxophone), unidentified (tenor saxophone) and Eddie Randle (trumpet). © Frank Driggs Collection.
p. 19
Poster for Eddie Randle's Blue Devils, about 1940.
p. 20
Left to right, top to bottom:
* Lucky Thompson, Dizzy Gillespie, Charlie Parker, and Billy Eckstine, on stage at the Aragon Ballroom, 1944. Photo Charles "Teenie" Harris. Carnegie Museum of Art, Heinz Family Fund. © 2004 Carnegie Museum of Art, Charles "Teenie" Harris Archive.
Menu and fixed fan for Club Plantation, St. Louis.
* The Billy Eckstine Orchestra in concert at the Aragon Ballroom: including Sarah Vaughan and Billy Eckstine, Lucky Thompson, Charlie Parker, Bob "Junior" Williams, Leo Parker, Charlie Rouse, Dizzy Gillespie, Marion "Boonie" Hazel, Howard McGhee, Howard Scott, Jerry Valentine, Taswell Baird, Linton Garner, Art Blakey, and Connie Wainwright, 1944. Photo Charles "Teenie" Harris. Carnegie Museum of Art, Heinz Family Fund. © 2004 Carnegie Museum of Art, Charles "Teenie" Harris Archive.
Menu and fixed fan for Club Plantation, St. Louis.
p. 21
Horn Players, 1983. Painting by Jean-Michel Basquiat. The Broad Art Foundation, Santa Monica. © Estate of Jean-Michel Basquiat/SODRAC (2010). Photo Douglas M. Parker Studio, Los Angeles.
p. 23
* Unidentified pianist, Miles Davis seated by the piano and Howard McGhee (trumpet), New York, about September 1947. Photo William P. Gottlieb. © William P. Gottlieb/www.jazzphotos.com.
pp. 24–25
Souvenirs from the jazz clubs on Fifty-second Street in New York (left to right, top to bottom): souvenir of the Three Deuces, about 1950; souvenir of the Onyx, 1937–39; menu for the Hickory House; souvenir of the Famous Door; flyer for Bop City; poster announcing a benefit for "Wild" Leo Parker on February 20, 1949, at the Royal Roost; program for the opening of Birdland, 1949; menu from Club Samoa; matchbook from the Three Deuces; souvenir of Jimmy Ryan's; souvenir of Kelly's Stable (with caricatures of owners Ralph Watkins and George Lynch); matchbook from the Royal Roost; souvenir of the Downbeat Club. © Collection of Norman Saks.
p. 26
* Charlie Parker Quintet, Three Deuces, New York, 1947 (left to right): Tommy Potter, Charlie Parker, Max Roach (hidden), Miles Davis and Duke Jordan (from the back). © Frank Driggs Collection.
p. 28
* Coleman Hawkins and Miles Davis on stage at the Three Deuces, New York, 1947. Photo William P. Gottlieb. © William P. Gottlieb/www.jazzphotos.com.
p. 29
* Dizzy Gillespie Big Band, Downbeat Club, New York (probably 1947). Photo William P. Gottlieb. © William P. Gottlieb/www.jazzphotos.com.
p. 30
* Charlie Parker, Miles Davis, Allen Eager, Kai Winding, on stage at the Royal Roost, New York, 1948. Photo Herman Leonard. © Herman Leonard Photography LLC/CTSIMAGES.COM.
p. 32
Group of labels for seventy-eights released by Dial Records and Savoy Records. Private collection.
p. 33
Untitled (Bird of Paradise), 1984. Painting by Jean-Michel Basquiat. Collection of Stéphane Samuel and Robert M. Rubin. © Estate of Jean-Michel Basquiat/SODRAC (2010). Photo Robert McKeever.
pp. 34–35
* "Fats" Navarro, Miles Davis, Kai Winding, Clique Club, New York, January 1949. © Frank Driggs Collection.
p. 36
* Miles Davis, about 1950. Rights Reserved.
p. 39
Left to right, top to bottom:
* The *Birth of the Cool* nonet for the Capitol recordings (left to right): Junior Collins (French horn), Bill Barber (tuba), Kai Winding (trombone), Max Roach (drums, behind a partition), Gerry Mulligan (baritone saxophone), Miles Davis (trumpet), Al Haig (piano), Lee Konitz (alto saxophone), Joe Shulman (double bass). New York, January 21, 1949. Photo William "PoPsie" Randolph. © 2010 Michael Randolph/www.PoPsiePhotos.com.
Miles Davis, first page of the trumpet part for "Conception," recorded as "Deception." Collection of MDP.
Classics in Jazz, first reissue on LP of the recordings known as Birth of the Cool, Capitol, mid-1950s.
* Original record cover for *Birth of the Cool*, Capitol, 1955. Private collection.
p. 40
* Miles Davis with Lee Konitz and Gerry Mulligan during one of the *Birth of the Cool* recording sessions, New York, January 21, 1949. Photo William "PoPsie" Randolph. © 2010 Michael Randolph/ www.PoPsiePhotos.com. Frank Driggs Collection.
pp. 42–43
Juliette Gréco and Miles Davis, Paris, May 1949. Photo Jean-Philippe Charbonnier. © Jean-Philippe Charbonnier/Rapho/Eyedea.
p. 44
Program for the Festival International de Jazz, Paris, May 1949. Illustration by Charles Delaunay. © BNF.
* Hot Lips Page, Tommy Potter, unidentified, "Big Chief" Moore, Sidney Bechet, Al Haig, Charlie Parker, Max Roach, Miles Davis, Kenny Dorham, Idlewild Airport, New York, May 1949. Collection of *Jazz Magazine*.
p. 45
* Miles Davis, James Moody, Tadd Dameron (hidden), Barney Spieler and Kenny Clarke, Salle Pleyel, Paris, May 1949. Photo Pierre Delord. © Pierre Delord/Médiathèque de Villefranche-de-Rouergue.
* Michèle Léglise-Vian, Miles Davis and Boris Vian, Paris, May 1949. Rights reserved.
pp. 46–47
* Miles Davis, backstage at the Shrine Auditorium, Los Angeles, September 15, 1950 (Billy Eckstine concert organized by Gene Norman for the series "Just Jazz"). Photo Bob Willoughby. © Bob Willoughby.
p. 48
Left to right, top to bottom:
* Oscar Pettiford, Miles Davis and Bud Powell, Clique Club, New York, January 1949. © Frank Driggs Collection.
* Milt Jackson, Oscar Pettiford, Graham Forbes, Miles Davis and J. J. Johnson, Downbeat Club, New York, 1952. Photo Marcel Fleiss. © Marcel Fleiss.
* From left to right, back to front: Roy Porter, Specs Wright, Bernie Peters, Jimbo Edwards (owner of the club Bop City), "Pat" (name?) (drums), Betty Bennett (vocals), Kenny Dorham, Dizzy Gillespie (at the piano), Miles Davis, "Don" (Lanphere?), Ernie Lewis, Sonny Criss, Milt Jackson, Carl Perkins, Jimmy Heath, Henry "Cowboy" Noyd, Oyama Johnson and Percy Heath, Bop City, San Francisco, September 1950. Collection of *Jazz Magazine*.
p. 51
Chet Baker, Miles Davis and Rolf Ericson, Lighthouse Cafe, Hermosa Beach, Los Angeles, August/September 1953. Photo Cecil Charles. © Cecil Charles/CTSIMAGES.COM.
p. 53
* Miles Davis in the studio for Blue Note, Rudy Van Gelder's studio, Hackensack, New Jersey, March 6, 1954. Photo Francis Wolff. © Mosaic Images LLC.
pp. 54–55
* Miles Davis in front of Prestige Records, New York, about 1955. Photo Esmond Edwards. © Esmond Edwards/CTSIMAGES.COM.
p. 56
* Jackie McLean, J. J. Johnson and Miles Davis rehearsing for Blue Note, May 1952. Photo Francis Wolff. © Mosaic Images LLC.
p. 57
* Jimmy Heath, Percy Heath, Miles Davis and Gil Coggins in the studio for Blue Note, WOR Studio, New York, April 20, 1953. Photo Francis Wolff. © Mosaic Images LLC.

p. 58
* Miles Davis and Horace Silver in the studio for Blue Note, Rudy Van Gelder's studio, Hackensack, New Jersey, March 6, 1954. Photo Francis Wolff. © Mosaic Images LLC.
p. 59
Flyer for a Miles Davis concert at the Open Door, New York, 1954. IJS.
pp. 60–61
* Group of Miles Davis LP covers (left to right, top to bottom): *Blue Haze*, Prestige, LP 7054; *Miles Davis and Horns*, Prestige, LP 7025; *Walkin'*, Prestige, LP 7076; *Bags' Groove*, Prestige, LP 7109; *Conception*, Prestige, LP 7013; *Dig*, Prestige, LP 7012; *Miles Davis* (Vol. 1), Blue Note, LP 1501; *Blue Moods*, Debut Records 120; *Miles Davis and the Modern Jazz Giants*, Prestige, LP 7150; *Miles Davis and Milt Jackson Quintet/Sextet*, Prestige, LP 7034; *The Musings of Miles*, Prestige, LP 7007; *Miles Davis* (Vol. 2), Blue Note, BLP 1502; *Collectors' Items*, Prestige, 7044. Private collection.
p. 63
* Oscar Pettiford, Miles Davis and Gil Coggins in studio for Blue Note, WOR Studio, New York, May 9, 1952. Photo Francis Wolff. © Mosaic Images LLC.
p. 64
* Percy Heath, Miles Davis and Gerry Mulligan, Newport Jazz Festival, Rhode Island, July 17, 1955. Photo Herman Leonard. © Herman Leonard Photography LLC/CTSIMAGES.COM.
p. 66
* Miles Davis in the studio at Columbia, 1956. Background: Philly Joe Jones and Paul Chambers. Photo Carole Reiff. © Carole Reiff Photo Archive.
p. 68
(Left to right) Red Garland, Miles Davis, Paul Chambers and Cannonball Adderley, Columbia Studios, New York, 1958. Photo Dennis Stock. © Dennis Stock/Magnum Photos.
Red Garland and Miles Davis, Columbia Studios, New York, 1958. Photo Dennis Stock. © Dennis Stock/Magnum Photos.
p. 69
* Miles Davis, Cannonball Adderley and John Coltrane, Columbia Studios, New York, 1958. Photo Dennis Stock. © Dennis Stock/Magnum Photos.
p. 70
* Miles Davis, Café Bohemia, New York, 1956. Photo Marvin Koner. © Marvin Koner/Corbis.
p. 71
Top to bottom:
Miles Davis and Cannonball Adderley, Café Bohemia, New York, April 1955. Photo Carole Reiff. © Carole Reiff Photo Archive.
* Miles Davis, Café Bohemia, New York, 1956. Photo Marvin Koner. © Marvin Koner/Corbis.
p. 72
* Record cover for *Miles* (a.k.a. *The New Miles Davis Quintet*), Prestige, LP 7014. Private collection.
Record cover for *'Round about Midnight*, Columbia, CL 949, released March 4, 1957. Private collection.
p. 73
* Group of record covers for LPs by Miles Davis (left to right, top to bottom): *Cookin' with the Miles Davis Quintet*, Prestige, LP 7094; *Relaxin' with the Miles Davis Quintet*, Prestige, LP 7129; *Steamin' with the Miles Davis Quintet*, Prestige, LP 7200; *Workin' with the Miles Davis Quintet*, Prestige, LP 7166. Private collection.
p. 75
* George Avakian and Miles Davis, Columbia Studios, New York, 1956. Photo Carole Reiff. © Carole Reiff Photo Archive.
pp. 78–79
* Miles Davis and Lester Young in concert, Amsterdam, November 1956. Photos Ed van der Elsken. © Ed van der Elsken/Nederlands Fotomuseum Rotterdam, courtesy Annet Gelink Gallery, Amsterdam.
p. 80
* Miles Davis and Sonny Rollins, 1957. Photo Bob Parent. © Bob Parent.
p. 82
* First and second versions of the record cover for *Miles Ahead*, Columbia, CL 1041. Private collection.
pp. 82–83
Gil Evans and Miles Davis (playing the flugelhorn) during the recording of *Miles Ahead*, Columbia Studios, New York, May 1957. Photo Don Hunstein. © Courtesy of SME.
p. 84
* Miles Davis and Louis Malle during the recording of the music for *Ascenseur pour l'échafaud* (a.k.a *Frantic*), Le Poste parisien, Paris, December 1957. Photo Vincent Rossell. © Vincent Rossell/Cinémathèque française.
* Jeanne Moreau and Miles Davis, Paris, December 1957. © Rue des Archives/AGIP.
p. 85
Miles Davis improvising in front of a projection from the film *Ascenseur pour l'échafaud* (a.k.a. *Frantic*) by Louis Malle for the television series "Cinépanorama" (ORTF), Paris, December 13, 1957. Photo Gérard Landau. © Institut National de l'Audiovisuel.
pp. 86–87
Miles Davis and, in the background, John Coltrane and Cannonball Adderley, probably 1957. Photo Bob Parent. © Bob Parent.
pp. 88–89
Left to right, top to bottom:
* Portrait of Miles Davis, about 1958. Rights Reserved.
* Images from the photo shoot for the *Milestones* record cover, February 1958. Photos Dennis Stock. © Dennis Stock/Magnum Photos.
* Record cover for *Porgy and Bess*, Columbia, CS 8085 (stereo), 1958. Private collection.
Record cover for *Milestones*, Columbia, CL 1193, released June 19, 1958. Private collection.
p. 90
* Miles Davis, Columbia Studios, New York, July 1958. Photo Don Hunstein. © Courtesy of SME.
pp. 92–93
* Miles Davis during the recording of *Porgy and Bess*, Columbia Studios, New York, summer 1958. Photo Don Hunstein. © Courtesy of SME.
p. 94
* Bill Evans and Miles Davis on stage, 1958. Photo Chuck Stewart. © Chuck Stewart.
p. 96
* Miles Davis smoking a cigarette during one of the recording sessions for *Kind of Blue*, Columbia Studios, New York, April 22, 1959. Photo Don Hunstein. © Courtesy of SME.
p. 97
John Coltrane, Cannonball Adderley, Miles Davis and Bill Evans during the recording of *Kind of Blue*, Columbia Studios, New York, April 22, 1959; Miles Davis during the recording of *Kind of Blue*, Columbia Studios, New York, April 22, 1959. Photos Don Hunstein. © Courtesy of SME.
pp. 98–99
Left to right, top to bottom:
Session sheet from March 2, 1959 (first session) corresponding to the pieces "Freddie Freeloader" (62290), "So What" (62291) and "Blue in Green" (62292). NYPL. © Courtesy of SME.
Two handwritten notes from producer Irving Townsend: one recapitulating the titles, order and length of the pieces on the record, April 1959, the other indicating the distribution of titles by side with master number. NYPL. © Courtesy of SME.
* Miles Davis, Paul Chambers and Bill Evans during one of the two recording sessions for *Kind of Blue*, Columbia Studios, New York, April 22, 1959. Photo Don Hunstein. © Courtesy of SME.
Bill Evans, handwritten liner notes for the cover of *Kind of Blue* (three sheets), 1959. NYPL. © Courtesy of SME.
* Record cover for *Kind of Blue*, Columbia, CL 1355, released August 17, 1959. Private collection.
p. 100
Miles Davis and Gil Evans during the recording of *Sketches of Spain*, Columbia Studios, New York, November 1959. Photo Vernon Smith. © Vernon Smith.
p. 101
* Record cover for *Sketches of Spain*, Columbia, CS 8271 (stereo), 1960. Private collection.
p. 103
Miles Davis and Gil Evans in the studio during a recording session for *Sketches of Spain*, Columbia Studios, November 1959. Photo Vernon Smith. © Vernon Smith.
p. 104
Miles Davis and Wayne Shorter on stage, Berlin, September 1964. Photo Jan Persson. © JazzSign/Lebrecht Music & Arts.
p. 106
Left to right:
* Miles Davis in handcuffs, shortly after he is assaulted by police officers in front of Birdland, New York, August 26, 1959. © Ullstein Bild.
Various press clippings, 1959.
Miles Davis and his lawyer Harold Lovett after Davis' release from prison, New York, August 1959. Photo Fred Klein. © Bettmann/Corbis.
p. 109
Left to right:
* Record cover for *Someday My Prince Will Come*, Columbia, CS 8456 (stereo), released in 1961. Private collection.
Frances Taylor and Miles Davis, London, September 25, 1960. © Rue des Archives/AGIP2.
p. 111
* Miles Davis in a raincoat, San Francisco, 1961. Photo Leigh Wiener. © Leigh Wiener.
p. 112
Record covers for *In Person at the Blackhawk, Friday Night* (Vol. 1), Columbia, LE 10018, and *In Person at the Blackhawk, Saturday Night* (Vol. 2), Columbia, P 17384, 1961. Private collection.
pp. 112–113
Front of the Black Hawk club with Miles Davis on the marquee, San Francisco, April 1961. Photo Leigh Wiener. © Leigh Wiener.
p. 114
* Record cover for *Miles Davis at Carnegie Hall*, Columbia, CL 1812, released in 1962.
* Record cover for *Quiet Nights*, Columbia, CL 2106, released in 1962. Private collection.
Hank Mobley (tenor saxophone) and Miles Davis with the Gil Evans Orchestra, Carnegie Hall, New York, May 19, 1961. Photo Vernon Smith. © Vernon Smith.
p. 115
* Miles Davis and Gil Evans during one of the recording sessions for *Quiet Nights*, August 1962. Photo Don Hunstein. © Courtesy of SME.
p. 117
Left to right, top to bottom:
Miles Davis and Tony Williams on stage, Berlin, September 1964. Photo Jan Persson. © JazzSign/Lebrecht Music & Arts.
* Record cover for *Seven Steps to Heaven*, Columbia, CS 8851, released in July 1963. Private collection.
Miles Davis and Ron Carter on stage, Berlin, September 1964. Photo Jan Persson. © JazzSign/Lebrecht Music & Arts.
pp. 118–119
Miles Davis, Herbie Hancock, Tony Williams and Ron Carter on stage, Berlin, September 1964. Photo Jan Persson. © JazzSign/Lebrecht Music & Arts.
p. 120
* Miles Davis, Philharmonic Hall, New York, February 12, 1964. Photo Vernon Smith. © Vernon Smith.
Record cover for *My Funny Valentine/In Concert*, Columbia, CL 2306 or CS 9106, released in February 1965. Private collection.
* George Coleman and Miles Davis, Philharmonic Hall, New York, February 12, 1964. Photo Vernon Smith. © Vernon Smith.
p. 122
Miles Davis, Salle Pleyel, Paris, 1964. Photo Philippe Gras. © Philippe Gras.
p. 125
Miles Davis, Orly airport, November 6, 1967. Photo Christian Rose. © Christian Rose.
pp. 126–127
* Front of the Plugged Nickel club, with Miles Davis on the marquee, Chicago, December 1965. © Courtesy of SME.
pp. 128–129
Left to right, top to bottom:
Record cover for *Sorcerer*, Columbia, CS 9532, released in 1967. Private collection.
Wayne Shorter, "E.S.P.," handwritten score (part for trumpet), n.d., probably 1965. © Miyako Music (Irving Music Inc.); Herbie Hancock, "The Sorcerer," handwritten score (part for bass), n.d., probably 1967 © 1981 Hancock Music; Wayne Shorter, "Capricorn," handwritten score (part for trumpet), probably 1967. © Miyako Music (Irving Music Inc.). Collection of MDP.
* Record cover for *Miles Smiles*, Columbia, CS 9401, released in 1967. Private collection. Record cover for *E.S.P.*, Columbia, CS 9150, 1965. Private collection.
Wayne Shorter, "Pinocchio," handwritten score, n.d., probably 1967. © Miyako Music (Irving Music Inc.). Collection of MDP.
* Record cover for *Nefertiti*, Columbia, CS 9594, released in 1968; record cover for *Filles de Kilimanjaro*, Columbia, CS 9750, released January 29, 1969. Private collection.

Herbie Hancock, "Little One," handwritten score (part for trumpet), n.d., probably 1965 © 1981 Hancock Music; Wayne Shorter, "Dolores," handwritten score (part for trumpet), n.d., probably 1966. © Miyako Music (Irving Music Inc.). Collection of MDP.

p. 130
* Miles Davis, Herbie Hancock and Wayne Shorter rehearsing for Columbia, about 1967–68. Photo Corky McCoy. © Cortez McCoy.

p. 132
Miles Davis at the Randall's Island music festival, n.d. Photo Hank Parker. © Courtesy of SME.
Cover of *Playboy*, September 1962. © Playboy Magazine.

p. 133
* Miles Davis at the wheel of his Ferrari, 1969. Photo Baron Wolman. © Baron Wolman.
* Miles Davis' Ferrari 275 GTB/4 parked in a parking lot. Photo Corky McCoy. © Cortez McCoy.

p. 134
* Miles Davis at home, portrait from a series taken for the cover for *In a Silent Way*, New York, 1969. Photo Lee Friedlander. Courtesy of the artist and Fraenkel Gallery, San Francisco.

p. 136
* Miles and Betty Davis in 1969. Photo Baron Wolman. © Baron Wolman.
* Record cover for *Miles in the Sky*, Columbia, CS 9628, released in 1968. Private collection.

p. 137
Miles Davis at Salle Pleyel, Paris, 1969. Photo Guy Le Querrec. © Guy Le Querrec/Magnum Photos.

pp. 138–139
* Miles Davis at his home on West Seventy-seventh Street, New York, June 1969. Photo Don Hunstein. © Courtesy of SME.

pp. 140–141
Left to right, top to bottom:
Scores for "Frelon Brun" parts for Miles Davis, Wayne Shorter, Herbie Hancock and Tony Williams, n.d., probably 1968. © Jazz Horn Music Corp. Collection of MDP.

p. 142
* Record cover for *In a Silent Way*, Columbia, CS 9875, released July 30, 1969. Private collection.

p. 143
Miles Davis, Antibes-Juan-les-Pins Jazz Festival, July 1969. Photo Jean-Pierre Leloir © Jean-Pierre Leloir.

pp. 144–145
Top:
* Miles Davis and Teo Macero, Columbia Studios, New York, January 1970. Photos Don Hunstein. © Courtesy of SME.
Bottom:
Miles Davis, Chick Corea, Dave Holland, Jack DeJohnette, Ronnie Scott's, London, November 2, 1969. Photo David Redfern. © Redferns/Getty Images.

p. 146
Left to right, top to bottom:
Painting by Mati Klarwein used to illustrate the cover of *Bitches Brew*, 1970. © Klarwein family.
Mati Klarwein, *Live*, painting used to illustrate the front of the cover of *Live-Evil*, 1971. Courtesy of Galerie Albert Benamou. © Klarwein family.
Mati Klarwein, *Evil*, painting used to illustrate the back of the cover of *Live-Evil*, 1971. Courtesy of Galerie Albert Benamou. © Klarwein family.

p. 147
Cover of *Rolling Stone* magazine, December 13, 1969. © Rolling Stone Magazine/Collection of Stéphane Samuel and Robert M. Rubin.

p. 148
* Miles Davis with boxer Sugar Ray Robinson, who is wearing a sweatsuit, 1969. Photo Corky McCoy. © Cortez McCoy.
* Record cover for *A Tribute to Jack Johnson*, Columbia, KC 30455, released February 24, 1971. Private collection.

p. 149
Miles Davis, Antibes, 1969. Photo Thierry Trombert. © Thierry Trombert.

p. 151
Miles Davis at the gym, about 1969. Photo Corky McCoy. © Cortez McCoy.

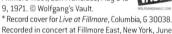

p. 152
Top to bottom, left to right:
Poster announcing the Grateful Dead and Miles Davis concerts at Fillmore West, San Francisco, April 9 to 12, 1970. © Wolfgang's Vault.
* Record cover for *Black Beauty: Miles Davis at Fillmore West*, CBS/Sony (Japan), SOPJ 39/40. Recorded at Fillmore West, San Francisco, April 10, 1970. Private collection.
Poster for the Berliner Jazztage festival, Germany, 1971. Collection Günther Kieser © Günther Kieser.
Poster announcing concerts by Miles Davis, Elvin Bishop and Mandrill at Fillmore West, San Francisco, May 6 to 9, 1971. © Wolfgang's Vault.
* Record cover for *Live at Fillmore*, Columbia, G 30038. Recorded in concert at Fillmore East, New York, June 1970. Private collection.

p. 153
Miles and Betty Davis, backstage at the Isle of Wight Festival, United Kingdom, August 1970. Photo Fred Lombardi. © Frederick Lombardi.

pp. 154–155
* Miles Davis in concert at Tanglewood, Berkshire, Massachusetts, August 18, 1970. Centre: Gary Bartz. Photo Amalie R. Rothschild. © Amalie R. Rothschild.

p. 156
Miles Davis, Koseinenkin Hall, Tokyo, Japan, June 19, 1973. Photo K. Abe. © K. Abe/CTSIMAGES.COM.

p. 158
Miles Davis at the barber, about 1969. Photo Corky McCoy. © Cortez McCoy.

p. 159
Miles Davis and Michael Henderson, Newport Festival, Paris, TNP, Paris, October 25, 1971. Photo Jean-Pierre Leloir. © Jean-Pierre Leloir.

pp. 160–161
* Miles Davis in various rooms and in front of his closet at his home on West Seventy-seventh Street, New York, 1971. Photos Anthony Barboza. © Anthony Barboza.

pp. 162–163
* Jackie Battle, Miles Davis and Betty Davis at the funeral of Jimi Hendrix, who passed away on September 18, 1970. Photo Bob Peterson. © Time & Life/Getty Images.

p. 164
* Miles Davis composing on the keyboard at home, about 1970. Photo Mark Patiky © Condé Nast Archive/Corbis.
Miles Davis' band in concert, Ahmanson Theatre, Los Angeles, May 2, 1973 (left to right): Reggie Lucas (guitar), Cedric Lawson (keyboard), David Liebman (saxophone), Pete Cosey (guitar), Miles Davis (trumpet), Michael Henderson (electric bass), Badal Roy (tabla), Mtume (percussion). Absent: Khalil Balakrishna (sitar) and Al Foster (drums). Photo Urve Kuusik. © Courtesy of SME.

p. 166
Ad for the record *On the Corner*, back cover of *Jazz Journal*, vol. 26, no. 3, March 1973. BNF. © Courtesy of SME.

p. 167
Left to right, top to bottom:
* Front of the record cover for *On the Corner*, Columbia, KC 31906, released October 11, 1972. Private collection.
Back of the record cover for *On the Corner*, Columbia, KC 31906, released October 11, 1972. Private collection.
* Front of the record cover for *Miles Davis in Concert: Live at Philharmonic Hall*, Columbia, KC 32092. Recorded in concert September 22, 1972, at Lincoln Center in New York. Private collection.
* Front and back covers of *Big Fun*, Columbia, PG 32866, released April 19, 1974. Private collection.

pp. 168–169
Miles Davis, Newport Festival, Paris, Palais des Sports, Paris, November 15, 1973. Photos Christian Rose. © Christian Rose.

p. 170
Left to right, top to bottom:
* Record cover for *Pangaea*, CBS/Sony, (J) SOPZ 96/7. Recorded in concert February 1, 1975, in Osaka, Japan. Private collection.
* Record cover for *Agharta*, Columbia, PG 33967 (American release). Recorded in concert February 1, 1975, in Osaka, Japan. Private collection.
* Front of the record cover for *Dark Magus*, CBS/Sony, (J) 40AP 741-2. Recorded in concert at Carnegie Hall, New York, March 30, 1974. Private collection.
* Record cover for *Agharta*, CBS/Sony, (J) 28AP 2167-8 (Japanese release). Recorded in concert February 1, 1975, in Osaka, Japan. Private collection.
* Front of the record cover for *Get Up with It*, Columbia, KG 33236, released November 22, 1974. Private collection.

p. 172
Miles Davis and David Liebman backstage, 1974; Mtume backstage, 1974; Reggie Lucas backstage, 1974. Photos Corky McCoy. © Cortez McCoy.

p. 175
Miles Davis' hands and trumpet, 1974.
Miles Davis, Dominique Gaumont (probably) and David Liebman (from the back) on stage, 1974. Photos Corky McCoy. © Cortez McCoy.

p. 176
* Recording session on March 2, 1978 (left to right): unidentified, Larry Coryell (guitar), Masabumi Kikuchi (keyboard), Eleana Steinberg, T. M. Stevens (electric bass), Miles Davis, George Pavlis (keyboard), Al Foster (drums) and Teo Macero (producer). Photo Don Hunstein. © Courtesy of SME.

pp. 178–179
* Miles Davis, at home, curtains closed, New York, about 1980. Photo Teppei Inokuchi. © Teppei Inokuchi.

p. 180
Portrait of Miles Davis, Montreal, Canada, 1985. Photo Anton Corbijn. © Anton Corbijn.

pp. 182–183
Rehearsing at Miles Davis' home, New York, spring 1981 (left to right): Al Foster (drums, hidden), Marcus Miller (electric bass), Mike Stern (guitar); Marcus Miller (electric bass); Marcus Miller (from the back) and Gil Evans; Marcus Miller (electric bass), Mike Stern (guitar), Mino Cinelu (percussion), Miles Davis; Bill Evans (soprano saxophone) and Miles Davis. Photos Teppei Inokuchi. © Teppei Inokuchi.

p. 184
Miles Davis in a pool, 1988. Photo Anthony Barboza. © Anthony Barboza.

p. 185
Miles Davis and Cicely Tyson next to his yellow Ferrari 308GTSi on his way to a concert at Kix in Boston, June 1981, New York. Photo Teppei Inokuchi. © Teppei Inokuchi.

p. 186
* Record cover for *The Man with the Horn*, Columbia, FC 36790, released in 1981.
* Record cover for *We Want Miles*, Columbia, C2 38005, released in 1982. Private collection.

p. 187
* Record cover for *Star People*, Columbia, FC 38657, released in 1983 (illustration by Miles Davis). Private collection.
Darryl Jones, Miles Davis and John Scofield in concert, Palais des Congrès, Paris, October 1983. Photo Didier Ferry. © Ferry/Dalle.

pp. 188–189
Left:
* Record cover for *You're under Arrest*, Columbia, FC 40023, released in 1985. Private collection.
Right:
* Photographs taken during a photo shoot for the record cover for *You're under Arrest*, 1985. Photos Anthony Barboza. © Anthony Barboza.

p. 190
Miles Davis and, in the background, Palle Mikkelborg during the recording of *Aura*, Denmark, 1985. Photo Kirsten Malone. © Kirsten Malone.

p. 193
Miles Davis during the recording of *Tutu*, 1986.
Marcus Miller, Miles Davis and, from the back, producer Tommy LiPuma during the recording of *Tutu*, 1986. Photos Teppei Inokuchi. © Teppei Inokuchi.

p. 194
* Miles Davis receiving a gold record award for *Tutu*, Paris, 1988. Photo Guy Le Querrec. © Guy Le Querrec/ Magnum Photos.

p. 195
Portrait of Miles Davis used on the front cover of *Tutu*, 1986. Photo Irving Penn. © 1986 by Irving Penn (Courtesy of Warner Bros.).

p. 197
Left to right, top to bottom:
Still from the documentary *The Making of Sun City* (dir. Steve Lawrence), 1986. © Artists United Against Apartheid.
Record cover for *Sun City*, Artists United Against Apartheid, Razor & Tie, RE 2007, released in 1985. Private collection.
Still from the feature film *Dingo* (dir. Rolf de Heer), 1991. © Les Films du Paradoxe.

WORKS IN THE EXHIBITION

Promotional postcard for the British rock group Scritti Politti with Miles Davis, probably 1988. Photo Ebet Roberts. Private collection.
Record cover for *Machismo* by Cameo, Atlanta Artists, 836 002-2, released in 1988. Miles Davis is featured on "In the Night."
Cover of the EP "Time after Time," CBS, 12AP3037 (Japan), released in 1985. B-side: "Katia."
Record cover for *Prisoner of Love* by Kenny Garrett, Atlantic Jazz, 782046-2, released in 1989. Miles Davis is featured on "Big Ol' Head" and "Free Mandela."
Record cover for the original film soundtrack of *Scrooged* (dir. Richard Donner), A&M Records, 393921-2, released in 1988. Miles Davis interprets "We Three Kings of Orient Are" with Larry Carlton, David Sanborn and Paul Shaffer.
Cover of the record *CK* by Chaka Khan, Warner Bros., 925707-2, released in 1988. Miles Davis is featured on "I'll Be Around." Private collection.
Still from the television series *Miami Vice* (season 2, episode 28, "Junk Love"), first broadcast on November 8, 1985. © Universal Studios.
Still from a television spot for Honda scooters, May 1986. © Honda Motors.

p. 198
* Miles Davis brandishing a sign inscribed with the name "Foley," Zénith, Paris, November 1989. Photo Annie Delory. © Dalle/APRF.

p. 200
Darryl Jones (bass guitar), Miles Davis (trumpet), "Foley" McCreary (lead bass), Kenny Garrett (alto saxophone) in concert at the "Jazz sur son 31" festival, Haute-Garonne, France, October 20, 1987. Photo Guy Le Querrec. © Guy Le Querrec/Magnum Photos.

p. 201
Miles Davis and Andy Warhol on the runway for designer Kohshin Satoh at the Tunnel club, New York, February 1987. Photo Susumu Shirai. © Susumu Shirai.

p. 203
I Can U Can't, painting by Miles Davis. Photo Alex Krassovsky. Collection of André Martinez and Odile Martinez de la Grange.
* Record cover for *Amandla*, Warner Bros., 25873, released in 1989. Private collection.

pp. 204–205
Miles Davis in concert, Tokyo, August 1988. Photos Shigeru Ushiyama. © Shigeru Ushiyama.

p. 207
Miles Davis at the "Jazz sur son 31" festival. Haute-Garonne, France, October 20, 1987. Photo Guy Le Querrec. © Guy Le Querrec/Magnum Photos.

p. 209
Miles Davis' hands as he draws. Photo Shigeru Ushiyama. © Shigeru Ushiyama.

pp. 210–211
* Miles Davis leaving Le Zenith, Paris, September 20, 1986. Photo Claude Gassian. © Claude Gassian.

p. 213
* Portrait of Miles Davis, 1989. Photo Annie Leibovitz. © Annie Leibovitz/Contact Press Images.

The photographs and record covers appearing in the exhibition and reproduced in the catalogue are not mentioned in the list below, but rather indicated by an asterisk in the list of illustrations.

INTRODUCTION

Audiovisual archives
Teffpunkt Jazz (excerpt), Miles Davis rehearsing with the Erwin Lehn Orchestra, Germany, 1957. © SWR.

Sound excerpts
Miles Davis' vocals edited with outtakes from the Columbia archives. © SME.

I. FROM ST. LOUIS TO FIFTY-SECOND STREET

Records and albums (seventy-eights)
Be-Bop, With All the Stars of the New Movement (Vols. 1 and 2), 1940s, Dial. IJS.
Charlie Parker, *The New Sound in Modern Music*, 1940s, Savoy Records. IJS.
New Sounds in Modern Music, 1940s, Savoy. IJS.
New Jazz/52nd Street Jazz, RCA, "Hot Jazz Series" (Vol. 9), 1940s. Courtesy LAJI.
Charlie Parker, *Bird of Paradise/Dexterity*, 1947, seventy-eight, Dial Records, no. 1032. Courtesy LAJI, www.lajazzinstitute.org.

Music
Jimmie Lunceford, *Uptown Blues* (Eldridge–C. Battle), 1939, OKeh.
Erskine Hawkins and His Orchestra, *Tuxedo Junction* (Dash–Hawkins–Johnson), 1939, Bluebird.
Coleman Hawkins and His Orchestra, *Body and Soul* (Green–Heyman–Sour–Eyton), 1939, RCA Victor.
Duke Ellington/Jimmy Blanton, *Mr. J. B. Blues* (Ellington–Blanton), 1940, RCA Victor.
Count Basie and His Orchestra, *Tickle-Toe* (L. Young), 1940, Columbia.
Louis Armstrong and His Orchestra, *Down in Honky Tonk Town* (Smith–McCarron), 1940, Decca.
Benny Goodman and His Sextet, *Air Mail Special* (Goodman–Mundy–Christian), 1941, Columbia.
Metronome All Stars, *One O'Clock Jump* (Basie), 1941, Victor.
Jay McShann and His Orchestra, *Hootie Blues* (McShann–Parker), 1941, Decca.
Billie Holiday with Eddie Heywood Orchestra, *All of Me* (Simons–Marks), 1941, OKeh.
Charlie Parker Quintet, "Groovin' High" (D. Gillespie), "Big Foot" (C. Parker) and "Ornithology" (C. Parker–B. Harris), in concert at the Royal Roost, New York, 1948, *The Complete Live Performances on Savoy*. © Savoy Jazz-Denon Records.

Printed matter
Menu from Club Plantation, St. Louis, n.d. Courtesy LAJI, www.lajazzinstitute.org.
Be-Bop Jazz catalogue, Dial Records, 1940s. Courtesy LAJI, www.lajazzinstitute.org.
"A Night in Manhattan," in *The Record Changer*, vol. 8, no. 2, February 1949. BNF.

Instruments
Three trumpet mouthpieces belonging to Miles Davis. Collection of MDP.

Paintings
Jean-Michel Basquiat, *Horn Players*, 1983, 243 x 190 cm. The Broad Art Foundation, Santa Monica. © Estate of Jean-Michel Basquiat/SODRAC (2010).
Jean-Michel Basquiat, *Untitled (Bird of Paradise)*, 1984, 152.5 x 106.5 cm. Collection of Stéphane Samuel and Robert M. Rubin, New York. © Estate of Jean-Michel Basquiat/SODRAC (2010).

Photographs (vintage prints)
Family photographs (anonymous): Portrait of Miles Davis at age eight or nine, 4.4 x 3.8 cm; Miles, Dorothy Mae, Vernon and Cleota Davis, Easter 1939, 6.3 x 8.9 cm; Four young boys, including Miles and Vernon Davis, Easter 1939, 8.9 x 6.3 cm; Edna and Dorothy Mae Davis, 8.9 x 6.3 cm; Edna and Vernon Davis, 6.3 x 8.9 cm; the members of the Violet Thimble Club, East St. Louis, 8 x 10 cm; Portrait of Miles Davis II graduating from the school of dentistry, Northwestern University, 1920s, 17 x 12 cm. Anthony Barboza Collection.
Portrait of Irene Birth, 1940s. Collection of MDP.

Photographs (reprints)
Anonymous, Andrew Preer's Cotton Club Orchestra, 1925. © Frank Driggs Collection.
Anonymous, Oliver Cobbe and his Brunswick Recording Orchestra, 1930. © Frank Driggs Collection.
Anonymous, Harry Sweets Edison in the Count Basie Orchestra, Famous Door, New York, 1938. © Frank Driggs Collection.
William P. Gottlieb, Miles Davis on piano and Howard McGhee on trumpet, New York, 1947. © William P. Gottlieb, www.jazzphotos.com.
William P. Gottlieb, the Charlie Parker Quintet at the Three Deuces, 1947. © William P. Gottlieb, www.jazzphotos.com.
Herman Leonard, Miles Davis at the Royal Roost (in the background: Max Roach and Kai Winding), 1948. © Herman Leonard Photography LLC/CTSIMAGES.COM.
William P. Gottlieb, billboard at the entrance to the Three Deuces announcing the Charlie Parker Quintet, New York, 1947. © William P. Gottlieb, www.jazzphotos.com.
Anonymous, Miles Davis at the Three Deuces, playing a muted trumpet, 1947. © Frank Driggs Collection.

Other
Facsimile of Miles Davis' high school diploma from Lincoln High School, East St. Louis, 1944. Collection of MDP.
Cathedral radio, Ohio Radio Corp., USA, 1930s. Collection of Klaus Blasquiz.

II. OUT OF THE COOL

Audiovisual archives
"L'existentialisme à Saint-Germain-des-Prés" (excerpt), *Les Actualités françaises*, first broadcast on September 20, 1951, ORTF. © INA.

Records and record covers
Acetate disc of the Tadd Dameron–Miles Davis Quintet concert at the Salle Pleyel made by Radiodiffusion française, May 8, 1949. Collection of Thierry Trombert.
L'Âge d'or de Saint-Germain-des-Prés, chansons, jazz, spectacles et souvenirs, LP box set with a book composed by Guillaume Hanoteau, Philips, P4L 0056. Private collection of Jacques-Prévert, Paris.
Miles Davis, *Classics in Jazz: Part 1*, forty-five, Capitol, EAP 1-459, 1950s. BNF.
Miles Davis, *Classics in Jazz: Part 2*, forty-five, Capitol, EAP 1-459. Archives Cohérie Boris Vian.

Music
The Miles Davis–Tadd Dameron Quintet, "Good Bait" (T. Dameron–C. Basie), *The Miles Davis/Tadd Dameron Quintet in Paris Festival International de Jazz; May, 1949*, Columbia, 1949. © SME.
Miles Davis, "Boplicity" (M. Davis) and "Deception" (M. Davis), *Birth of the Cool*, 1949. © Capitol Records.
Miles Davis, "Dig" (M. Davis), *Dig*, Prestige, 1951. © Concord Music Group.
Miles Davis, "Tempus Fugit" (B. Powell), *Miles Davis* (Vol. 2), Blue Note, 1954. © Capitol Records.
Miles Davis, "Blue Haze" (M. Davis), *Blue Haze*, Prestige, 1954. © Concord Music Group.
Miles Davis, "Walkin'" (R. Carpenter), *Walkin'*, Prestige, 1957. © Concord Music Group.
Miles Davis, "Bags' Groove" (M. Jackson), *Bags' Groove*, Prestige, 1955. © Concord Music Group.
Miles Davis, "My Funny Valentine" (R. Rodgers–L. Hart), *Cookin' with the Miles Davis Quintet*, Prestige, 1956. © Concord Music Group.
Miles Davis, "Oleo" (S. Rollins), *Relaxin' with the Miles Davis Quintet*, Prestige, 1958. © Concord Music Group.

Printed matter
Reproduction of the 1949 Festival International de Jazz de Paris poster, 1949. Collection of Sarah Tenot.
Program for the 1949 Festival International de Jazz de Paris (Illustration by Charles Delaunay), 1949. BNF.
Program for the opening night of the 1949 Festival International de Jazz de Paris (Tuesday, May 8, 1949). BNF.
America, no. 5 "Jazz 47," including contributions by Jean-Paul Sartre, Jean Cocteau, Hughes Panassié, Charles Delaunay, Boris Vian, Robert Goffin, André Hodeir, Frank Ténot, C. de Razinsky, A. Bétonville, J.-L. Bédouin, Henri Bernard. Illustrations by Fernand Léger, Félix Labisse and Jean Dubuffet, 1947. Collection of Roger Lajus.
Marian McPartland, "Crowds Jam Paris Jazz Festival," in *Down Beat*, vol. 16, no. 12, July 1, 1949. BNF.
Boris Vian, "Quelques mots sur Miles Davis," in *Jazz News*, no. 5, May 1949. Archives Cohérie Boris Vian.
"Trois jeunes vedettes" (referring to Charlie Parker, Miles Davis and Max Roach), in *La Revue du jazz*, no. 5, May 1949. BNF.
"Le Festival de Pleyel, les impressions de Johnny 'Scat' James," in *La Revue du jazz*, no. 6, June–July 1949. BNF.
André Hodeir, "Miles Davis l'insaisissable," in *Jazz Hot*, no. 32, April 1949. Private collection.
Catalogue Debut Records, about 1954. IJS.
Catalogue Blue Note Records, about 1954. IJS.
Catalogue Prestige Records, 1957. IJS.
Flyer for a Miles Davis concert at the Open Door, New York, 1954. IJS.
"Dope Menace Keeps Growing," in *Down Beat*, vol. 17, no. 23, November 17, 1950. Courtesy LAJI, www.lajazzinstitute.org.

Instrument
Miles Davis' Harmon mute. Collection of MDP.

Handwritten scores
John Lewis, "Rouge," group of nine scores written in ink (parts for trumpet, trombone, French horn, tuba, baritone saxophone, double bass and drums), about 1949. Collection of MDP.
Miles Davis, "Deception," group of seven scores written in pencil (parts for trumpet, trombone, tuba, alto saxophone, baritone saxophone, double bass, conductor), about 1949. Collection of MDP.

Photographs (vintage prints)
Jean-Philippe Charbonnier, Jam session at the Salle Pleyel, Paris, 1949, 18.2 x 24 cm. BNF.
Daniel Filipacchi, Miles Davis and Kenny Clarke, Paris, 1949, 23.5 x 18 cm. © Frank Driggs Collection.
Jean-Philippe Charbonnier, Juliette Gréco and Miles Davis, 1949, series of three photographs, 11 x 17 cm (for one), 24 x 18 cm (for the others). Galerie Agathe-Gaillard.
Cecil Charles, Chet Baker, Miles Davis and Rolf Ericson at the Lighthouse in Hermosa Beach, 1953, colour print, 8.5 x 8.5 cm. Courtesy LAJI, www.lajazzinstitute.org.

Photographs (reprints)
Anonymous, Hot Lips Page, Miles Davis and Kenny Dorham at the counter of a French café, Paris, 1949. © Frank Driggs Collection.
Anonymous, Tommy Potter, Boris Vian, Kenny Dorham, Juliette Gréco, Miles Davis, anonymous, Michèle Vian and Charlie Parker, Paris, May 1949.
Pierre Delord, Tadd Dameron–Miles Davis Quintet at Salle Pleyel, May 1949, series of seven photographs. © Médiathèque de Villefranche-de-Rouergue.
Willy Ronis, scene at Saint-Germain-des-Prés, 1955. © Willy Ronis/Rapho/Eyedea Illustration.
Anonymous, Popsie Randolph, Miles Davis and Al Haig during a recording session for *Birth of the Cool*, 1949. Photo William "PoPsie" Randolph. © 2010 Michael Randolph/www.PoPsiePhotos.com. Frank Driggs Collection.
Anonymous, Miles Davis playing trumpet during a recording session for *Birth of the Cool*, 1949. © Frank Driggs Collection.
Francis Wolff, Miles Davis, Art Blakey, Jimmy Heath, April 1953. © Mosaic Images LLC.
Francis Wolff, Miles Davis in the studio for Blue Note, March 1954. © Mosaic Images LLC.
Anonymous, Thelonious Monk, Miles Davis, Gigi Gryce and Max Roach, about 1954. Rights reserved.

III. MILES AHEAD

Audiovisual archives
Louis Malle in a postsynchronization booth for *Ascenseur pour l'échafaud* [a.k.a. *Frantic*] (excerpt), "Cinépanorama" television series, 1957. © INA.
The Sound of Miles Davis (excerpt), television show, CBS, presented by Robert Herridge, 1959.

Archival documents
Handwritten note by Marcel Romano informing Janet Urtreger of Miles Davis' appointment at the Nouvelles Éditions du Film's offices to sign the contract for the music for *Ascenseur pour l'échafaud*, 1957, 15 x 10 cm. Collection of J. de Mirbeck-Urtreger.
Note with handwriting on the front and back from Marcel Romano, serving as a payment receipt for the recording of the music for *Ascenseur pour l'échafaud* [a.k.a *Frantic*], and signed by Miles Davis, 1957, 15 x 10 cm. Collection of J. de Mirbeck-Urtreger.
Group of documents pertaining to the production of the record *Kind of Blue*: session sheet from March 2, 1959 (job no. 43079); session sheet from April 22, 1959 (job no. 43079); three handwritten notes by producer Irving Townsend: one with the titles, order and duration of the pieces on the record, the second with the distribution of tracks per side with their final titles, the third listing the musicians on the record and the order in which they appear on the record cover; handwritten version of Bill Evans' notes for the cover; internal correspondence sent by I. Townsend (May 21, 1959) justifying his request to pay an additional $100 to three musicians. NYPL.
Handwritten note establishing the order of tracks on the record *Porgy and Bess* (approved by Gil Evans), 1958. NYPL.
Pannonica de Koenigswarter, *Les Musiciens de jazz et leurs trois vœux* [*Three Wishes: An Intimate Look at Jazz Greats*], two Hermès notebooks containing the manuscript. Collection of Shaun de Koenigswarter.
Duplicate of the playlist for a Miles Davis concert at Carnegie Hall, New York, 1961. Collection of MDP.

Record covers
Miles Davis, *Ascenseur pour l'échafaud*, original soundtrack of the film by Louis Malle, LP Fontana, 33/25 660.213, 1958. Archives Cohérie Boris Vian.
Collective, *Music for Brass*, 1956, Columbia, CL 941. Courtesy of Paris Jazz Corner.

Music
Miles Davis, "The Duke" (D. Brubeck), *Miles Ahead*, Columbia, 1957. © SME.
Miles Davis, "Gone, Gone, Gone" (G. Gershwin–I. Gershwin–D. Heyward), *Porgy and Bess*, Columbia, 1958. © SME.
Miles Davis, "Will o' the Wisp" (M. de Falla), *Sketches of Spain*, Columbia, 1960. © SME.
Miles Davis, *Kind of Blue* (in extenso), 1959. © SME.

Film
Louis Malle, *Ascenseur pour l'échafaud* [a.k.a *Frantic*] (excerpt), 1957. © NEF/Pyramide.

Printed matter
Poster for the film *Ascenseur pour l'échafaud* [a.k.a. *Frantic*] by Louis Malle, designed by Willy Mucha, 1958. Cinémathèque française.
Poster for the film *Ascenseur pour l'échafaud* [a.k.a. *Frantic*], photomontage, 1958. Cinémathèque française.
Original sheet music for *Ascenseur pour l'échafaud* [a.k.a. *Frantic*] by Miles Davis, Éditions Continental, 1958. Collection of MDP.
Program for the Newport Jazz Festival, 1955. IJS.
Program for the Birdland '56 tour, November 17 and 18, 1956. Courtesy LAJI, www.lajazzinstitute.org.
Program for the Miles Davis Quintet concert, December 8, 1957, Amsterdam, Concertgebouw, 1957. IJS.
Jazz Hot, no. 126, November 1957. BNF.
"Louis Malle : le problème de la musique de film est un problème horriblement compliqué," in *Jazz Hot*, no. 155, June 1960. Private collection.
Miles Davis and Group, fascicle published by Columbia to promote Miles Davis, 1959. IJS.
"Miles Davis Looks at Alter Ego Gil Evans," *Down Beat*, vol. 28, no. 24, February 16, 1961. BNF.
"It Ain't Necessarily So," excerpt of *Porgy and Bess*, 1935, printed score for voice and piano, Gershwin Publishing Corp., New York. Collection of Philippe Baudoin.
Ted Joans, *All of Ted Joans and No More: Beat Generation Jazz Poems* (revised edition). Excelsior Press Publishers, New York, September 1961. Collection of Robert M. Rubin.

Instruments
Martin Committee trumpet owned by Miles Davis in the 1950s. University of North Carolina at Greensboro, UNCG School of Music.
Selmer Balanced Action tenor saxophone owned by John Coltrane in the 1950s. Collection of Ravi Coltrane.
Martin Magna flugelhorn used by Miles Davis between about 1957 and 1959. Collection of Wallace Roney, gift of Miles Davis.

Handwritten scores
Miles Davis, "So What" (sheet with some notes), probably 1961. Collection of MDP.
Gil Evans, "Gone Gone Gone," group of orchestra scores (eighteen musicians) and solo trumpet arranged by Gil Evans, excerpt of *Porgy and Bess*, 1958. Collection of MDP.
Gil Evans, "[There's a] Boat That's Leaving," solo part for trumpet arranged by Gil Evans, excerpt of *Porgy and Bess*, 1958. Collection of MDP.
Gil Evans, "The Song of Our Country," part for trumpet, 1960. Collection of MDP.

Photograph (vintage print)
Pannonica de Koenigswarter, Miles Davis at "Cathouse," Polaroid, 12 x 8 cm. Collection of Shaun de Koenigswarter.

Photographs (reprints)
Vincent Rossell, Miles Davis and Louis Malle during the recording of the music for *Ascenseur pour l'échafaud* [a.k.a *Frantic*], 1957. Vincent Rossell/Cinémathèque française.
Janet Urtreger, Portrait of Miles Davis in Paris, 1957. © Jeanne de Mirbeck-Urtreger.
André Sas, René Urtreger, Barney Wilen, Kenny Clarke, Pierre Michelot and Miles Davis, on stage at the Club St Germain, Paris, November 1957. © Dalle.
Don Hunstein, group of photographs taken in studio during the recording session of *Porgy and Bess*, April 22, 1959. © SME.
Dennis Stock, Miles Davis listening in the booth during a recording session, 1958. © Magnum Photos.
Don Hunstein, View of an empty Columbia studio, Thirtieth Street in New York. © SME.
Don Hunstein, Miles Davis in the studio directing John Coltrane, Cannonball Adderley and Philly Joe Jones, March 1958. © SME.
Don Hunstein, Miles Davis in the studio with the Gil Evans Orchestra during the recording of *Porgy and Bess*, 1958. © SME.
Don Hunstein, Gil Evans and Miles Davis, flugelhorn under his elbow, during the recording of *Porgy and Bess*, 1958. © SME.
Don Hunstein, Miles Davis from the back, at the trumpet chair, during the recording of *Porgy and Bess*, 1958. © SME.
Don Hunstein, Miles Davis sound editing *Porgy and Bess* with Gil Evans and Cal Lampley, July 1958. © SME.
Don Hunstein, Miles Davis and Gil Evans examining a score during the recording of *Miles Ahead*, 1957. © SME.

Other
Neumann microphone M49/M50, 1950s. Collection of Klaus Blasquiz.

IV. MILES SMILES

Audiovisual archives
Jazz—gehört und gesehen F: 51—Das Miles Davis Quintett, televised concert by the Miles Davis Quintet at the Stadthalle de Karlsruhe, Germany, November 7, 1967. © SWR.
Miles and Frances Davis arriving at the train station in Paris, July 25, 1963, ORTF. © INA.

Music
Miles Davis, "Someday My Prince Will Come" (F. Churchill–L. Morey), *Someday My Prince Will Come*, Columbia, 1961. © SME.
Miles Davis, "Stella by Starlight" (V. Young–N. Washington), *My Funny Valentine*, Columbia, 1964. © SME.
Miles Davis, "Filles de Kilimanjaro" (M. Davis), *Filles de Kilimanjaro*, Columbia, 1968. © SME.

Printed matter
Down Beat, vol. 31, no. 23, August 13, 1964.
Down Beat, vol. 29, no. 23, August 30, 1962. Collection of Robert M. Rubin.
Down Beat, vol. 33, no. 5, March 10, 1966. BNF.
Down Beat, vol. 34, no. 7, April 6, 1967, 1967. BNF.
Down Beat, vol. 34, no. 26, December 28, 1967, 1967. BNF.
Down Beat, vol. 35, no. 26, December 26, 1968. Collection of Robert M. Rubin.
Down Beat (Japanese Edition), November 1960. Collection of Kiyoshi Koyama.
Down Beat (Japanese Edition), October 1961. Collection of Kiyoshi Koyama.
Down Beat (Japanese Edition), April 1962. Collection of Kiyoshi Koyama.
Jazz, vol. 13, no. 3, March 1968. BNF.
Jazz Hip, no. 36, summer 1963. BNF.
Jazz Hip, no. 37, 1964. BNF.
Jazz Hot, no. 189, July?August 1963. Private collection.
Jazz Hot, no. 236, November 1967. Private collection.
Jazz Journal, vol. 13, no. 10, October 1960. BNF.
Jazz Magazine, no. 57, March 1960. Private collection.
Jazz Magazine, no. 64, November 1960. Collection of *Jazz Magazine*.
Jazz Magazine, no. 98, September 1963. Private collection.
Metronome, vol. 78, no. 10, October 1961. BNF.
Orkester Journalen, no. 4, April 1960. BNF.
Playboy, September 1962. Collection of Robert M. Rubin.
Rytmi, no. 9–10, 1960. BNF.
Swing Journal, July 1964. Collection of Kiyoshi Koyama.
Swing Journal, spring 1965 (Special Issue). Collection of Kiyoshi Koyama.
Swing Journal, June 1966 (Special Issue). Collection of Kiyoshi Koyama.
Swing Journal, August 1968. Collection of Kiyoshi Koyama.

Official program of "The World Jazz Festival," 1964, Tokyo, Japan. Collection of Kiyoshi Koyama.

Instruments
Parts of a black Gretsch drum kit used by Philly Joe Jones and Tony Williams: bass drum, tom, floor tom, 1960s. Collection of Cindy Blackman.
Black Gretsch snare drum, 1960s. Collection of Cherie Willoughby.
Turkish K Zildjian 22" ride cymbal belonging to Tony Williams in the 1960s. Collection of Cindy Blackman, gift of Jimmy Cobb.
Pair of Charleston Turkish K Zildjian 14" cymbals and Turkish K Zildjian 18" crash cymbals. Collection of Cindy Blackman.
Blue-green lacquered Martin Magna trumpet used by Miles Davis in the mid-1960s. Collection of Wallace Roney, gift of Miles Davis.

Photographs (reprints)
Corky McCoy, Wayne Shorter on saxophone and Herbie Hancock at the piano during a rehearsal in the studio, about 1967–68. © Cortez McCoy.
Vernon Smith, Miles Davis, George Coleman and Ron Carter, New York, Philharmonic Hall, 1964. SME.

Handwritten scores
Anonymous [J. J. Johnson?], "From St. Louis," parts for trumpet, trombone, tenor saxophone annotated with "Miles [Davis]," "Hank [Mobley]," "J. J. [Johnson]," probably 1962. Collection of MDP.
Miles Davis/Gil Evans, "Filles de Kilimanjaro," parts for trumpet, tenor saxophone, double bass and drums, 1968. Collection of MDP.
Herbie Hancock, "Little One," part for trumpet, 1965 (© 1981 Hancock Music). Collection of MDP.
Herbie Hancock, "The Sorcerer," part for bass, 1967 (© 1982 Hancock Music). Collection of MDP.
Wayne Shorter, "Capricorn," part for trumpet, 1967. Collection of MDP.
Wayne Shorter, "Dolores," part for trumpet, 1966. Collection of MDP.
Wayne Shorter, "E.S.P.," part for trumpet, with the dedication "For Miles," 1965. Collection of MDP.
Wayne Shorter, "Footprints," part for double bass, 1966. Collection of MDP.
Wayne Shorter, "Pinocchio," 1967. Collection of MDP.

Records
Miles Davis, *Someday My Prince Will Come*, group of five forty-fives for juke-boxes, with reproductions of the cover and labels, 1961. Collection of Robert M. Rubin.

Archival documents
Correspondence from Michel J. Vermette to Stanley West, dated January 27, 1964, informing him that Miles Davis would like to spend two of the summer months on the French Riviera and give a weekly concert. NYPL.
Letter from Teo Macero, dated November 20, 1968, indicating the track list on the record *Filles de Kilimanjaro* and Miles Davis' wish to translate all the titles into French. NYPL.

Record covers
Miles Davis in Europe, Columbia, CL 2183 (mono), 1963. Private collection.
Miles in Tokyo, CBS/SONY, SONX60064, 1969. Private collection.
Miles in Berlin, CBS, SBPG62976, 1969. Private collection.

V. ELECTRIC MILES

Music
Miles Davis, "Spanish Key" (M. Davis), *Bitches Brew*, Columbia, 1969. © SME.

Films
William Clayton, *Jack Johnson* (excerpt), 1970. © ESPN, London.
Olana DiGirolamo, *Play That Teo* (excerpt), 2009. © Olana DiGirolamo, Los Angeles.
Murray Lerner, *Miles Electric: A Different Kind of Blue* (excerpt), 1970. © Eagle Rock Entertainment, Paris.

Printed matter
Poster announcing concerts by Miles Davis and the Grateful Dead at Fillmore West, April 1970, 53.4 x 35.5 cm. Wolfgang's Vault.
Poster announcing the concerts of Miles Davis and Leon Russell at Fillmore West, October 1970, 53.4 x 35.5 cm. Wolfgang's Vault.
Poster announcing the concerts of Miles Davis, Elvin Bishop and Mandrill at Fillmore West, May 6 to 9, 1971, 53.4 x 35.5 cm. Wolfgang's Vault.
Rolling Stone, no. 48, December 13, 1969, with Miles Davis on the cover. Collection of Robert M. Rubin.
Down Beat, "Yearbook 1969," 1969. BNF.
Down Beat, vol. 36, no. 25, December 11, 1969. BNF.

Instruments
Martin Committee trumpet with black-copper finish, engraved with the name "Miles Davis" on the bell, used by Miles Davis between 1969 and 1974. Collection of Wallace Roney, gift of Miles Davis.
Fender Rhodes 73 suitcase electric piano, 1967. Collection of Olivier Grall.
"Echoplex" tape delay effect, (early) 1970s. Musée de la Musique, Paris.

Handwritten scores
Hermeto Pascoal, "Nem Um Talvez," group of three scores (parts for trumpet, piano and bass), 1970. Collection of MDP.
Hermeto Pascoal, "Igrejinha" (alias "Little Church"), group of five scores (parts for trumpet, piano and bass), 1970. Collection of MDP.
Wayne Shorter, "Paraphernalia," part for guitar, 1968. Collection of MDP.
Wayne Shorter, arrangement of "Guinnevere," song by David Crosby, group of eight scores (parts for trumpet, soprano saxophone, bass clarinet, two electric pianos, double bass and electric bass), 1970. Collection of MDP.
Joe Zawinul, "Direction" [*sic*], 1968. Collection of MDP.

Photographs (reprints)
Guy Le Querrec, Miles Davis at the Salle Pleyel, Paris, 1969. © Magnum Photos.
Don Hunstein, Miles Davis at home, 1969. © SME.

Photographs (vintage prints)
Amalie R. Rothschild, *Miles Davis multi, Tanglewood, August 18, 1970*, signed print numbered 7/250, stamp on the back. Collection of Amalie R. Rothschild, Florence.
Lee Friedlander, Portrait of Miles Davis, 1969, 43.2 x 43.2 cm. Fraenkel Gallery, San Francisco.

Paintings
Mati Klarwein, *Live*, oil on canvas, painting used for the front cover of *Live-Evil*, 1971, 70 x 70 cm. Galerie Albert Benamou.
Mati Klarwein, *Evil*, oil on canvas, painting used for the back cover of *Live-Evil*, 1971, 70 x 70 cm. Galerie Albert Benamou.

Archival documents
Copy of correspondence from Bruce Lundvall, dated April 1, 1969, recommending that Miles Davis be promoted in the "underground" press. NYPL.
Copy of correspondence from Corinne Chertok, dated August 8, 1969, mentioning that Miles Davis was asking to be recognized as co-author of "In a Silent Way." NYPL.
Sheet from a notebook mentioning the rental of bells, two Fender electric pianos and a bass clarinet for the recording sessions on August 19, 20 and 21, 1969. NYPL.
Session sheet from August 19, 1969. NYPL.
Session sheet from August 21, 1969. NYPL.
Teo Macero's handwritten notes for the editing of "Pharoah's Dance" and "Miles Runs the Voodoo Down," 1969. NYPL.
Handwritten note from Teo Macero outlining the track list for *Bitches Brew* by side and composers, 1969. NYPL.
Proof for the cover of *In a Silent Way* with the rejected title *Mornin' Fast Train from Memphis to Harlem*, 1969. SME.
Typed correspondence from Teo Macero to Clive Davis, dated October 23, 1969, with additional handwritten notes concerning the advances paid out to Miles Davis. NYPL.
Memo from Teo Macero, dated November 14, 1969, informing his managers of Miles Davis' wish to entitle his record *Bitches Brew*. NYPL.
Correspondence from Clive Davis, dated November 17, 1969, asking Bill Graham to book Miles Davis at the Fillmore. NYPL.
Correspondence from Miles Davis, dated January 8, 1970, to Clive Davis asking to be on Columbia's payroll. NYPL.
Copy of a telegram, dated January 9, 1970, from Miles Davis to Walter Dean expressing his displeasure at the cancellation of a recording session. NYPL.
Columbia sales report, dated September 18, 1972. NYPL.

VI. ON THE CORNER

Audiovisual archives
Teppei Inokuchi, *Miles Davis in Studio*, 1972, with, notably, Al Foster, David Liebman, Badal Roy, Michael Henderson. © Teppei Inokuchi.
Miles Davis' band in concert in Japan, 1973. Courtesy of the Eleana S. Tee Cobb Jazz Heritage Collection.
Corky McCoy, Miles Davis training in the boxing ring, 1969. © Cortez McCoy.

Drawings
Corky McCoy, *On the Corner*, illustration for front of record cover, pencil on tracing paper, 1972, 39.5 x 35 cm. Collection of Cortez McCoy.
Corky McCoy, *Water Babies*, series of three drawings representing characters, pencil, 124 x 31 cm, 224 x 31 cm and 324 x 31 cm. Collection of Cortez McCoy.
Corky McCoy, *Water Babies*, illustration used for record cover, pencil on tracing paper, 48 x 34 cm. Collection of Cortez McCoy.
Corky McCoy, *Live & Electric*, proposed record cover design, about 1973, 35.5 x 28.5 cm. Collection of Cortez McCoy.

Records
Miles Davis, "Molester" [Parts 1 and 2], forty-five, for commercial release. Private collection.
Miles Davis, "Holly-Wuud," stereo and mono versions, forty-five for radio. Private collection.
Miles Davis, "Vote for Miles," forty-five, stereo and mono versions. Private collection.

Archival documents
Proof for an ad for the launch of the record *Jack Johnson*, 1971. NYPL.
Session sheet from June 1, 1972. NYPL.
Session sheet from June 6, 1972. NYPL.
Teo Macero's handwritten notes concerning the sound editing of the record *On the Corner*, 1972. NYPL.
Memo from John Berg to Teo Macero, dated March 13, 1973, regarding Miles Davis' request to withdraw the names of the musicians from the credits on the record *In Concert*, 1973. NYPL.

Music
Miles Davis, "Great Expectations" (excerpt) (M. Davis–J. Zawinul), *Big Fun*, Columbia, 1969. © SME.
Miles Davis, "Ife" (excerpt) (M. Davis), *Big Fun*, Columbia, 1972. © SME.
Miles Davis, "On the Corner" (M. Davis), *On the Corner*, Columbia, 1972. © SME.
Miles Davis, "Black Satin" (M. Davis), *On the Corner*, Columbia, 1972. © SME.

Printed matter
Promotional poster of Miles Davis in a boxing ring, about 1971. Collection of Robert M. Rubin.
Poster for the Berliner Jazztage '71 festival, illustration by Günther Kieser, 119 x 84 cm. Private collection.
Ad for *On the Corner*, back cover of *Jazz Journal*, vol. 26, no. 3, March 1973. BNF.
Down Beat, vol. 41, no. 18, July 18, 1974. BNF.

Instruments, amplifiers and sound effects
Yamaha amplifier, model RA-200, bearing Miles Davis' name, used between about 1973 and 1975, Japan. Collection of MDP.
Vox wah-wah pedal, Jen Ellettronica, Italy, 1960s. Collection of Klaus Blasquiz.
Customized green-painted Martin Magna C trumpet, engraved with the name of Miles Davis, Elkhart, Indiana, 1970s. IJS.
EMS Synthi Aks synthesizer, 1970s. Collection of Olivier Grall.
Yamaha YC 45 D electric organ, 1970s. Collection of Olivier Grall.
Dominique Gaumont's Gibson SG electric guitar, 1970s. Collection of Michèle Codin.

Handwritten scores
Paul Buckmaster, "On/Off," three-page original score: the composition inspired the tunes "Black Satin," "One and One," "Helen Butte," "Mr. Freedom X," 1972. Collection of Paul Buckmaster.

Paul Buckmaster, "Piece #3," two-page original score: the composition inspired the tune "Ife," 1972. Collection of Paul Buckmaster.

Photograph (vintage print)
Takashi Arihara, Miles Davis' band backstage, Tokyo, August 2, 1975, photograph autographed by each musician in the group, 33 x 40 cm. Collection of Kiyoshi Koyama.

Photograph (reprint)
Don Hunstein, Miles Davis and Teo Macero, Columbia Studios, November 1971. SME.

Other
Miles Davis' Everlast punching bag, 1980s. Collection of MDP.

VII. SILENCE

Archival documents
Copy of correspondence, dated December 11, 1975, from Teo Macero to Miles Davis in the hospital. NYPL.
Handwritten note from Teo Macero regarding plans for a Miles Davis record that would be entitled *The World & the Light*, 1976. NYPL.
Letter contracting Yomiuri Shimbun for Miles Davis' planned twenty-one-day tour of Japan (May 23–June 12, 1977), 1977. NYPL.

Music
Miles Davis, "He Loved Him Madly" (M. Davis), *Get Up with It*, 1974. © SME.

Photograph (reprint)
Don Hunstein, Miles Davis in the studio, March 1978. SME.

VIII. STAR PEOPLE

Costumes
Kohshin Satoh, Miles Davis' red studded jacket, about 1988. Collection of MDP.
Nancy and Lélia Campbell (Davis called them "Samething"), red cotton jacket with silk embroidey on West African loincloth worn by Miles Davis on the back cover of *Amandla*, 1987. Collection of MDP.
Kohshin Satoh, jacket and trousers worn by Miles Davis on the book cover of *The Best to Best*, about 1989. Collection of MDP.
Kansai, black jacket with a dragon motif on the front, worn by Miles Davis on the cover of *You're under Arrest*, about 1985. Collection of MDP.
Kansai, white jacket with rhinestones worn by Miles Davis in the music video for "Tutu Medley," about 1986. Collection of MDP.
Gianni Versace, jacket worn by Miles Davis during the concert Miles & Friends, about 1991. Collection of MDP.

Audiovisual archives
60 Minutes (excerpt), 1989. © CBS News Archive/BBC Motion Gallery.
Arsenio Hall Show (excerpt), 1989. © CBS.
Conspiracy of Hope for Amnesty International (excerpt), 1986. © MTV Network/Amnesty International.
Days with Miles (dir. Per Møller Hansen), documentary about the making of the record *Aura*, 1989. © Danmarks Radio.
"Decoy" (music video) (dir. Annabel Jankel/Rocky Morton), 1984. © SME.
Fashion show for Kohshin Satoh's 1987–88 collection at the Tunnel club, New York, with the participation of Miles Davis and Andy Warhol (excerpts), 1987. © Kohshin Satoh.
Dingo (excerpt) (dir. Rolf de Heer), 1989. © Les Films du Paradoxe.
"The Doo-Bop Song" (music video), 1992. © Warner Music Group.
"Miles noir sur blanc" (dir. Jérôme Habans), *Les Enfants du rock*, 1986. INA.
"Fantasy" (music video), 1992. © Warner Music Group.
The Hot Spot (dir. Dennis Hopper), 1990. MGM.
The Making of Sun City (excerpt) (dir. Steve Lawrence), 1985. © Global Vision Inc.
Miami Vice (season 2, episode 28, "Junk Love") (excerpt), 1985. © Universal Studios.
Miles and Friends (dir. Renaud Le Van Kim), 1991. © Grande Halle.
Miles Davis & Quincy Jones Live at Montreux (excerpt), 1991. © Warner Music Group.
The New Alfred Hitchcock Presents (season 1, "Prisoners" episode) (excerpt), 1985. © Universal Studios.
Night Music (excerpts), 1989. © Broadway Video.
Saturday Night Live (excerpt), 1981. © Broadway Video.
Television spot for Honda Scooters, 1986. © Honda Motor Europe (South) S.A.S.
Television spot for Van Aquavit (dir. Anthony Barboza). © Anthony Barboza.
The Today Show (excerpt), 1982. © NBC Universal, New York.
"Tutu Medley" (music video) (dir. Spike Lee), 1986. © Warner Music Group.

Record cover
Miles Davis, *We Want Miles*, LP autographed by Miles Davis. IJS.

Printed matter
Kohshin Satoh and Miles Davis, *The Best to Best*, Kamakura, Japan, Yobisha, 1992. Private collection.
Kohshin Satoh, fall–winter catalogue, 1987. Collection of Kohshin Satoh.

Instruments
Red-lacquered Martin Committee trumpet engraved with Miles Davis' name, about 1985. Collection of MDP.
Silver Martin Committee trumpet engraved with Miles Davis' name, about 1985. Collection of MDP.
Purple Yamaha drum kit: snare drum, mid-tom, floor tom, bass drum (bearing Al Foster's name on the skin) and a set of Paiste cymbals, early 1980s. Collection of Al Foster.
Fodera "Monarch Deluxe" bass guitar. Collection of Marcus Miller.
Black Kramer "The Duke" bass guitar. Collection of Foley McCreary.
Pro Co RAT effects pedal, 1980s. Collection of John Scofield.
Ibanez CS9 chorus effects pedal, 1980s. Collection of John Scofield.
Black Schecter Jazz bass guitar, 1980s. Collection of Darryl Jones.
Oberheim OB-Xa programmable polyphonic synthesizer, used on stage by Miles Davis. Collection of MDP.
Roland D50 programmable polyphonic synthesizer, used on stage by Miles Davis. Collection of MDP.

Manuscript
Miles Davis/Quincy Troupe, *Miles: The Autobiography*, first annotated pages of the typescript, 1989, 21.5 x 28 cm. Schomburg Center For Research in Black Culture, The New York Public Library for the Performing Arts, Astor, Lenox and Tilden Foundation, New York.

Works of art
Miles Davis, *Twelve Things*, painting on wood, 1984, 65 x 90 cm. Collection of MDP.
Miles Davis, *Fourteen Things*, painting on wood, about 1984, 45 x 60.5 cm. Collection of MDP.
Miles Davis, *Santa Fe*, painting on wood, about 1984, 45 x 60.5 cm. Collection of MDP.
Miles Davis and Jo Gelbard, *Amandla*, designed for the record cover (not used), 1989, 65.5 x 50.5 cm. Collection of Warner Music Group.
Miles Davis and Jo Gelbard, *Amandla*, designed for the record cover (used), 1989, 76.5 x 50.5 cm, painting and drawing. Collection of Warner Music Group.
Miles Davis, *Untitled*, painting on wood, about 1990, 58 x 114 cm. Collection of MDP.
Miles Davis, *Untitled*, painting on wood, about 1990, 114 x 58 cm. Collection of MDP.
Miles Davis, *I Can U Can't*, 1990, 118 x 172 cm. Collection of André Martinez.
Miles Davis and Jo Gelbard, *Untitled*, mixed media, 1990, 122 x 66 cm. Collection of André Martinez and Odile Martinez de la Grange.
Miles Davis and Jo Gelbard, *1991 Paris Set*, painting that served as a model for hangings used at a Miles Davis concert at the Grande Halle de La Villette, 1991, 106.7 x 142.2 cm. Collection of Jo Gelbard.

Photograph (vintage print)
Irving Penn, three photographs taken for the record *Tutu* (front, back and inside), 1986, 52.5 x 50.5 cm. Collection of Warner Music Group.

Other
Tutu gold record, 1988, France. Collection of MDP.
Six signs used to introduce the musicians on stage: "Kenny" (Garrett), "Foley" (McCreary), "Deron" (Johnson), "Richard" (Patterson), "Ricky" (Wellman) and "Me" (Miles Davis), 1991. Collection of MDP.
Miles Davis' leather trumpet case. Collection of MDP.
Backstage pass with Miles Davis' portrait, 1989. Collection of MDP.
Toy machine gun appearing on the cover of *You're under Arrest*, about 1985. Courtesy of Anthony Barboza Collection.

MONTREAL ONLY

Works of Art
Jean-Michel Basquiat, *With Strings Two*, 1982, acrylic and mixed media on canvas, 244 x 152.5 cm. The Broad Art Foundation, Santa Monica. © Estate of Jean-Michel Basquiat/SODRAC (2010)
Miles Davis, *Self-portrait*, undated, coloured pencil on paper, 39 x 28 cm. Festival International de Jazz de Montréal Collection.
Miles Davis and Jo Gelbard, *Butter Beans*, 1990, acrylic and pastel on canvas, 178 x 152.5 cm. Collection of Jo Gelbard.
Miles Davis and Jo Gelbard, *Blackboard*, 1990, acrylic and pastel on canvas, 142 x 107 cm. Collection of James Rabito.
Mati Klarwein, *Zonked* or *Miles over Machu Pichu*, about 1971, oil on canvas, 45.7 x 94 cm. Stella Benabou Shapiro and Dorian Shapiro Collection. © Klarwein family.
Mati Klarwein, *Earth, Wind and Fire/Last Days and Time*, 1969, 50.8 x 50.8 cm. Private Collection. © Klarwein family.
Niki de Saint Phalle, *Miles Davis*, 1999, polyester resin, polyurethane foam on steel framework, mirror mosaic, coloured stones, glass paste, ceramic, gold leaf, 270 x 130 x 100 cm. Niki Charitable Art Foundation, Santee, California. © 2010 Niki Charitable Art Foundation/ ADAGP/SODRAC
Kazuya Sakai, *Filles de Kilimanjaro III (Miles Davis)*, 1976, acrylic on canvas 200.6 x 200 cm. The Blanton Museum of Art, The University of Texas at Austin, Archer M. Huntington Museum Fund (1977.21).

Audiovisual archives
Excerpt of Miles Davis' concert at the Festival International de Jazz de Montréal, Théâtre Saint-Denis, June 28, 1985. Festival International de Jazz de Montréal Collection.

Printed matter
Poster for the 9th edition of the Festival International de Jazz de Montréal, July 1–10, 1988. Festival International de Jazz de Montréal Collection.
Poster for Miles Davis' concerts at the Spectrum, Montreal, December 8–10, 1989 (postponed). Festival International de Jazz de Montréal Collection.
Miles Davis and Quincy Troupe, *Miles: The Autobiography*, Simon and Schuster, New York, 1989, 1990, with first page autographed by Miles Davis. Private collection.
Coda, vol. 6, no. 8 (December 1964–January 1965), cover photograph: Miles Davis at Monterey. Siegfried H. Mohr, courtesy CODA JazzMedia Group Inc., Toronto, Ontario.

Photographs (vintage prints)
Anonymous, Hot Lips Page and Big Chief Moore examining plans and etchings of Paris, 1949, 13 x 18 cm. Private collection.
Anonymous, Big Chief Moore signing the guest book at Paris City Hall, 1949, 13 x 18 cm. Private collection.
Anonymous, Miles Davis with Sidney Bechet and Big Chief Moore, 1949, 13 x 18 cm. Private collection.

Photographs (reprints)
Miles Davis's Hand, Malibu, California, 1989. Photo Herman Leonard. © Herman Leonard Photography LLC/CTSIMAGES.COM.
Miles Davis, Malibu, California, 1989. Photo Herman Leonard. © Herman Leonard Photography LLC/CTSIMAGES.COM.
« Bop City, New York City, NY, 1953 », about 1948. Photo Herman Leonard. © Herman Leonard Photography LLC/CTSIMAGES.COM.

Record covers (selection)
Collection of Paul Marechal

SELECTED BIBLIOGRAPHY

Bergerot, Franck. *Miles Davis, introduction à l'écoute du jazz moderne.* Paris: Le Seuil, 1996.

Carner, Gary. *The Miles Davis Companion: Four Decades of Commentary*. New York: Schirmer Books, 1996.

Carr, Ian. *Miles Davis: The Definitive Biography*. New York: Harper Collins, 1999.

Chambers, Jack. *Milestones I: The Music and Times of Miles Davis to 1960*. Toronto: University of Toronto Press, 1983.

———. *Milestones II: The Music and Times of Miles Davis since 1960*. Toronto: University of Toronto Press, 1985.

Cole, George. *The Last Miles: The Music of Miles Davis, 1980–1991*. Ann Arbor: University of Michigan Press, 2004.

Cugny, Laurent. *Électrique Miles Davis, 1968-1975*. Reprint, Marseille: Tractatus & Co, 2009.

———. *Las Vegas Tango, une vie de Gil Evans*. Paris: POL, 1989.

Davis, Gregory. *Dark Magus: The Jekyll and Hyde Life of Miles Davis*. San Francisco: Backbeat Books, 2006.

Davis, Miles and Quincy Troupe. *Miles: The Autobiography*. New York: Simon & Schuster, 1989.

Fisher, Larry. *Miles Davis and David Liebman: Jazz Connections*. New York: Edwin Mellen Press, 1996.

Gerber, Alain. *Miles*. Paris: Fayard, 2007.

———. *Miles Davis and le blues du blanc*. Paris: Fayard, 2003.

Kahn, Ashley. *Kind of Blue: The Making of the Miles Davis Masterpiece*. New York: Da Capo Press, 2000.

Lohmann, Jan. *The Sound of Miles Davis: The Discography, a Listing of Records and Tapes, 1945–1991*. Copenhagen: JazzMedia APS, 1991.

Owsley, Dennis. *City of Gabriels: The History of Jazz in St. Louis, 1895–1973*. St. Louis: Reedy Press, 2006.

Satoh, Kohshin and Miles Davis. *The Best to Best*. Kamakura, Japan: Yobisha, 1992.

Szwed, John. *So What: The Life of Miles Davis*. New York: Simon & Schuster, 2004.

Tingen, Paul. *Miles Beyond: The Electric Explorations of Miles Davis, 1967–1991*. New York: Billboard Books, 2001.

Troupe, Quincy. *Miles and Me*. Berkeley: University of California Press, 2000.

Vail, Ken. *Miles' Diary: The Life of Miles Davis, 1947–1961*. London: Sanctuary Publishing Ltd, 1996.

Williams, Richard. *Miles Davis: The Man in the Green Shirt*. New York: H. Holt, 1993.

Yudkin, Jeremy. *Miles Davis, Miles Smiles, and the Invention of Post Bop*. Bloomington: Indiana University Press, 2008.

Please visit Peter Losin's website, a comprehensive reference for both the discography and the recording sessions: www.plosin.com/milesAhead/

ABOUT THE AUTHOR

Editor-in-chief of *Jazz Magazine*, Franck Bergerot is the author of *Miles Davis, introduction à l'écoute du jazz moderne* (Le Seuil, 1996) as well as *Jazz dans tous ses états : histoire, styles, foyers, grandes figures* (Larousse, 2006). He oversaw the first volumes of the complete works of Miles Davis released by the Masters of Jazz label. He also wrote the 53 liner notes contained in the box set *Miles Davis: Complete Columbia Album Collection*.

ACKNOWLEDGEMENTS

The biography included in this catalogue would not have seen the light of day without the work or the testimonials of André Hodeir, Ian Carr, Jack Chambers, Laurent Cugny, Quincy Troupe, Jan Lohmann, Enrico Merlin, Bob Belden, David Liebman, Larry Fisher, Paul Tingen, Ken Vail, Peter Losin, John Szwed, Ashley Kahn, George Porter and Jeremy Yudkin. It was also made possible by the information gathered during the listening sessions that preceded the writing of my book *Miles Davis, introduction à l'écoute du jazz moderne*, published by Le Seuil in 1996, and my involvement in the reissue in CD format of Miles Davis' first recordings with Masters of Jazz, "Young Miles" (Vols. 1 to 3). I would also like to thank Vincent Bessières, Christian Bonnet, Claude Carrière, Marion Challier, Guillaume de Chassy, Christophe Devillers, Marc Ducret, François-Marie Foucault, Patrick Fradet, Frédéric Goaty, Gisèle and Christian Lhernault, Jean-Pierre Lion, Jeanne de Mirbeck, Patrick Raffault, Jean-Charles Richard and Malo Vallois. F.B.